Croydon's

Railways

©M.W.G. Skinner & Kingfisher
Railway Productions
ISBN 0 946184 14 3
December 1985

Typesetting by:
Alphaset
65A The Avenue,
Southampton SO1 2TA

Printed by:
Netherwood Dalton & Co.
Bradley Mills,
Huddersfield,
Yorks.

Croydon's
Railways

M.W.G. Skinner

Published by

Kingfisher Railway Productions
188 Bitterne Road, Southampton SO2 4BE
Tel. (0703) 222032

Acknowledgements

I would like to thank the many individuals and organisations who have helped me compile this history, particularly the invaluable assistance received from John Howard-Turner (who allowed access to his considerable library, records and files) and his assistants, the Misses C. Eastland and D. Smith.

Sincere thanks go to the many photographers who loaned their prints and to R.C. Riley, Reg Randall, Kevin Robertson, Graham Long, Ian Kerr and other friends and colleagues for their assistance. The facilities of the public libraries at Croydon, Coulsdon and St. Pancras, the Public Records Office at Kew and the Department of Transport were very helpful to me. I would like to record my appreciation for all the assistance and co-operation afforded by these many sources.

Bibliography

To enable this book to be as comprehensive as possible considerable research was necessary. The following books (listed alphabetically by Publisher) were consulted, some to a greater, others to a lesser degree.

History of the Southern Railway, C.F. Dendy Marshall and R.W. Kidner, Ian Allan
Southern Electric 1909-1979, G.T. Moody, Ian Allan
The London Brighton and South Coast Railway, C. Hamilton Ellis, Ian Allan
The Southern Eastern and Chatham Railway, O.S. Nock, Ian Allan
Brighton Line Album, R.C. Riley, Ian Allan
Southern Album, P. Ransome Wallis, Ian Allan
Railways before the Grouping:
    L.B. & S.C.R. No. 1, O.J. Morris, Ian Allan
    L.B. & S.C.R. Locomotives, F. Burtt, Ian Allan
    S.E. & C.R. Locomotives, F. Burtt, Ian Allan
Clinkers Registry of closed Passenger stations and Goods Depots in England, Scotland and Wales 1830-1977, C.R. Clinker, Avon Anglia
The London, Brighton and South Coast Railway (3 volumes), J.T. Howard-Turner, B.T. Batsford
Souvenir Programme of the Centenary of the Caterham Railway, Bourne Society and Railway and Canal Historical Society
Bourne Society Local Historical Records, Bourne Society
A Regional History of the Railways of Great Britain:
Vol. 2. Southern England, H.P. White, David and Charles
Vol. 3. Greater London, H.P. White, David and Charles
Londons Termini, Alan A. Jackson, David and Charles
Londons Local Railways, Alan A. Jackson, David and Charles
Locomotive and Train Working in the Latter Part of the Nineteenth Century, E.L. Ahrons, W. Heffer
The Story of Londons Underground, John R. Day, London Transport
The London to Brighton Line 1841-1977, Adrian Gray, Oakwood Press
The Oxted Line, R.W. Kidner, Oakwood Press
The Reading to Tonbridge Lines, R.W. Kidner, Oakwood Press
The Tattenham Corner Branch, N. Owen, Oakwood Press
The Bricklayers Arms Branch and Loco Shed, M. Jackman, Oakwood Press
The S.E. & C.R. in the 1914-1918 War, David Gould, Oakwood Press
The Caterham Railway, J. Spence, Oakwood Press
A Pictorial Record of Southern Signals, G. Pryer, Oxford Publishing Co.
An Historical Survey of Southern Sheds, Chris Hawkins and George Reeve, Oxford Publishing Co.
An Historical Survey of Selected Southern Stations, G.A. Pryer and G.J. Bowring, Oxford Publishing Co.
Locomotives of the L.B. & S.C.R. (3 volumes), D.L. Bradley, Railway Correspondence and Travel Society
Londons Lost Railways, Charles Clapper, Routledge and Kegan Paul
War on the Line, Bernard Darwin, Southern Railway

Various editions of the 'Railway Magazine', 'Railway World', 'Modern Railways', and 'Croydon Advertiser' provided further sources of reference, as did Department of Transport Accident Reports and Railway Timetables (Public and Working).

Introduction

The present day railway scene in the Croydon area, with ubiquitous electric and diesel electric multiple unit trains and Gatwick Expresses running in close succession and largely controlled by electrically operated colour light signals, does not give the casual observer, or the majority of commuters, the impression of an interesting subject for a book.

In fact the railways of Croydon have had a more varied and fascinating history, and greater variation in operation, than many of the lines more beloved by railway enthusiasts which as a result receive considerably greater coverage journalistically.

Throughout its long railway history – which began long before Stephenson and the 'Rocket' – the area has been in the forefront with the latest technical developments in the fields of traction, signalling and civil engineering, sometimes achieving a 'first'. Unusually there have been no less than six distinct forms of train power:- Horse, steam, atmospheric, A.C. overhead wire electric, D.C. conductor rail electric and diesel, plus numerous variations within those general headings.

The development of railways and the places they serve have invariably been synonymous with one another – railways being originally provided to link the existing isolated towns whilst also serving the scantily populated places in between. This encouraged residential development along the route, resulting in other railways being opened, leading to further development. This was certainly the case in Croydon and the surrounding area and as trains became more popular and their speed increased, shortening journey times, residential building spread progressively further from London, commuting as we know it resulted, and still more new lines and stations were needed.

Catering for vast numbers of passengers has always played a prominent part in Croydon's railway story, influencing the number and pattern of train services, the number of tracks and stations on each route and the signalling requirement.

Travelling habits too have changed from time to time, affected by changes in working hours, competition from other forms of transport, and trends in excursion, holiday and other leisure activities.

Croydon has always been rated high among the towns and boroughs of Great Britain served by the largest number of overground railway stations, invariably being 'top of the league'. At the start of 1983 there were twenty-four within the Borough, the highest ever figure, but this had been reduced to twenty by the end of that year. With regular, and in most cases frequent, through services to and from widespread locations it is undoubtedly among the best rail served places in the world.

Numerous books have been written about the railways which serve the Borough but these have been devoted either to an entire railway company or to one section of line, rather than specifically to the railways of Croydon, a situation which this book sets out to rectify. Five intensive, but interesting, years of perusing such books, researching hitherto unpublished data, recalling from ones own memory and collating, checking and compiling has resulted in a wide ranging and detailed book, divided into sections, each devoted to a facet of the overall story and presented in chronological order, thus giving the reader a sequence of events as they occurred.

'Croydon', in the title of the book, relates throughout to the present day London Borough of Croydon in order to maintain consistency, and wherever possible the text keeps within these limits. However, as few of the routes or branch lines are entirely within the Borough boundaries and few trains start and finish their journeys completely in this limited area, it was found necessary to venture beyond to adequately cover the subject.

The Development of Routes and Historical section, whilst basically covering the lines within the Borough – the area included on the accompanying maps – unavoidably refers to some routes further afield, but only those which are significant.

Similarly, in chapter two, as nine of the present day London termini (including Euston, Liverpool Street and Paddington) and others long since closed are, or have been, served by direct services (this also applies to many other places including the majority of suburban stations in between a wide spectrum of the coast from Margate to Portsmouth, the Midlands and the North of England) these have to be referred to.

In an attempt to avoid the book appealing only to railway enthusiasts and B.R. staff, the use of railway terminology and jargon is, wherever possible, avoided and items such as acts of parliament, financial authorities, abortive proposals, disagreements and agreements between rival companies etc., which are of little interest other than to historians, are not elaborated in detail.

It is hoped that the result will be a serious comprehensive railway reference book, with maps and diagrams to assist the reader, and interesting illustrations, which will appeal, and be readable to, a large proportion of the half million people who reside and/or work in, or travel to, from, or through the Borough daily.

M.W.G. Skinner
Coulsdon, Surrey.
November 1985

Contents

Chapter One   Page

Development of Routes and Historical Section

To 31st December 1839 7
1st January 1840 – 31st December 1859 10
1st January 1860 – 31st December 1879 14
1st January 1880 – 31st December 1899 18
1st January 1900 – 31st December 1919 23
1st January 1920 – 31st December 1939 27
1st January 1940 – 31st December 1959 32
1st January 1969 – 31st December 1979 35
1st January To Date 37

Chapter Two
Part One – 19th Century Passenger Services . . . 41
Part Two – 20th Century Passenger Services . . . 45
Part Three – Other Traffic 71
Chapter Three
Signalling 77
Chapter Four
Accidents
Part One – 19th Century 100
Part Two – 20th Century 104
Chapter Five
Miscellaneous Section 111

The name of 'Croydon' is to be seen in many parts of the region in the form of a nameplate on ED No. 73121 *Croydon 1883-1983*.
John Scrace

Chapter One

Development of Routes and Historical Section
To 31st December 1839

At the start of the 19th century the population of Croydon and the surrounding district was considerably lower than today. The market town of Croydon had 5,743 inhabitants in the 1801 census, whilst the village of Coulsdon could boast but 420 souls.

Nevertheless, Croydon was one of the largest and most important towns in the south east. In 1799 a horse tramway from London to Portsmouth, via Croydon, was planned and in 1800 a canal connecting the River Thames at Rotherhithe with Croydon was proposed. The tramway started at Ram Field (by the Ram Brewery) in Wandsworth and ran via Mitcham to Pitlake

An extension known as the Croydon, Merstham and Godstone Railway was opened on 24th July 1805. It ran from Pitlake Meadow parallel with, and just to the west side of, the Brighton Road almost to the present day southernmost boundary of the Borough near Hooley, where, after following a wriggly route for a short distance, it eventually took up a route on the east side and into the Greystone Limeworks at Merstham. The traffic dealt with included farm produce, stone, chalk and Fullers Earth. The continuation onward to Godstone, also the Surrey Iron Railway's Portsmouth line, were never proceeded with.

A very early scene (c. 1830) in Croydon with the town's second town hall forming the main part of the picture.
Pamlin Prints

Meadow (near Croydon Parish Church) and opened for traffic on 26th July 1803. It was known as the 'Surrey Iron Railway' and was the first publicly owned railway in the world. The traffic, conveyed in the horse drawn wagons over a 4ft. 2in. gauge double track, was largely coal from boats on the Thames and dung and charcoal produced in the Croydon area in the opposite direction, although 38 mills and factories were served too. One horse could haul 50 to 60 tons without difficulty on the level sections. The Railway owned no vehicles, but charged tolls to its users, varying from 1d per ton mile for dung, to 3d per ton mile for coal.

The Surrey Iron Railway differed from railways as we know them today. Flangeless wheels ran on the top of the flat surface of angle plates, being guided by vertical flanges on the inside edge of the plates.

The Croydon Canal took a fairly direct route from its connection with the Grand Surrey Canal (north of New Cross) to Croydon, albeit with 26 locks between New Cross and Honor Oak Park, and swing bridges towards the Croydon end. It commenced business on 23rd October 1809, whereupon a short branch line to serve it was soon provided from Pitlake Meadow. This was, however, the property of the Canal authorities.

In April 1823 a railway starting from Waterloo Bridge was proposed. It would have run to Tooting thence over the route of the Surrey Iron Railway to Croydon and the Croydon, Merstham and Godstone Railway to Merstham, both railways being modified to suit. From Merstham it would have traversed new ground to New Chapel near East Grinstead, where it would have connected with another proposed route from Strood (near

Chatham) to Portsmouth, afterwards running via Holmbush (near Crawley) and Nuthurst (south east of Horsham) and Shoreham to Southwick (for Brighton). This was the first of many contenders for a London - Brighton railway hauled by steam locomotives.

More London - Brighton lines were proposed in 1825. One was from Nine Elms (Battersea) via Wandsworth, Dorking, Horsham and Shoreham, not passing through the Borough, whilst another was a variation in route through the same places. Another alternative took a route through Croydon and direct to Brighton. This, too, had variants including a more easterly route to Lewes and Newhaven with a line to Brighton branching off near Ardingly and another branch from near Reigate to Portsmouth. The promoting company was known by the grandiose title of the Surrey, Sussex, Hants, Wilts and Somerset Railway, it being their intention to continue through Portsmouth, Southampton and Salisbury to the Bristol coalfields.

A railway between London and Croydon only was also being considered. In 1826 more possibilities were being put forward for railways between London and Brighton, including routes via Oxted or Dorking or Guildford.

Another direct proposal, its route slightly more westerly than before, put forward in 1829 failed to attract interest.

The first half of the 1830s was very active. Not only were several London - Brighton routes being progressed, some with optional variants, but Dover and Tunbridge Wells were being looked upon as desirable destinations. Some of the routes being planned would have passed through the Borough, others would not.

The population of Croydon in 1831 had reached 12,500, making it even more attractive than hitherto to railway developers.

The London - Croydon railway was again in prominence during 1833, as was a direct route from Kennington to Brighton via Croydon. The promoters of the London and Brighton railway asked Robert Stephenson to look at the various schemes. He favoured the direct route, but it was deferred owing to difficulty in raising capital.

It was resurrected again in 1834 and two more proposals were forthcoming - from Elephant & Castle via Brixton, Croydon, Charlwood, West Grinstead and Shoreham, and from Nine Elms via Wandsworth, Dorking, Horsham and Shoreham again.

An extension of the proposed London - Croydon railway south westwards via Betchworth, Horsham and Shoreham was also being planned. This, too, had its variants - to run southwards via Merstham and Newdigate to Horsham, and there was a branch from the proposed London - Southampton railway at Wandsworth to join the latter near what is now Purley.

Later in the year Robert Stephenson was again brought in to assist the promoters. It had become obvious that whichever of the many proposals was eventually progressed there were two obvious routes, either direct via Croydon or via Dorking, Horsham and Shoreham. This time he favoured the latter route, but decided to have it properly calculated.

Up to this time none of the proposed railways had obtained an Act of Parliament. However, on 12th June 1835 the London and Croydon Railway obtained their's, to build the first passenger carrying railway into Croydon, from a junction with the forthcoming London and Greenwich Railway at Corbetts Lane 1¾ miles out of London Bridge to what is now West Croydon station. Trains would use London Bridge station running over the London and Greenwich line.

During 1835 not only were the numerous Brighton proposals still current but on 15th September a Bill was prepared

for a line from Kennington running practically straight to Croydon then down the Caterham Valley, to the west of Oxted, and on to Dover via Tonbridge (spelt Tunbridge until 1893), followed on 30th October by another Bill. This time a more circuitous route via Wandsworth and passing through Croydon by a more westerly route before gaining the Caterham Valley was proposed. Both these schemes not only went to Dover, but included branches to Tunbridge Wells, running direct in the first instance from near Oxted and in the second from Tonbridge. Also from Oxted, routes onward to Brighton were included, the first running practically straight, and the second via Worth, Lindfield, Wivelsfield and Clayton. Although the South Eastern Railway Company was not incorporated until the following year they were behind these proposals, and used their name to head the Bills. These were early attempts by that Company to have their own railway between London and Brighton, which they were to pursue unsuccessfully for many more years. A further Bill varying these routes was put forward by the South Eastern Railway in February 1836.

So far as the other Brighton routes were concerned the extension of the London and Croydon Railway had been withdrawn and interest had waned in the case of some of the other proposals. The direct route had also been altered to use the London and Croydon route from London Bridge instead of eminating from Kennington.

The desire to serve Brighton was obvious. The fishing village of Brighthelmstone had begun to expand by the early 1800s to become the fashionable seaside resort of Brighton. It owed much of this to a Doctor Russell of Lewes, who had advertised the medicinal properties of sea water as a relief from, and a cure for, glandular diseases as early as 1752. The Prince of Wales (later George IV) also popularised the resort by visiting it from 1783.

By 1815 the Brighton road was one of the busiest in the land, 100,000 people a year travelling along it by horse carriage. In 1819 there were 52 public coaches. The population of Brighton had soared to 24,429 by 1821 and 40,634 by 1831. During 1835, 117,000 travelled by horse carriage and by the following year there were licensed coaches capable of accommodating 3,400 passengers daily. There was obvious railway potential.

A House of Commons Committee closely examined the various Brighton routes from 16th March to 26th April 1836 and on 13th May it was announced that Sir John Rennies' direct route had been selected. It would use the London and Greenwich Railway to Corbetts Lane and the London and Croydon Railway to a junction south of Jolly Sailor (now Norwood Junction) called Brighton Junction (but sometimes referred to as Croydon Junction) from whence it would become a new railway. They considered the route via Dorking, Horsham and Shoreham to be the best from an engineering viewpoint but the direct route, using London Bridge as its terminus and sharing the route to Brighton Junction conformed with Parliament's opinion that it was undesirable to have more than one route into and out of London southwards. Being 5 miles shorter was another feature to its advantage and it was considered that these combined benefits outweighed the heavy engineering works. Tolls would be payable to the other companies for the use of their routes.

On 30th May 1836 the South Eastern Railway put forward yet another Bill to Parliament, and on 21st June they obtained their Act - for a continuation from the London and Croydon Railway at Croydon (West) through the Caterham Valley to Dover via Oxted and Tonbridge. They, too, would share the route from London Bridge to Croydon. Their line from Oxted to Brighton was not included.

Movements on the Croydon Canal with its locks and swing bridges were slow even for those days. and it was not a success.

Moreover the London and Croydon Railway required some of the canal bed for their route. The London and Brighton Railway would also require part of the route of the Croydon, Merstham and Godstone Railway. In consequence both ceased operations, along with the canal branch line, from 22nd August 1836.

During 1836 the first conventional railway (with flanged wheels guided by the rails) which was to play a part in Croydon's railway history had opened in stages. This was the London and Greenwich Railway with its terminus at London Bridge, later to be used by the other companies.

The South Eastern Railway's Act was amended on 3rd July 1837. Instead of the continuation from Croydon (West) it would now start at a junction south of Penge, then run just to the east side of the proposed London and Brighton Railway to Purley, there taking up the original route via the Caterham valley.

However, by the time the London and Brighton Railway received its Act of Parliament on 15th July the Committee considered that it might be better for the South Eastern Railway to use the London and Brighton route to near Reigate (now Redhill), whence it could run practically straight to Dover avoiding both the duplication of tracks for more than 5 miles and heavy engineering work through the North Downs. Accordingly the Act made provision for such eventuality, with a caveat that should the South Eastern Railway decide to adopt the idea within two years the London and Brighton Railway should be required to sell the Brighton Junction - Reigate portion of the line to them at cost price. However, an agreement between the two companies on 25th April 1839 amended this, the northern half of that portion to remain in the ownership of the London and Brighton Railway and the southern half to be transferred to the South Eastern Railway, provided an Act was passed before July 1841 for the diversion. Tolls were to be exempted between the two companies over this portion. The South Eastern Railway soon adopted the idea and on 19th July its Act was revised accordingly.

In the meantime, on 5th June, the London and Croydon Railway had opened. With running powers over the London and Greenwich Railway for the first 1¾ miles from London Bridge to a junction at Corbetts Lane, upon payment of tolls, their line ran to a terminus at Croydon (now West Croydon) with intermediate stations at New Cross (now New Cross Gate), Dartmouth Arms (now Forest Hill), Sydenham, Penge (now Penge West), Annerley (now spelt Anerley) and Jolly Sailor (now Norwood Junction). The route as far as possible followed the course of the old canal. Between New Cross and Croydon there was more or less open countryside so the potential for traffic was not good. The intermediate stations were provided to serve the small communities and to give them a means of travelling from place to place. It was not envisaged that London workers in any numbers would live outside the city and travel to and fro daily. Prior to the coming of the railways it must be remembered that the only means of transport had been by horse or on foot – even bicycles had not been invented – and those who worked in London had been obliged to live near their workplace. The use of inn names for naming the stations gives an indication of the size of some of the places.

However, the main thing was that the town of Croydon was served by a passenger railway linking it with the City of London! Moreover, it would not be long before links were made with Brighton and Dover, the two other main centres of the south east at the time.

The new railway quickly showed its capabilities, success-fully conveying 11,000 passengers to and from the annual Croydon Fair with a ten minute interval service, on only its second day of operation.

At about this time a Select Committee was set up to look into the many problems envisaged in a few years time when four separate companies would be running their trains intermingled over the two tracks between London Bridge and Corbetts Lane Junction. The South Eastern Railway proposed new lines to a separate London terminus at Elephant and Castle – one from Dartmouth Arms via Nunhead and Peckham, the other from Jolly Sailor via Herne Hill, to avoid congestion (and, no doubt, also with a view to avoid paying the high tolls proposed by the London and Greenwich Railway). The London and Croydon Railway realised that they stood to lose tolls too, so they did not support the proposals, and nothing more was heard of them.

Some relics of the period covered by this chapter can still be seen. An example of the flanged rail track of the Croydon, Merstham and Godstone Railway is preserved in Rotary Field, Purley, more or less on the actual route, some earthworks can be traced in the Coulsdon area, whilst beside the Happy Eater Restaurant at Hooley, just outside the Borough, a bridge remains which took that railway under Dean Lane.

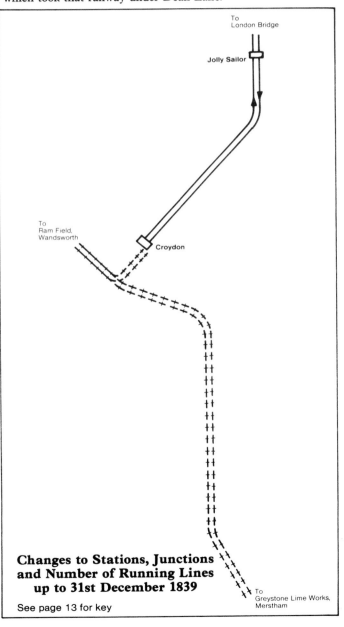

Changes to Stations, Junctions and Number of Running Lines up to 31st December 1839

See page 13 for key

1st January 1840 - 31st December 1859

During 1840 it was reported that 6,206 men, 960 horses and 5 locomotives were employed on building the London and Brighton Railway. Work progressed so well that it was opened to Haywards Heath on 12th July 1841, and to Brighton on 21st September. Within the Borough, stations were provided at Croydon (now East Croydon) and Godstone Road (now Purley).

Whilst the former station was opened as Croydon the author can find little evidence available to indicate exactly when and how its title gradually changed to become East Croydon. Through the years it is variously and intermittently referred to as Croydon, Croydon (East) and East Croydon, even in official timetables, documents and maps. A map produced in 1847 already shows it as East Croydon, yet luggage labels of Southern Railway vintage are worded Croydon (East) and reference books listing changes in station names do not cover this aspect. Because of this uncertainty it is referred to as East Croydon henceforth.

The population of Croydon had now reached 13,627 whilst Coulsdon had topped the thousand mark with 1,041.

The benefits of the coming of the railways can be seen from the fact that 7,191 passengers used the London and Brighton Railway in the first week.

A station was opened by that company at Stoats Nest (Coulsdon) on 1st December 1841. In these early days trains called only if required at both Godstone Road and Stoats Nest, the latter being served in this manner even before it was completed. Stoats Nest was regarded as the station for Epsom Racecourse (it was, of course, the nearest), racegoers completing the intervening 7 or 8 miles by horse carriage or on foot.

The South Eastern Railway opened as far as Tonbridge on 26th May 1842. It had the tracks of the London and Greenwich, London and Croydon, and London and Brighton to traverse before reaching its own, with tolls to pay where applicable. There were, however, other compensating factors. They had acquired the most expensive half of the Brighton Junction – Reigate 'joint' line for half the overall cost and they controlled the junction at Reigate and could, when it suited them, give preference to their own trains over those of the London and Brighton Railway – a practice they were not slow to adopt.

This, coupled with the problems associated with four companies intermingling over the same tracks, the tolls, and competitiveness generally, was a recipe for arguments and aggravation, some of which were to linger on in one form or another for at least the next 80 years until the grouping of the companies into the Southern Railway.

During 1842 the London and Croydon and the South Eastern Railway made economies by pooling their locomotives and rolling stock. The London and Brighton Railway joined in from 1st March 1844.

The financial burden of the tolls caused problems and various suggestions were made between the four companies to lease to one another in an effort to ease things. Nothing however came of them and the South Eastern and the London and Croydon decided that the answer was to build a new line to a terminus of their own. A branch line was provided nearly 1¾ miles long leaving the London Bridge line about ¾ mile north of New Cross whence it ran in a westerly direction to their self styled 'West End' terminus at Bricklayers Arms – the station again being named after a nearby hostelry! The opening of the new line was on 1st May 1844, two thirds of the London and Croydon trains and half of the South Eastern's being diverted to and from the new station instead of London Bridge, thereby avoiding the London and Greenwich tolls. Omnibuses met all trains to convey passengers to the City and West End. The remaining trains, including all those of the London and Brighton continued to serve London Bridge.

Although the South Eastern had regarded the Stoats Nest to Reigate section of line to be theirs previously, this was not the case. They did not pay their share before 1844, albeit because the London and Brighton did not forward the account until this late date. The London and Brighton had therefore operated the line until 19th July 1844 when the South Eastern assumed control.

New proposals were made around this time for yet another London – Brighton route via Epsom and Horsham, also a line from the entrance to the Grosvenor Canal (near Victoria) to Godstone Road (Purley) during 1844, followed by a Croydon – Wandsworth line and a direct West End – Croydon link in 1845. None came to fruition.

The South Eastern Railway leased the London and Greenwich from 1st January 1845 from which date the latter ceased to exist effectively, although it actually continued to be a separate undertaking until the formation of the Southern Railway in 1923. The South Eastern improved their finances in two ways – they did not have to pay tolls to the London and Greenwich and they received the tolls of the 'Croydon' and 'Brighton' for that section.

The problems of operating the expresses of both the South Eastern and the London and Brighton and their own unrenumerative stopping services over the double line between Corbetts Lane and Brighton Junction had caused the London and Croydon to consider ceasing to run their own services and to rely entirely on the tolls collected from the other companies. It decided, however, on an alternative – to extend its line to Epsom, along which route there was traffic potential, and to explore ways of reducing working expenses. One of the latter was the Atmospheric system. By this method a train would be headed by a special vehicle known as a piston carriage instead of a steam locomotive. This had an arm underneath which passed through a slot along a circular iron tube laid between the rails. A piston was attached to the leading end of the arm and a counterweight to the rear. The slot was normally covered by a leather flap to make it airtight. The flap moved aside immediately before the arm and closed mechanically behind it. Pumping stations were provided at intervals of up to 3 miles beside the line to create vacuum in the tube. Electric telegraph circuits were provided between pumping stations so that messages could be passed to ensure that the necessary vacuum was partially created prior to the approach of a train. Vacuum ahead of the piston and atmospheric pressure behind it caused it to move forward. Advantages claimed for the system were reduced permanent way costs, freedom from smoke and dirt, ability to work on steeper gradients and sharper curves and at greater speeds, reduced operating costs and the absence of collisions (two trains could not work simultaneously between two pumping stations).

The London and Croydon proposed to carry out conversion in four stages – (1) Dartmouth Arms – Croydon, (2) Dartmouth Arms – New Cross, (3) New Cross – London Bridge and (4) the new line Croydon – Epsom.

An additional line was specially provided on the east side and Stage 1 was to be used as a proving ground. This section was flat except for a wooden fly-over at Brighton Junction (the first fly-over in the world) necessary due to the impracticability of the atmospheric tube crossing other lines on the level.

Whilst these preparations were going on Dartmouth Arms station was renamed Forest Hill from 3rd July 1845.

The first atmospheric trial was on 22nd August. The train reached 60 mph and on a later trial run 70 mph. The trials also proved that the trains could work without the pumping station at Norwood. Failures, however, occurred with the pumping equipment and the public introduction of the system was delayed until 19th January 1846, after more trials had been satisfactorily carried out. Failures in the pumping engines occurred again from the first day.

After disagreements and misunderstandings in interpretation the locomotive and rolling stock pool was ended on 31st January 1846.

The London and Croydon Railway had not found Bricklayers Arms a good proposition, so as from March 1846 they reverted to using London Bridge. The tolls had been reduced and this allowed them to charge the same fare to London Bridge as they had to Bricklayers Arms.

By Easter 1846 modifications to the atmospheric equipment had resulted in reasonably satisfactory performance and work was commenced on Stage 2. However, as Summer approached a new hazard arose – the mixture of tallow and beeswax used to seal the tube flap melted and the leather hardened. In addition rubbish, including rats, were sucked through the pipes clogging up the air valves. From the end of May until 13th July atmospheric working was suspended whilst modifications were carried out.

Another problem with the system was the excessive turnround time at termini. The piston carriage could not reverse, neither could the iron pipe cross other rails, so to get the piston carriage to the other end of the train it had to be manhandled out of the tube, have its piston and counter weight removed, then be taken round its train by further manhandling or possibly horse towing, have the piston and counterweight replaced the opposite way round and then re-inserted in the tube.

On 27th July 1846 the London and Brighton, London and Croydon and three smaller companies amalgamated to become the London, Brighton and South Coast Railway. (Now that the number of companies serving the Borough was reduced to two the opportunity is taken from this point henceforth to refer to the new company as the L.B. & S.C.R. and the South Eastern Railway as the S.E.R.)

The Surrey Iron Railway ceased operations on 31st August and the Jolly Sailor was renamed Norwood in October.

In December owing to the uncertainties of the atmospheric system it was decided that Stage 3 would be dropped and work on Stage 4 stopped. Stage 2 was in operation with locomotive changing at New Cross in either direction. The Winter of 1846/7 was a hard one and this caused the leather to crack. It is not surprising that the atmospheric system did not appeal to the Board of the newly formed L.B. & S.C.R. and they condemned it from 4th May 1847. As the extension from Croydon (now West Croydon) to Epsom did not open until the following day it was never operated under atmospheric conditions. This new line conveyed 32,000 passengers on Derby Day that year, Epsom station, although 1½ miles away, being much closer to the racecourse than Stoats Nest.

Godstone Road station closed on 30th September 1847 as uneconomical, the platform shelter going to Bexhill.

On 10th July 1848 the L.B. & S.C.R. and S.E.R. produced an agreement concerning their territorial rights and other differences. The principle resolutions taken were that tolls would be abolished and any future lines would be toll free provided that the L.B. & S.C.R. did not become involved in any line to the east of the Corbetts Lane – Reigate Junction line and north of the Reigate Junction – Tonbridge line and the S.E.R. similarly to the west and south of those lines. Moreover S.E.R. trains would be permitted to call only at East Croydon, Norwood, Forest Hill and New Cross on the L.B. & S.C.R. owned section north of Stoats Nest, and then only on condition that they did not compete with the L.B. & S.C.R. for the London traffic from those stations.

A Reading, Guildford and Reigate Railway opened a line from Reigate (now Redhill) where it made a junction with the 'joint' Dover and Brighton main lines, the station being renamed Reigate Junction. It reached Reading on 20th August 1849.

During 1849 the L.B. & S.C.R. established a Goods Depot at Willow Walk, alongside Bricklayers Arms, the latter place having been acquired by the S.E.R. a few years earlier.

An alteration between Brighton Junction and Corbetts Lane took place during that year. By replacing the redundant atmospheric line with normal track three lines were made available. These were allocated as two 'up' lines, one each for the L.B. & S.C.R. and S.E.R., an arrangement which was strictly enforced, and a joint 'down' line.

Quite good passenger traffic had built up during the 1840s, particularly between London, Brighton, Reigate and the suburban area. Moreover, the coastal towns in an arc from Margate to Portsmouth, plus the Reading line were, or were about to be, served by the S.E.R. or L.B. & S.C.R., all services sharing the one route out of London Bridge southwards. As a result East Croydon was provided with an excellent variety of services.

Outside the Borough, but significant to future developments, was the opening of another New Cross station, on the line from London Bridge to Lewisham, by the S.E.R. during 1850.

The original London and Croydon Railway station at Croydon was renamed West Croydon in April 1851.

The London terminus at Bricklayers Arms was not proving a success as a passenger station and all regular passenger services were withdrawn from January 1852, although limited special passenger services were to use it spasmodically until 1939. It continued as a parcels and freight depot.

During 1852 the Reading, Guildford and Reigate Railway was absorbed into the S.E.R.

By 1854 a fourth line had been provided between Bricklayers Arms Junction and Brighton Junction, permitting two 'up' and two 'down' lines to be operated. A permanent flyover had also replaced the timber structure at the latter place.

Just over the borders of the Borough the L.B. & S.C.R. opened a line from Sydenham to Crystal Palace for freight only on 27th March 1854, no doubt a good deal of the materials and furnishings from the Great Exhibition held in Hyde Park in 1851, which was transferred to the Crystal Palace, were conveyed along it. The line and Crystal Palace station opened to passengers ten weeks later on 10th June, the day the Crystal Palace itself opened to the public. At least 10,000 passengers a day were being carried shortly after the opening, the majority from London Bridge.

Next came a connecting link between the London and South Western Railway (L.S.W.R.) at Wimbledon and the L.B. & S.C.R. at West Croydon via Mitcham. This started as an independent company. There were no intermediate stations within the Borough, but there was one just outside at Beddington (later Beddington Lane Halt and now Beddington Lane). It opened on 20th October 1855 and largely followed the route of the former Surrey Iron Railway. The L.B. & S.C.R. leased the line from 1856.

Caterham was next on the scene. With a population of 487 in 1851 passenger traffic could not have offered much of a prospect. However, quarries providing excellent firestone were located to the south of Caterham and were thought to be a potential source of revenue so a railway was under consideration.

The obvious route both geographically and for serving London was along the Caterham Valley to where Godstone Road station had been. The L.B. & S.C.R. and S.E.R. were both interested but problems would arise whichever provided the line. Under the terms of the 1848 agreement this route would be entirely within the S.E.R. territory so they should provide it. The junction would, unfortunately, connect up with the L.B. & S.C.R. portion of the main line with obvious repercussions, and even if Godstone Road was re-opened the S.E.R. main line trains were not permitted to call there and thus provide connecting services. If the more logical solution was adopted – the L.B. & S.C.R. providing a branch from its own main line – this would be a complete breach of the agreement and the S.E.R. would object.

Plans were drawn up for a separate line to run from East Croydon alongside the main line to the site of Godstone Road then via Caterham to Godstone, serving the quarries along the way, but it was not proceeded with. A similar fate befell proposals both to provide a proper junction at Godstone Road, or to run under the Brighton line south of Godstone Road without making a physical connection and continue on to join the Sutton-West Croydon line.

During discussions between companies the L.B. & S.C.R. proposed moving Stoats Nest station to a point just south of the junction with the Caterham line, but instead, by July 1856, they agreed to re-open Godstone Road station and stop four trains daily to provide connections. By the end of the month it was agreed that the S.E.R. could also stop their trains there.

Despite considerable discussion and argument it could not be agreed who should provide the branch and it was left to a local independent company, the Caterham Railway Company, to be formed to sponsor it. After a ceremonial opening on 4th August 1856 it was opened to the public the following day. Within the Borough there was an intermediate station at Coulsdon (re-named Kenley on 1st December). The re-opened Godstone Road was renamed Caterham Junction from the opening. Through running was not possible between the branch and the main line.

The L.B. & S.C.R. leased the trains to the independent company, in itself contrary to the 1848 agreement.

They closed Stoats Nest station to passengers on 1st December although it continued as a freight depot and an additional siding was laid in at about this time to facilitate the conveyance of building materials in connection with the Reedham Orphanage development.

The Caterham Railway Company were in financial difficulties from the start. Their working expenses for the first year were £1,700 and their income £874. They could not afford to pay the L.B. & S.C.R. for the use of the trains and ran up other debts as well, resulting in much wrangling.

The crowds visiting the Crystal Palace indicated that a line linking it with the West End would be advantageous. A West End of London & Clapham & Norwood Junction Railway was given powers, but was abandoned when the nominally independent West End of London and Crystal Palace Railway Company opened a line on 1st December 1856 between Crystal Palace, where it was a continuation of the Sydenham line, and Wandsworth where it was temporarily terminated. Wandsworth station was just to the north of the road overbridge at the present Wandsworth Common station. To reach the West End at this stage it was necessary to walk across the common to the L.S.W.R. Clapham Common station, thence to Waterloo. The independent company's trains were operated by the L.B. & S.C.R.

Another significant opening outside the Borough was the Mid Kent Railway from Lewisham, where the suffix Junction was added, to Beckenham (now Beckenham Junction) on 1st January 1857. This was the start of the Mid Kent line which was eventually to provide Croydon with another route to London.

From 1st October the West End of London and Crystal Palace Railway was extended to Norwood. The new section made a junction with the existing line immediately west of Crystal Palace station so additional separate platforms were required. At the Norwood end the double line separated, the 'down' line passing over the four tracks of the London–Brighton line by a bridge, thus gaining the 'down' side of the line before connecting up. Norwood station was probably renamed Norwood Junction at this time.

Croydon's population had now reached 20,355.

Wandsworth station was renamed Wandsworth Common in January 1858 only a couple of months before it closed upon the line being extended towards the West End, albeit only to Pimlico on the south bank of the Thames. The extension ran parallel with the L.S.W.R. Waterloo lines on the east side until dropping down to pass under them. It opened on 29th March and the L.B. & S.C.R. leased the line throughout from Norwood Junction to Pimlico during the year.

They could not, however, show such interest in the West End of London and Crystal Palace Railway's Farnborough extension which commenced at Bromley Junction between Crystal Palace and Norwood Junction, just to the west of the bridge over the main lines, and opened as far as Bromley (now Shortlands) via Beckenham, where it made a junction with the Mid Kent Railway, as this would have been contrary to the 1848 agreement. As it was the S.E.R. considered that there had been L.B. & S.C.R. connivance. It opened on 3rd May 1858.

Other happenings during 1858 were the renaming of Reigate Junction to become Redhill Junction and Bromley to become Shortlands. An extension of the Mid Kent Railway to the Fair Field at Croydon was also under consideration, but this came to nothing.

During 1859 the L.B. & S.C.R. purchased the Norwood Junction – Pimlico line which they had leased, whilst an East Kent Railway leased the Farnborough extension, seeing it as part of a through route from Victoria to Dover which they were trying to achieve in stages.

On 1st June Norwood Junction Station was resited on the south side of Portland Road underline bridge.

The area between New Cross and Norwood Junction was still not built up to any extent. Guide books published for railway travellers at the time include such quotes as:- 'Leaving New Cross passengers cannot fail to admire the ingenuity with which the declivities on each side have been converted to flower and kitchen gardens', 'Leaving Forest Hill to the left lies the village of Sydenham celebrated for its beauty and salubrity', 'Sydenham station is situated in the midst of beautiful scenery', 'Penge has half finished streets', 'Anerley, a holiday resort . . . .' and 'Crystal Palace has suburban villas'.

The Caterham Railway Company's difficulties continued. Not only were the L.B. & S.C.R. being unsuccessful in obtaining their costs for running the trains, but the S.E.R. were angered by the L.B. & S.C.R.'s involvement within their territory as laid down in the 1848 agreement. Moreover, the L.B. & S.C.R. were showing interest in territory to the east of the Brighton line at Norwood Junction too.

In the end the whole affair was taken to court where it was ruled that the L.B. & S.C.R. could retain its Norwood Junction encroachment but the S.E.R. would take over the Caterham Railway from 21st July 1859. The latters intentions of extending the line to the quarries south of Caterham were never carried out although connecting tramways were provided.

On 1st August the East Kent Railway became the London, Chatham and Dover Railway (L.C.D.R.), soon to become a serious competitor to the S.E.R. for London - Dover traffic.

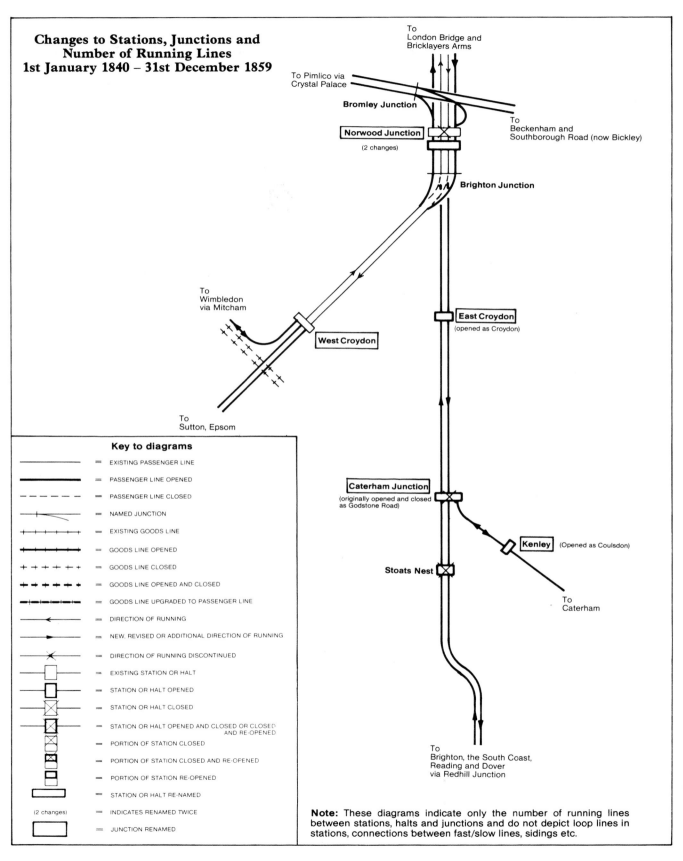

Changes to Stations, Junctions and Number of Running Lines 1st January 1840 – 31st December 1859

To London Bridge and Bricklayers Arms

To Pimlico via Crystal Palace

Bromley Junction

To Beckenham and Southborough Road (now Bickley)

Norwood Junction

(2 changes)

Brighton Junction

To Wimbledon via Mitcham

West Croydon

East Croydon

(opened as Croydon)

To Sutton, Epsom

Caterham Junction

(originally opened and closed as Godstone Road)

Kenley (Opened as Coulsdon)

Stoats Nest

To Caterham

To Brighton, the South Coast, Reading and Dover via Redhill Junction

Key to diagrams

—————	= EXISTING PASSENGER LINE
——————	= PASSENGER LINE OPENED
– – – – –	= PASSENGER LINE CLOSED
—+—	= NAMED JUNCTION
+++++++	= EXISTING GOODS LINE
━+━+━+━	= GOODS LINE OPENED
+ + + + +	= GOODS LINE CLOSED
━ + ━ + ━	= GOODS LINE OPENED AND CLOSED
━┼━┼━┼━	= GOODS LINE UPGRADED TO PASSENGER LINE
◄——	= DIRECTION OF RUNNING
——►	= NEW, REVISED OR ADDITIONAL DIRECTION OF RUNNING
—✕—	= DIRECTION OF RUNNING DISCONTINUED
☐	= EXISTING STATION OR HALT
▢	= STATION OR HALT OPENED
⊠	= STATION OR HALT CLOSED
⊠	= STATION OR HALT OPENED AND CLOSED OR CLOSED AND RE-OPENED
⊠	= PORTION OF STATION CLOSED
⊠	= PORTION OF STATION CLOSED AND RE-OPENED
▢	= PORTION OF STATION RE-OPENED
▭	= STATION OR HALT RE-NAMED
(2 changes)	= INDICATES RENAMED TWICE
▭	= JUNCTION RENAMED

Note: These diagrams indicate only the number of running lines between stations, halts and junctions and do not depict loop lines in stations, connections between fast/slow lines, sidings etc.

13

1st January 1860 - 31st December 1879

On 1st October 1860 the West End proper was at last reached with the opening of Victoria Station. To reach the new terminus a line branched off from the Pimlico line about ½ mile short of that station and climbed steeply to the south end of Grosvenor Bridge over the River Thames. After crossing the river the line dropped steeply down into the new terminus. Grosvenor Bridge was the first railway bridge across the Thames. The line into Pimlico was closed to passengers but remained to serve Battersea Wharf Goods Depot.

On 25th August the L.C.D.R. opened the first stage of their own main line from their own terminus at Victoria (on the eastern side of the original one) through Brixton to Herne Hill.

During 1862 relations between the S.E.R. and L.B. & S.C.R. were at their worst and any opportunity to aggravate one another was taken. The L.B. & S.C.R., in particular, placed restrictions on S.E.R. passengers in the Croydon area including insistence that Caterham line passengers to East Croydon must hold L.B. & S.C.R. tickets. To conform with this passengers were

Victoria station yard in Victorian times.   *Pamlin Prints*

The new line was a separate company – The Victoria Station and Pimlico Railway and both the L.B. & S.C.R. and L.C.D.R. used it. Between the junction near Pimlico and Bromley Junction the L.B. & S.C.R. granted running powers to the L.C.D.R. on condition that they paid a toll and did not serve the intermediate stations. The latter, having acquired the Farnborough extension by this time, reached their own tracks at Bromley Junction. Their route throughout to Dover was not, however, completed until 22nd July 1861, being 6½ miles less than the S.E.R.'s route from London Bridge to Dover via East Croydon and Redhill Junction.

Additional lines were provided from the West Croydon lines south of Brighton Junction (the new junction being called Gloucester Road Junction) to a point ½ mile north of East Croydon (later known as Windmill Bridge Junction) from 1st May 1862. These were extended during the year to terminal platforms beside East Croydon station. The terminus was regarded as their own separate station by the L.B. & S.C.R. who called it New Croydon.

A half mile long double line spur, known as the Norwood Spur, connecting the Farnborough extension and Norwood Junction, and permitting through running between the latter station and Beckenham and beyond, was opened by the L.B. & S.C.R. on 18th June, although the L.C.D.R. provided the trains.

obliged to re-book at Caterham Junction, whereupon the L.B. & S.C.R. timed their connecting trains so that there was insufficient time to do so! There were occasions when they physically restrained Caterham passengers from joining S.E.R. trains at Caterham Junction. All this resulted in the scandalous treatment of Caterham passengers being highlighted in no less a place than the leading article of 'The Times'. Following this things quietened down.

Up to this time trains between East or West Croydon and Victoria ran via Crystal Palace – the only route. A more direct route was achieved on 1st December 1862 by the opening of a double track line from Windmill Bridge Junction (½ mile north of East Croydon) to Balham Hill (now Balham) where it made a junction with the former route. The area through which the new line passed was not particularly populated. There were resultantly only two intermediate stations – Thornton Heath (originally called Colliers Water Lane for a short time, according to the 'Railway Gazette' at the time) and Streatham Common, the latter being outside the Borough. The new line was not at this stage connected with West Croydon, but a spur line was provided linking it with Brighton Junction (renamed Norwood Fork Junction simultaneously).

A new station was opened during February 1863 at Waddon on the West Croydon – Epsom line.

The West London Extension Railway (often referred to as the West London Line or WLL) opened on 2nd March 1863 linking the Great Western Railway and the London & North Western Railway with the railways south of the Thames. Making triangular junctions with both the L.B. & S.C.R. lines between Victoria and Balham Hill and the L.S.W.R. Waterloo lines, direct running was possible between the new line and Waterloo, Windsor, Victoria and Balham Hill, and, therefore, Croydon. A new station serving all three companies was provided. It was known as Clapham Junction.

The L.C.D.R.'s new main line was extended from Herne Hill to a junction with the Farnborough extension short of Beckenham on 1st July. This shortened their Victoria – Dover distance by another 3 miles, making it even shorter in comparison with the S.E.R. route, and effectively reduced the status of the Bromley Junction – Beckenham line – the Farnborough Extension – which never did reach Farnborough (Kent).

A link up between the Mid Kent Railway and the Caterham branch, providing a London-Caterham route avoiding the L.B. & S.C.R. altogether was under consideration, but it got no further.

An independent company opened a line from London Bridge to Charing Cross on 11th January 1864, providing Croydon with another London terminus across the Thames. It was soon taken over by the S.E.R. who also absorbed the Mid Kent Railway later in the year, extending it from New Beckenham (just short of Beckenham) to a terminus at Croydon (Addiscombe Road), with a view to extending it to Brighton in due course. This gave Croydon another route to London. Beckenham was suffixed 'Junction', at this time.

The ownership of the Wimbledon – West Croydon line was established on 29th July 1864, that within the Borough was L.B. & S.C.R. property.

On 21st December 1864 the L.C.D.R.'s City line from Herne Hill crossed the Thames to reach a terminus at Ludgate Hill. Whilst this line was to feature as a route serving Croydon, in later years it could not be reached at this time.

A station was provided at Selhurst on the new Croydon – Victoria line on 1st May 1865 and on the 22nd of that month a branch line was opened between Sutton on the West Croydon – Epsom line and Epsom Downs, providing Croydon passengers with closer access to the famous racecourse than did the Epsom station. On the same day a spur was opened linking the West Croydon lines with the new main lines at Selhurst, the junction on the former lines being known as St. James Junction.

The S.E.R. had for years been endeavouring to obtain a more direct route to Dover than that from London Bridge via East Croydon and Redhill Junction, particularly as the L.C.D.R. had reduced their distance. They made a start on 1st July by opening the first stage – from a junction with the Lewisham line (where St. Johns station now is) to Chislehurst.

Just outside the Borough boundary at Crystal Palace a new route opened on 1st August. This was the Crystal Palace and South London Junction Railway. From a higher level terminus at Crystal Palace this line ran via Nunhead to near Brixton where it linked up with the L.C.D.R. lines into Victoria and Ludgate Hill.

The L.B. & S.C.R. line was extended beyond New Croydon to a terminus at South Croydon on 1st September.

Another line began construction during 1865. This was the Surrey and Sussex Junction Railway whose intended route was from a junction with the Brighton main line at South Croydon to link up with the lines under construction or proposed between Tunbridge Wells and East Grinstead, Brighton and Eastbourne to the south of Ashurst.

It was supported by the L.B. & S.C.R. which aggravated the S.E.R. for not only was part of it contrary to the 1848 agreement,

but also another agreement made between the two companies in 1864 concerning Tunbridge Wells and Eastbourne traffic was considered to have been breached. The L.B. & S.C.R. informed the S.E.R. that they considered it to be simply a linking up of L.B. & S.C.R. lines, but the S.E.R. saw it as a scheme to obtain more than their fair share of Tunbridge Wells and Eastbourne traffic.

The S.E.R. responded by proposing a line which would have given them their much desired access to Brighton. This would have taken a route from near Beckenham Junction via Hayes, Tatsfield, East Grinstead, Sheffield Park and Rottingdean. It was similar to a proposal they had put forward in 1863. Nothing was to become of either.

Another link by tunnel, from the L.C.D.R. station at Ludgate Hill via Farringdon Street to the Great Northern and the Midland Railways, was provided from 1st January 1866. It was still not, however, possible to reach it from Croydon at this stage.

The S.E.R. opened another terminus in London, this time not only across the Thames but right in the City, at Cannon Street, on 1st September 1866. This could be reached from East or West Croydon or Croydon (Addiscombe Road) via London Bridge.

During 1866 the L.C.D.R. went bankrupt and set about re-organising itself.

The approach to Victoria from Clapham Junction up to this time was still via the original Pimlico route, running parallel to, and on the east side of the Waterloo lines before descending to make a junction with a leg of the West London Extension Railway before curving left to pass under the L.B. & S.C.R. South London line from London Bridge via Peckham Rye, the S.E.R. new main line, the Waterloo lines and the S.E.R. new main line again before climbing back up to Grosvenor Bridge. A new L.B. & S.C.R. main line, running at a higher level, was provided from 1st December 1867. This branched off to the right of the former route about ½ mile on the Victoria side of Clapham Junction, the junction being called Pouparts. It passed over the leg of the West London Extension Railway then climbed and turned left to pass over the junction of that railway and the original route, then the Waterloo lines, before connecting with the South London line at York Road (now Battersea Park) and then the original route. This is still the main line today, the original route losing much of its importance so far as passenger traffic was concerned, although Stewarts Lane Depot and some goods yards were served by it. It still remains today and can be used as a passenger line should the need arise.

A short branch line from New Croydon to a small new terminus called Central Croydon was opened by the L.B. & S.C.R. on 1st January 1868. The terminus, which had two platforms and two centre lines, was situated in the area now occupied by the Croydon Town Hall, the line running approximately through what are now the sunken gardens on the south side of Katherine Street, under Park Lane and through the underground car park between the Ashcroft Theatre and College of Art to connect up with the South Croydon line just south of New Croydon station.

The S.E.R.'s new main line to Dover was extended in stages during that year – from Chislehurst to Sevenoaks on 3rd March, from Sevenoaks to Tonbridge for freight only on the same day, for local passenger services on 1st May, and for expresses on 1st June. This completed the link up with the original route via East Croydon and Redhill Junction, which became only a secondary main line henceforth, over 12 miles having been cut off the distance from London Bridge to Tonbridge, thus making the S.E.R. and L.C.D.R. more equal in distance from Dover.

On 1st October 1868 the L.B. & S.C.R. opened a new line between Peckham Rye (making a junction with the South London line, and consequently linking it with London Bridge) and Sutton on the West Croydon – Epsom line. It passed under the L.B. & S.C.R. Crystal Palace line west of Tulse Hill and

Central Croydon
station.
Croydon Libraries

consideration was given to providing a spur towards Crystal Palace at this point, also a spur towards Croydon where it passed over the Victoria – Brighton main line north of Streatham Common (actually renamed Greyhound Lane a month earlier until reverting from 1st January 1870) but neither was provided at this stage. Connections between Sutton and Victoria were, however, provided at the latter place. Immediately west thereof another line branched off to Wimbledon. Junctions were made with the Wimbledon – West Croydon line on either side of a new station at Mitcham Junction.

The East London Railway, often known as the East London Line (ELL), opened on 7th December 1869 from Wapping to New Cross (L.B. & S.C.R.) where they had their own station on the east side. By changing trains there Croydon passengers could now reach the East End of London.

Work on the Surrey and Sussex Junction Railway ceased during 1869: there had been wrangling over land deals, arguments with the S.E.R. and a riot over the importation of Belgian navvies. The Duke of Richmond was appointed to arbitrate and he transferred ownership to the L.B. & S.C.R. who, being financially over-extended at the time, paid a £32,250 penalty rather than complete building the line.

The L.C.D.R. proposed to extend their line beyond their terminus at Crystal Palace, providing junctions with the L.B. & S.C.R.'s Crystal Palace line east of Lower Norwood (now West Norwood) station, then running southwards to cross the Victoria-Brighton main line west of Thornton Heath before bearing left to join the Wimbledon-West Croydon line and enter West Croydon along that line. A spur would have been provided to the main line at Thornton Heath to allow access to East Croydon, with running powers over the L.B. & S.C.R. through to Stoats Nest from where a new line would branch off along the Chipstead Valley. This would continue on to Banstead where it would join

the Epsom Downs branch with a triangular junction, thus allowing through running to Epsom Downs or Sutton. A surprisingly brave proposal from a bankrupt company. None of it materialised.

At the start of the 1870s Britain was beginning to recover from a severe financial recession. This having coincided with the second half of a decade of considerable investment on expansion of route and other improvements, notably in signalling methods, had proved disastrous for the railways south of the Thames. The L.C.D.R. had been bankrupt and the other companies were nearing that condition. The Franco-Prussian War of 1870 brought a wave of prosperity to Britain which proved to be a saving grace. However, the railway companies were in no mood to consider large scale investment and contented themselves with minor improvements and alterations. As a result this decade was the least active of the Victorian era.

The spur line between Tulse Hill and the Crystal Palace line near Lower Norwood station opened on 1st November 1870. This spur, and another opened the previous year between Tulse Hill and the L.C.D.R. main line at Herne Hill, made it possible for through running between Croydon and Ludgate Hill and the routes via Farringdon Street to be achieved.

The 1871 census showed the population of Croydon to be 55,652, but despite this increase and its convenient position the Central Croydon station had not attracted sufficient custom and it was closed on 1st December.

Woodside station on the Mid Kent line to Croydon (Addiscombe Road) had opened during 1871, being partly provided to serve Stroud Green racecourse.

On 2nd March 1874 another London terminus was opened by the L.C.D.R. This was Holborn Viaduct, served by a short extension from Ludgate Hill, and consequently available for through running to and from Croydon.

During 1874 a South Caterham Railway was proposed to link Caterham Junction and Caterham-on-the-Hill. It would have deviated eastwards from the Brighton line about ½ mile south of Caterham Junction to take a route approximately to that now taken by Old Lodge Lane and Caterham Drive, skirting the village of Coulsdon (now Old Coulsdon), and on to a terminus at Money Pit (now Money Road).

During 1875 the aforementioned proposed railway from Beckenham Junction to Brighton was again revived as an independent company. It was not progressed.

On 10th April 1876 the East London Railway was extended from Wapping to Shoreditch with a connection onward to Liverpool Street on the Great Eastern Railway. By this time the East London Railway had been connected to the main lines at both New Cross stations so it was possible to run direct from East or West Croydon or Croydon (Addiscombe Road) to yet another London terminus!

A new station was opened in January 1878, at Norbury on the Victoria – Brighton main line and on 17th June an Act of Parliament was granted authorising the building of a Croydon, Oxted and East Grinstead Railway and work soon commenced.

Problems in dealing with the increasing traffic at Beckenham Junction caused the L.C.D.R. to open a spur line prior to 1879 between their main line and the former Farnborough extension to permit trains from Victoria via Herne Hill to be diverted into Crystal Palace to turn round there instead of at Beckenham Junction.

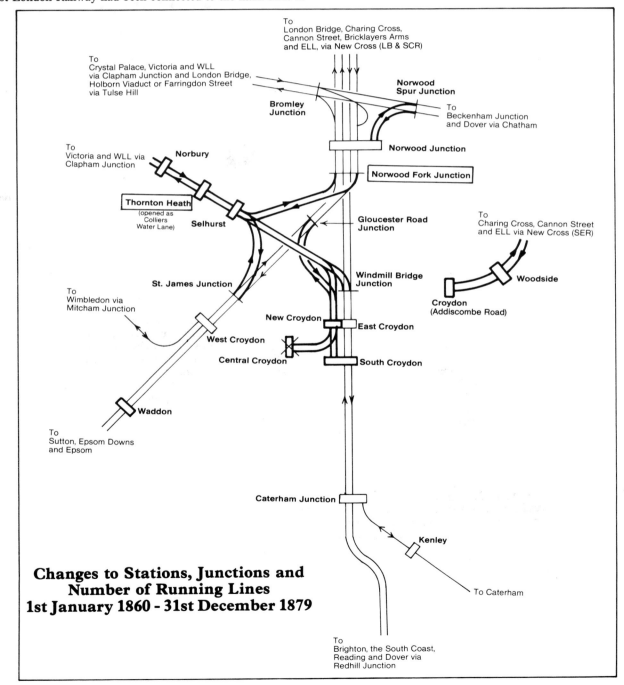

Changes to Stations, Junctions and Number of Running Lines 1st January 1860 - 31st December 1879

1st January 1880 - 31st December 1899

Notwithstanding progress on the Croydon, Oxted and East Grinstead Railway, during 1881 the Oxted & Groombridge Railway, who were promoting a line between those places, also sought powers to extend to Croydon, join the Brighton line, run through East Croydon and then branch off to Beckenham. Parliament threw it out, the L.B. & S.C.R. objecting on the grounds that there was insufficient accommodation at East Croydon for what was already required.

The population of Croydon had now reached 78,953, whilst Coulsdon could boast 2,539.

In 1882 the railway from Caterham Junction to Caterham-on-the-Hill was resurrected, this time under the title of the Coulsdon and Upper Caterham Railway. It was to take a similar route as before but was to continue a little further to Willey Heath.

An alternative, known as the Upper Caterham Railway, was also proposed. This would have left the Brighton line about a mile further south (near todays Coulsdon South station) to run along the eastern edge of Farthing Down, through Happy Valley and to the east of Chaldon village to terminate close to the Willey Heath site. Both routes passed through sparsely inhabited terrain and were soon abandoned. It is believed that a temporary light railway had followed part of the latter route during the 1870s in connection with the construction of Caterham Guards Barracks.

A few tradesmen of Croydon High Street formed themselves into a syndicate during the Spring of 1882, engaging Mr. Floyd, the L.C.D.R. engineer, to prepare surveys for a 'Croydon & London Direct Railway'. Their aim was for a direct line taking Croydon passengers 'across the water' into the City of London, which, in the opposite direction, would attract customers to their shops. They expressed dissatisfaction with existing services run by the L.B. & S.C.R. to Victoria and the S.E.R. to Charing Cross and Cannon Street, all 'across the water' – the latter being also in the City.

In the meantime, just outside the Borough, a branch from the Mid Kent line at Elmers End serving Eden Park, West Wickham and Hayes opened on 29th May. At this time the area was rural and the new branch was looked upon as a means for Londoners to spend a day in the country rather than for commuting in the opposite direction. The Mid Kent line generally was not heavily built up. Most stations had a few terraced houses nearby, New Beckenham being an exception in that it served an area with bigger houses.

Mr. Floyd's surveys for a route from Crown Hill, Croydon via Thornton Heath to join the L.C.D.R. main line either at Herne Hill or Dulwich, using their City Line onwards, were almost ready when, at the end of the year the Oxted & Groombridge produced almost identical plans, except that there was no station in the centre of Croydon, but one in the Old Town instead. Their line also continued southwards wide of South Croydon, across the Brighton line, thence to Oxted.

The syndicate accused them of stealing their plans for the part north of Croydon, also objecting to the fact that there was to be no station in the centre of the town. Agreement could not be reached and the syndicate decided to have nothing more to do with the Oxted & Groombridge, whereupon the latter attempted to obtain Parliamentary Powers for their proposal. They were again unsuccessful, and the syndicate instructed Mr. Floyd to complete his plans. On 3rd October 1883 these were presented at a meeting in the small Public Hall, Croydon. The route was from a terminus to be known as Croydon Central (not to be confused with Central Croydon) near the theatre close to Crown Hill, on the east side of Church Street, to a junction with the L.C.D.R. at Dulwich, from whence trains could run to and from the L.C.D.R.

Middle Row in Croydon c. 1890. Most of the houses are offering 'good lodgings for travellers'. Middle Row was considered as a possible site for the Croydon terminus of the Croydon and London District Railway.
Pamlin Prints

station at Victoria or via the City line to their 'new station forming in Queen Victoria Street' (St. Pauls, now Blackfriars) where access would be available to the Midland and Great Northern Railway via Farringdon Street. Middle Row had been considered as the Croydon terminus but this would have meant crossing Church Street and Surrey Street at a very high level, so it was discounted. The first two intermediate stations would be at Mitcham Road and Thornton Heath Pond, both in the Borough.

The meeting agreed to proceed with the line as presented, but this scheme, like so many others, never got very far and the railway was never built. Neither was the Brighton Direct Railway launched the same year. This was to run from Kensington via the WLL, Wimbledon and Morden to Sutton where it would link up with another route from Blackfriars which would also have used the L.C.D.R. route to Dulwich and then bear off, passing to the west of Crystal Palace and over the Brighton main line in the Norbury/Thornton Heath area. From Sutton it would have stayed to the west of the existing route.

The former Surrey and Sussex Junction Railway's route was largely used for the Croydon, Oxted and East Grinstead Railway, built by the L.B. & S.C.R. but run as a joint venture with the S.E.R., the latter seeing it as yet another possible way of gaining access to Brighton and also as another route from London Bridge to Tonbridge, a spur being included to connect the new line with the Redhill Junction-Tonbridge line, permitting

Purley station c.1890 before quadrupling. The platforms depicted are the present day numbers 3, 4 and 5 from left to right. *Pamlin Prints*

direct running between Oxted and Tonbridge, at Crowhurst, 3 miles south of Oxted. The line from Crowhurst Junction onward to East Grinstead passed under the Redhill Junction - Tonbridge line and was solely L.B. & S.C.R. property. Connection was made with the L.B. & S.C.R. Brighton main line at South Croydon.

The only station on the new line within the Borough was at Sanderstead, which had a population of about 200. Just outside the Borough boundary there was a station at Upper Warlingham. (A suffix 'and Whyteleafe' was added from 1st January 1894 to 1st January 1900.) The line was opened on 10th March 1884, although the Crowhurst Spur, which provided a diversionary route to Dover in the event of blockages on the S.E.R. main line via Sevenoaks and/or the original route via Redhill Junction, was not available to passenger trains until 1st August.

The joint L.B. & S.C.R./S.E.R. extended their territory a little further when, on 10th August 1885, they opened the Woodside and South Croydon Railway. This connected the Mid Kent line at Woodside, where a 'down' bay platform was provided, with the Croydon, Oxted and East Grinstead line about ½ mile south of South Croydon, where a new station – Selsdon Road (later Selsdon) was provided with platforms on both lines. There was one intermediate station – Coombe Lane (later Coombe Road). Once again the S.E.R. gained a diversionary route to Dover – via the Mid Kent line, Oxted and Crowhurst Junction, and hopefully, another means of reaching Brighton.

On 1st January 1886 a spur line (first considered in 1868 when the Peckham Rye – Sutton line opened) was opened between that line and the Victoria – Brighton main line at Streatham Common, enabling trains from the Thornton Heath route to run to and from Tulse Hill and beyond.

St. Pauls (now Blackfriars) station, just to the north of the Thames on the L.C.D.R. City line, opened on 10th May 1886,

providing another London terminus which could be reached from Croydon, and Central Croydon was re-opened on 1st June to give it a second chance.

Also during that year the East London Railway's separate station at New Cross (L.B. & S.C.R.) was closed, their trains being diverted into the main station.

Caterham Junction was renamed Purley on 1st October 1888, and exactly a year later a new station was provided on the S.E.R. portion of the Brighton line at Coulsdon (now Coulsdon South).

The second chance given to Central Croydon station did not prove to be successful and it was finally closed on 1st September 1890, although the tracks to the east of Park Lane

The present town hall and sunken gardens now covering the former station site and trackbed of the Central Croydon branch. *Author*

London Road, Croydon c. 1890. The horse-drawn tramlines can just be seen in the road.   *Pamlin Prints*

were retained, being converted to an Engineers Department Depot, known as Fairfield Yard. The remainder was sold to Croydon Corporation, the Town Hall being built on part of it. The sunken gardens beside Katherine Street are situated on the former trackbed.

Croydon's population had reached 102,795 in 1891. A spectacular increase in population in the inner suburbs was beginning, some places were to treble in the next 20 years. This was largely attributable to the success of the railways which encouraged what was referred to as 'country living'.

There had been further proposals for a railway to serve the Chipstead Valley. An extension of the Epsom Downs line from Banstead to Tadworth and a line from Purley to link up with it to make a circular route, actually received their Acts of Parliament in 1892 and 1893 respectively, but the first was never to be built. One of the biggest problems would have been the considerable variation in levels between the stations at either end. A rise of 240ft. in just under 3 miles would have required a gradient of 1 in 50 throughout.

During 1894/5 East Croydon was rebuilt with three island platforms.

The spur between the Penage and Crystal Palace lines near Beckenham Junction had been little used and was severed by 1895.

Coulsdon station was renamed Coulsdon & Cane Hill from March 1896.

During that year an Act of Parliament was obtained to permit the West Croydon-Wimbledon line to be doubled, but it was not acted upon.

A fifth line was opened between East Croydon and South Croydon during 1896, probably on 28th July. It was on the east side and was called the 'down' relief line. A similar line on the east side from Norwood Junction to link up with it at East Croydon opened on 4th July 1897. This was also known as the 'down' relief line south of Windmill Bridge Junction, but north thereof it was only a Goods line.

Cosmo Bonsor, an M.P. and Director of the Bank of England, resided in Kingswood Warren and naturally supported the idea of a railway to serve the Chipstead Valley. Having joined the S.E.R. board in 1894 and become its Deputy Chairman by 1897, he was no doubt able to use his influence there, as it was the S.E.R. which supported the Chipstead Valley Railway Company and had taken it over by the time the line opened.

Prior to the opening, the S.E.R. realised that if its trains were to be able to run to and from London they would have to alter the layout at the north end of Purley to permit, and this would lead to congestion on the already busy double line between that station and South Croydon. They gave thought to providing their own station at Purley and their own line from it, with a 580

An 'up' Royal Train approaching South Croydon on 17th July 1899. Note the new local lines under construction on the right.

Railway Magazine

yard long tunnel under the Downs, to join the Oxted line at Sanderstead.

The L.B. & S.C.R. in the meantime put forward a proposal to provide their own additional two lines (see later) whereupon the S.E.R. simply provided a normal junction at the north end of Purley on 31st October 1897.

The Chipstead Valley line made a junction with the Caterham line at the south end of Purley station and opened as far as Kingswood & Burgh Heath (now Kingswood), with one intermediate station – Chipstead and Banstead Downs (now Chipstead) – just outside the Borough on 2nd November. It was a single line at first, as was the Caterham line.

On 1st November 1898 the L.C.D.R. Crystal Palace station became Crystal Palace (High Level) & Upper Norwood.

The S.E.R. and L.C.D.R. formed a working union, the South Eastern & Chatham Railway (S.E.C.R.), from 1st January 1899. During that year they doubled the Caterham line.

On 5th November the L.B. & S.C.R. overcame the problem of the S.E.C.R. delaying their trains on the Redhill line by extending their own lines from the former terminus at South Croydon to Earlswood (just beyond Redhill Junction), completely avoiding the S.E.C.R. section from Stoats Nest to Redhill Junction. A new station was provided at Purley Oaks on the new lines only, also additional platforms at Purley. Stoats Nest Goods station was abolished and a new Stoats Nest passenger terminus and depot (later Coulsdon North) leading off the new lines was opened. Platforms were also provided on the new lines opposite the terminus and a junction was made with the original lines, thus giving the L.B. & S.C.R. the use of four lines throughout, two shared with the S.E.C.R. and two of their own.

The new line which, south of Stoats Nest, soon acquired the name 'Quarry line' opened for a short period only for freight traffic. This was due to some of the signal boxes not having been commissioned in time. Upon completion of the signalling the majority of the L.B. & S.C.R. trains were routed by the new line.

It contained some interesting engineering features. Leaving Stoats Nest it first passed over the London – Brighton road by a girder bridge at the far end of which it immediately plunged into a 'tunnel' (actually a covered cutting – the Cane Hill Asylum Authorities insisting on an earth covered roof being placed over the cutting through their grounds to avoid the trains aggravating the inmates). In official terms it was called a covered way. At the further end the London – Brighton road was again immediately crossed by another girder bridge. This combination of under-bridges and 'tunnel' butting on to one another is unusual in this country. It is, however, common in mountainous areas such as the Alps, where ravines are crossed in this manner between tunnels in adjacent mountainsides. Beyond the second girder bridge the Quarry line ran on the higher shelf of a two level cutting, the S.E.C.R. line running at the lower level. At the present Borough boundary near the village of Hooley the Quarry line passed over the S.E.C.R. line by another iron girder bridge to run on the east side of it. Other interesting features onward included duplicating the chalk cuttings and Merstham tunnel, parallel with the S.E.C.R. line but at a higher level, and another tunnel passing under Redstone Hill and the Redhill Junction – Tonbridge line before rejoining the original Brighton line just before Earlswood.

The practicability of electric railway traction had been established by this time and a scheme for a new electrified line from London to Brighton was proposed. It did not materialise though.

Croydon (Addiscombe Road) station was rebuilt and remodelled in 1899. When completed it had a new and impressive frontage and three platforms.

Most of Britain's railways had by now acquired affectionate nicknames, usually by the humorous misuse of their initials or by a form of rhyming slang, and the railways within the Borough were no exception. Using such parlance the position as the century closed could be summed up as 'The Land 'em, Smash' em and over' (a wicked title for one of the most safety conscious railways in the country) had become part of the 'Slow, Easy and Comfortable', now the only rival to the 'Longtime Blighted and Slow Coach Railway' for the Borough's traffic!

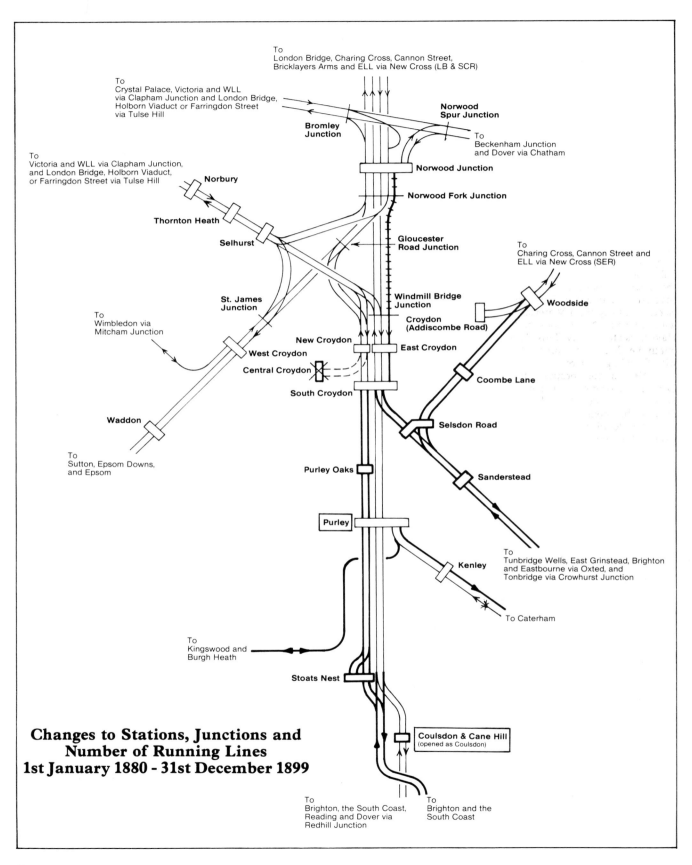

To
London Bridge, Charing Cross, Cannon Street,
Bricklayers Arms and ELL via New Cross (LB & SCR)

To
Crystal Palace, Victoria and WLL
via Clapham Junction and London Bridge,
Holborn Viaduct or Farringdon Street
via Tulse Hill

Norwood
Spur Junction

Bromley
Junction

To
Beckenham Junction
and Dover via Chatham

Norwood Junction

To
Victoria and WLL via Clapham Junction,
and London Bridge, Holborn Viaduct,
or Farringdon Street via Tulse Hill

Norbury

Norwood Fork Junction

Thornton Heath

Gloucester
Road Junction

Selhurst

To
Charing Cross, Cannon Street and
ELL via New Cross (SER)

St. James
Junction

Windmill Bridge
Junction

Woodside

Croydon
(Addiscombe Road)

To
Wimbledon via
Mitcham Junction

New Croydon

East Croydon

West Croydon

Coombe Lane

Central Croydon

South Croydon

Waddon

Selsdon Road

To
Sutton, Epsom Downs,
and Epsom

Sanderstead

Purley Oaks

Purley

To
Tunbridge Wells, East Grinstead, Brighton
and Eastbourne via Oxted, and
Tonbridge via Crowhurst Junction

Kenley

To Caterham

To
Kingswood and
Burgh Heath

Stoats Nest

**Changes to Stations, Junctions and
Number of Running Lines
1st January 1880 - 31st December 1899**

Coulsdon & Cane Hill
(opened as Coulsdon)

To
Brighton, the South Coast,
Reading and Dover via
Redhill Junction

To
Brighton and the
South Coast

1st January 1900 - 31st December 1919

As the new century began the separation of workplace and residence had become commonplace for the middle classes and some working class families, and the railway network had almost reached its present day extent routewise. So far as the Borough was concerned it had, although there were many other changes still to come. On 1st January 1900 a new station was provided on the Caterham line at Whyteleafe, only a matter of yards outside the Borough and from 1st July the Chipstead Valley line was extended to Tadworth & Walton-on-the-Hill and was converted to double line throughout. It was further extended to Tattenham Corner on 4th October 1901. This, yet again, provided a nearer station to Epsom Racecourse, this one only a matter of yards away.

A novel proposal was put forward in September 1901 – The London & Brighton Electric Railway Company's high speed system from a terminus in Lupus Street, Pimlico, with no intermediate stations on its direct line, but with places such as Croydon being served by short branch lines – their trains following the Brighton ones closely. By thus virtually assuring the Brighton trains a clear run, the 48 miles was aimed to be covered in 32 minutes! This was later altered to a conventional electric railway from Waterloo to Brighton taking 40 minutes with intermediate stations at Croydon, Redhill, Horley and Haywards Heath only. This Company's application was thrown out in the House of Commons because of their failure to comply with Standing Orders.

Yet another proposal for an electric railway between London and Brighton came in 1902. It's London terminus was to have been in the Aldwych. A monorail system was also put forward, but none of the proposals materialised.

The double line between Streatham Junction and Windmill Bridge Junction was quadrupled from 6th July 1903, the additional two 'local' lines being laid on the east side of the main lines as far as Selhurst whence they dived under them to run on the west side. To permit the new 'local' lines to run to and from West Croydon as well as East Croydon, the London Bridge – West Croydon line was re-aligned, the resultant junctions taking over the title of Gloucester Road Junction - the former one having disappeared, the 'local' lines between Windmill Bridge Junction and Norwood Fork Junction now running independently from the West Croydon line, although trains could run via Gloucester Road Junction if required.

The services between West Croydon and Victoria, being predominantly of a local nature would, from now onwards, usually run via the new 'local' lines. In view of this the connections between St. James Junction and the Victoria main lines were designated as the 'Emergency Spur'.

The London Bridge/Victoria – Brighton line was now quadrupled throughout the Borough, assuming the Redhill and Quarry lines as four tracks.

Smitham station, on the Tattenham Corner line, a matter of yards as the crow flies from Stoats Nest station was opened on 1st January 1904, whilst new halts were provided at Bandon (a short distance outside the Borough between Waddon and Wallington) on 11th June 1906 and both Bingham Road (between Woodside and Coombe Lane) and Spencer Road (between Coombe Lane and Selsdon Road) on 1st September of the same year. These were among several new stations and halts being provided in the suburban area to compete with the convenience of the electric trams and to a lesser degree the early omnibuses. Their effect on railway receipts had been considerable, particularly for short distance journeys.

The 'down' goods line from the south end of Norwood Junction station to Windmill Bridge Junction was upgraded to a

Thornton Heath station, just after the quadrupling.   *Lens of Sutton*

Selhurst station before the quadrupling, looking towards Croydon. Note the separate 'up' signals ie. one ex-Norwood Fork and the other (clear) ex-East or West Croydon, located after the junction!
R.C. Riley Collection

Looking towards Victoria from Selhurst station platform about the same period.   *Pamlin Prints*

Norbury station during the quadrupling of the line, 5th December 1901.
R.C. Riley Collection

passenger line from 3rd January 1908, thus completing a 'down' relief line throughout from Norwood Junction to South Croydon.

A minor renaming took place on 1st October, Woodside being lengthened to Woodside & South Norwood.

East Croydon and New Croydon became regarded as one station in name alone from 1st January 1909. The former was now referred to as the 'Main' station and the latter as the 'Local' station, the S.E.R. still being unable to use it.

For some years electric trains had been prophesied as the real answer to tram and bus competition. Some inner suburban stations had suffered most, many having lost more than half of their passengers. The South London line (London Bridge to Victoria via Peckham Rye) for example attracted 18 million passengers in 1902 but only 4 million in 1908. It is not surprising that this line was selected as the first to be electrified. The L.B. & S.C.R. chose a 6,600 volts A.C. overhead wire system. Services commenced on 1st December 1909 under the legend of 'Elevated Electric'. It was an immediate success, the drop in passenger receipts being recovered in little over a year, with the increase continuing.

Norwood Junction was renamed Norwood Junction & South Norwood on 1st October 1910, and a halt was provided at Reedham (between Purley and Smitham) on the Tattenham Corner line on 1st March 1911.

Croydon's population had now reached 170,165.

No doubt encouraged by the successful introduction of electric traction on the South London line, the L.B. & S.C.R. went ahead with plans to extend it, the next section being Battersea Park (linking with the South London line) via Crystal Palace to Selhurst Depot (provided in conjunction). This was worked electrically from 12th May 1911 in time for the opening of the Festival of Empire at Crystal Palace by King George V that day.

On 1st June 1911 Stoats Nest was renamed Coulsdon & Smitham Downs. It is a popular belief that this was done to eliminate memories of the serious train disaster there on 29th January 1910 (see Chapter Four). This may have hastened the renaming but the author's opinion is that the L.B. & S.C.R. wished to include the growing villages of Coulsdon and Smitham

in their timetables. Any stranger looking up timetables for a train to either place would have found them only in the S.E.C.R. services.

In 1913 the L.B. & S.C.R. decided to electrify all their remaining suburban routes out to Coulsdon & Smitham Downs and Cheam (just beyond Sutton) with a few exceptions, one of which was the West Croydon – Wimbledon line.

Bandon Halt had not been a success and it was closed on 7th June 1914.

By this time urban building had extended to cover the majority of the area within the triangle formed by the Victoria and London Bridge to Croydon main lines. The middle classes were moving progressively further out and as a result the inner South London suburbs were becoming predominantly working class.

A good deal of work had been carried out towards electrifying between Balham and West Croydon (via Thornton Heath) before the outbreak of the First World War but the crisis caused its completion to be held back.

By this time the 'down' relief line at Norwood Junction had been extended to start at the north end of the station, by upgrading the remainder of the 'down' goods line.

The need for wartime economies, and the failure of many of the halts to attract sufficient customers, resulted in some of them being closed, along with other lightly used stations – some permanently, others temporarily. Spencer Road Halt and Bingham Road Halt were the first casualties within the Borough, closing on 1st March 1915. Coombe Lane, Selsdon Road, Reedham Halt and Smitham following suit on 1st January 1917. On that day services were withdrawn between Crystal Palace and Beckenham Junction and over the Norwood Spur line, also at several other suburban stations outside the Borough including the Crystal Palace High Level line. Where a line was completely closed to passenger traffic the tracks were still available for other traffic.

Reedham Halt and Smitham re-opened on 1st January 1919, the Oxted line platforms only at Selsdon Road also the Crystal Palace High Level line being brought back into use on 1st March.

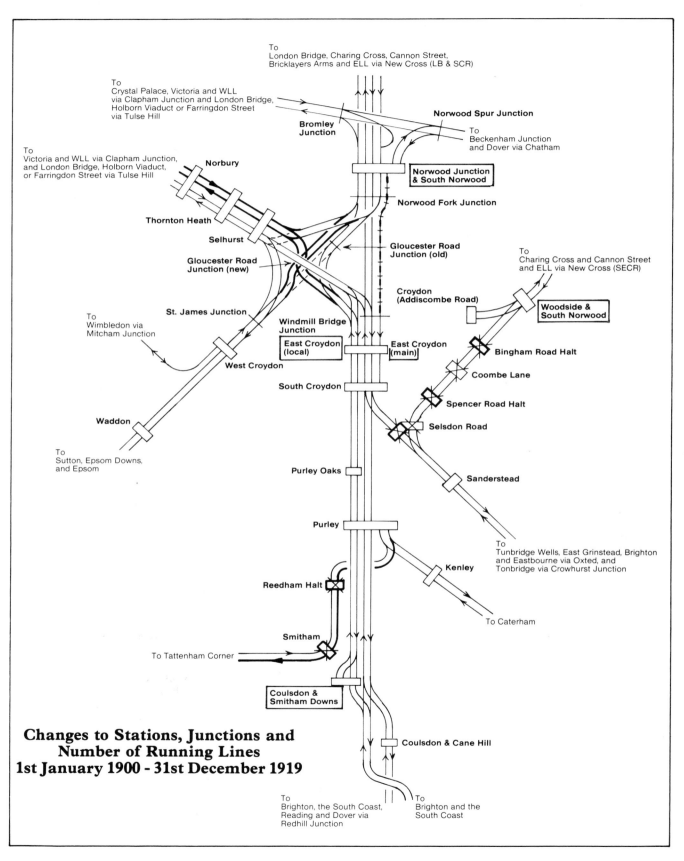

To
London Bridge, Charing Cross, Cannon Street,
Bricklayers Arms and ELL via New Cross (LB & SCR)

To Crystal Palace, Victoria and WLL
via Clapham Junction and London Bridge,
Holborn Viaduct or Farringdon Street
via Tulse Hill

Norwood Spur Junction

**Bromley
Junction**

To
Beckenham Junction
and Dover via Chatham

To
Victoria and WLL via Clapham Junction,
and London Bridge, Holborn Viaduct,
or Farringdon Street via Tulse Hill

Norbury

**Norwood Junction
& South Norwood**

Norwood Fork Junction

Thornton Heath

Selhurst

Gloucester Road
Junction (old)

Gloucester Road
Junction (new)

To
Charing Cross and Cannon Street
and ELL via New Cross (SECR)

**Croydon
(Addiscombe Road)**

St. James Junction

**Woodside &
South Norwood**

To
Wimbledon via
Mitcham Junction

Windmill Bridge
Junction

**East Croydon
(local)**

**East Croydon
(main)**

Bingham Road Halt

Coombe Lane

West Croydon

South Croydon

Spencer Road Halt

Selsdon Road

Waddon

To
Sutton, Epsom Downs,
and Epsom

Purley Oaks

Sanderstead

Purley

To
Tunbridge Wells, East Grinstead, Brighton
and Eastbourne via Oxted, and
Tonbridge via Crowhurst Junction

Kenley

Reedham Halt

To Caterham

Smitham

To Tattenham Corner

**Coulsdon &
Smitham Downs**

Changes to Stations, Junctions and
Number of Running Lines
1st January 1900 - 31st December 1919

Coulsdon & Cane Hill

To
Brighton, the South Coast,
Reading and Dover via
Redhill Junction

To
Brighton and the
South Coast

1st January 1920 - 31st December 1939

By 1921 Croydon's population was 190,684 and Coulsdon's 5,823.

Work on the L.B. & S.C.R. 6,600 volts A.C. overhead electrification was resumed in 1922. The S.E.C.R. were, in the meantime, proposing electrification of their lines, including from Croydon to Tadworth, Caterham, and Tonbridge via both Redhill Junction and Oxted, and the Mid Kent lines, with 1,500 volts D.C. on the conductor rail system. The need for electrification was becoming greater, suburban traffic having increased by 26% over a period of ten years.

The L.B. & S.C.R., S.E.C.R. and L.S.W.R. became the Southern Railway (S.R.) in the grouping of railways as from 1st January 1923. Right up to that time competitive features had continued – e.g. an instruction that should a S.E.C.R. locomotive require the assistance of an L.B. & S.C.R. locomotive anywhere between London Bridge and Purley the station master at Purley must arrange for a fresh S.E.C.R. locomotive to be provided there.

The overhead electrification was eventually opened from Balham and Norwood Junction to Coulsdon North and Sutton (via West Croydon) on 1st April 1925.

On the same day Croydon (Addiscombe Road) station was reduced in name to Croydon (Addiscombe).

Just outside the Borough the Crystal Palace High Level branch was publicly electrified on the third rail system from 12th July, although it had been used for trials and staff training before that date.

In November a new railway, the Southern Heights Railway, applied for a Light Railway Order. It proposed a railway 15¾ miles long which would connect the Dover main line 180 yards south of Orpington station and the Oxted line ½ mile south of Sanderstead station, both junctions facing London and consisting of a single line with eight intermediate stations – Green Street Green, Downe & Keston, Cudham & Biggin Hill, Westerham Hill, Tatsfield, Chelsham, Hamsey Green and Mitchley Wood, with passing loops at Westerham Hill, Tatsfield and Hamsey

A.C. overhead (left) and D.C. conductor rail suburban trains side by side in Coulsdon North carriage sidings.   *Croydon Libraries*

In their first year the S.R. sold 198,000,000 ordinary tickets and 170,000 season tickets. On Derby Day 37,000 passengers were conveyed to the races and 40,000 returned.

The grouping resulted in the renaming of several stations, particularly at places formerly served by more than one company – New Cross (L.B. & S.C.R.) for example becoming New Cross Gate from 9th July 1923. Within the Borough Coulsdon & Smitham Downs became Coulsdon West and Coulsdon & Cane Hill became Coulsdon East on the same day. In the case of these two stations the new names lasted but three weeks – Coulsdon West and East becoming Coulsdon North and South on 1st August.

East Croydon Main and Local became finally regarded as one station proper in July 1924.

Green. There would be a 450ft difference in height between Tatsfield and Sanderstead which would have required some steep gradients.

It was the intention that the S.R. would electrify the line and work it for 75% of the receipts. It was basically a revival and extension of an earlier scheme for a light railway from Orpington to Tatsfield, known as the Orpington, Cudham & Tatsfield Light Railway, which had first been proposed in 1898 but which had lapsed.

The Hayes branch was electrified from 21st September for staff training until 28th February 1926 when public electric services using conductor rails were introduced on the Mid Kent lines to both Hayes and Addiscombe (Croydon), the latters

West Croydon station prior to rebuilding.   *Croydon Libraries*

West Croydon station during rebuilding 1932/33. The Wimbledon line bay platform is on the right.   *Lens of Sutton*

name having been reversed concurrently. On the Hayes branch, traffic was destined to increase twelve fold in the next nine years!

The population of Coulsdon and Purley had now reached 24,000.

On 9th August the S.R. management decided to standardise electrification throughout their system, the 660 volts D.C. conductor rail type being selected.

Suburban development had now reached the Oxted line, a new station being opened at Riddlesdown on 5th June 1927. An indication of the development resulting largely from the success of electrification can be gained from the fact that 7¼ million more passengers were carried by the S.R. in 1927 than in 1926.

From 25th March 1928 the lines from London Bridge to Tattenham Corner, Caterham and Crystal Palace via Sydenham were provided with electric services. At Purley Oaks platforms were provided on the main lines, and Tattenham Corner was re-opened on an every day basis.

The Epsom Downs branch had electric trains from 17th June. By now several of the overhead routes had been provided with conductor rails, and overhead electric working was gradually suspended.

The Norwood Spur was reduced to one line during 1928. This was done in an unusual way. It was not a single line for use in both directions but instead was available only for movements from Beckenham Junction to Norwood Junction, anything in the opposite direction having to run to Crystal Palace to reverse.

The combined S.R. London termini were now dealing with 102,000 passengers in the busiest peak hour.

On 3rd March 1929, electric services were introduced on the Crystal Palace – Beckenham Junction route which was re-opened to passenger traffic.

In April the Southern Heights Light Railway proposal was slightly amended to join the 'local' lines at Orpington instead of making a junction south of that station. This lengthened it to 16 miles.

Redhill Junction was shortened in title to Redhill in July.

Overhead A.C. electric trains ceased in the early hours of 22nd September, the last passenger train being 00.10 from Victoria to Coulsdon North.

By this time the middle classes employed in London were moving further out, the electric trains attracting them to reside 10 to 20 miles distant, and housing estates quickly sprang up to meet the demand.

A line outside the Borough, but playing a large part in the Borough's train services, was that from Wimbledon to Sutton completed on 5th January 1930. It was electrified from the beginning.

The first year of electric working over the Crystal Palace – Beckenham Junction line must have proved successful, a new station being opened at Birkbeck, just outside the Borough, on 2nd March.

From 25th May a single goods line was opened beside the single Passenger line between West Croydon and Waddon Marsh. From the latter place it continued to Beddington Lane but only as a siding. Industries along this stretch were rail served by connections from the new line instead of from the passenger line as hitherto, and new industries were also served as they appeared. Shunting could now be performed without interference with the passenger trains. This was in readiness for the electrification of the Wimbledon – West Croydon line. A new halt was provided at Waddon Marsh from 6th July, the day of the first, and more frequent, electric services.

In 1931 the population of Croydon had reached 233,032 and during that year East Croydon dealt with 1.3 million passengers, 20,000 of which were season ticket holders.

Norwood Spur Junction, showing the singled line to Norwood Junction in the foreground. *J.J. Smith*

Willow Walk was absorbed as part of Bricklayers Arms from 7th March 1932.

From 17th July 1932 electrification was extended from Purley to Reigate and Three Bridges. On the same day a new station was opened at Woodmansterne on the Tattenham Corner line to serve another developing area. Electrification reached Brighton on 30th December.

During 1932 the S.R. carried 208,000,000 passengers and there were 183,000 season tickets sold.

The Surrey Heights Light Railway experienced difficulty in raising capital, also the S.R. demanded proper standards which proved expensive, so the light railway gave up during 1932.

Fairfield Yard, the remaining part of the long-closed Central Croydon branch was closed during February 1933.

Consideration was given to providing a loop line off the West Croydon – Sutton line, just west of Waddon, to serve Croydon Airport, but it was rejected.

A 6% increase (4,000 passengers a week) was needed to justify the investment on the Brighton line electrification. In the first month 5% was obtained, and there was a 78% increase over the Easter period with a 'high' of 127% on Easter Monday when 129,000 passengers went to Brighton. Between 17.00 and 22.00 on that day 102 trains conveyed 75,000 passengers on their homeward journey. During the whole of 1933 the total passenger traffic on the newly electrified lines south of Coulsdon went up by a third!

West Croydon station had been rebuilt during 1932 and 1933. This had removed the remains of the old London & Croydon Railway terminus – the overall roof over the buffer stops end of what is now No. 1 platform, also the station entrance which had hitherto been midway along the 'down' platform leading to and from Station Road, opposite where the bus station is now located.

An example of the increase in passenger traffic following electrification can be obtained from the figures at one station within the Borough – Kenley – 28,000 tickets, 600 seasons in 1928, and 68,000 tickets, and 1200 seasons in 1934.

Following the success of previous electrification, the Woodside & South Norwood – Selsdon Road line was re-opened, electrified, on 30th September 1935. Bingham Road Halt was upgraded to a station, Coombe Lane became Coombe Road station and Selsdon Road was shortened in name to Selsdon. Spencer Road Halt was not re-opened. Through trains were provided to and from Charing Cross and Cannon Street and Sanderstead where connection could be made with Oxted line trains without the need to change platforms, as would be necessary at Selsdon. Another probable reason for the extension at Sanderstead was that originally it was planned that the trains would continue via

29

Hastings excursion passing Spencer Road halt, 13th September 1931. Although the halt had been closed for 16 years it is in good condition; vandalism was not so prevalent in those days!

H.C. Casserley

the Southern Heights Light Railway back to London without reversing, had that line been built.

By 1936 the population of Coulsdon and Purley had reached 51,500 (more than doubled in 10 years). In recognition Reedham Halt was promoted to a station on 5th July.

At about this time Waddon station was rebuilt, providing a station of the most modern type.

St. Pauls station was renamed Blackfriars on 1st February 1937.

During 1938 over the entire S.R. 237,000,000 passenger journeys were made and 223,000 season tickets were sold. An average of 370,000 passengers arrived daily at the London termini, over 120,000 of them in the busiest hour. Between 1930 and 1939 there had been a 12½ million rise in the number of passengers carried by the S.R. per year. The Borough's stations could take credit for many of them.

The Second World War was declared on 3rd September 1939. Between the two wars the density of population in the inner London suburbs had remained fairly stagnant but henceforth it commenced to fall.

Charing Cross – Tadworth train at Reedham Halt, 22nd May 1926. *Pamlin Prints*

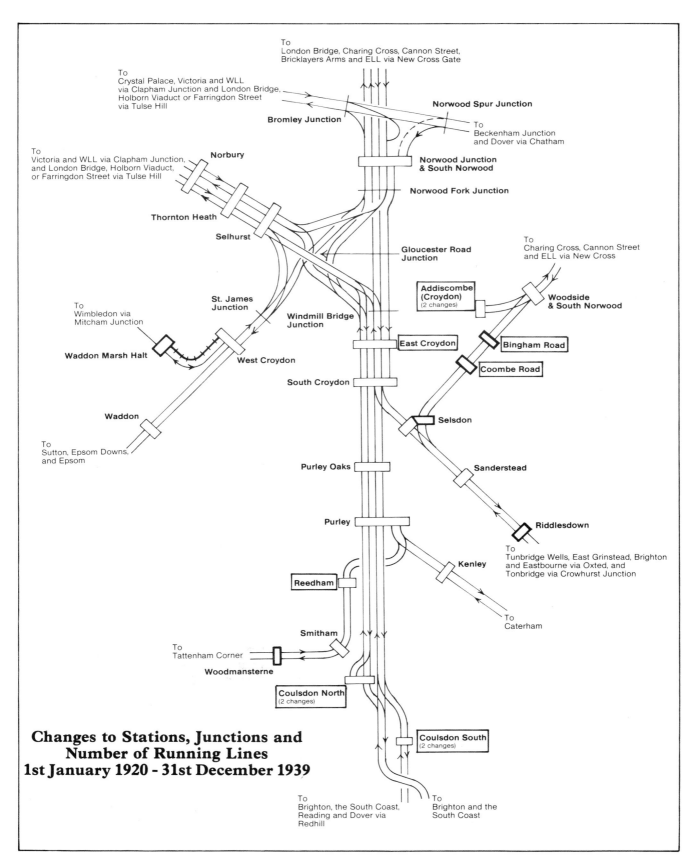

To
London Bridge, Charing Cross, Cannon Street,
Bricklayers Arms and ELL via New Cross Gate

To
Crystal Palace, Victoria and WLL
via Clapham Junction and London Bridge,
Holborn Viaduct or Farringdon Street
via Tulse Hill

Norwood Spur Junction

Bromley Junction

To
Beckenham Junction
and Dover via Chatham

To
Victoria and WLL via Clapham Junction,
and London Bridge, Holborn Viaduct,
or Farringdon Street via Tulse Hill

Norbury

Norwood Junction
& South Norwood

Thornton Heath

Norwood Fork Junction

Selhurst

Gloucester Road
Junction

To
Charing Cross, Cannon Street
and ELL via New Cross

St. James
Junction

Addiscombe
(Croydon)
(2 changes)

Woodside
& South Norwood

To
Wimbledon via
Mitcham Junction

Windmill Bridge
Junction

Waddon Marsh Halt

East Croydon

Bingham Road

West Croydon

Coombe Road

South Croydon

Waddon

Selsdon

To
Sutton, Epsom Downs,
and Epsom

Sanderstead

Purley Oaks

Purley

Riddlesdown

To
Tunbridge Wells, East Grinstead, Brighton
and Eastbourne via Oxted, and
Tonbridge via Crowhurst Junction

Kenley

Reedham

To
Caterham

Smitham

To
Tattenham Corner

Woodmansterne

Coulsdon North
(2 changes)

Coulsdon South
(2 changes)

Changes to Stations, Junctions and
Number of Running Lines
1st January 1920 - 31st December 1939

To
Brighton, the South Coast,
Reading and Dover via
Redhill

To
Brighton and the
South Coast

1st January 1940 - 31st December 1959

The Second World War caused a slight slump in the number of passenger journeys on the S.R. The figure for 1941 was down to 230 million but in 1942 it had increased again to 292 million.

Throughout the War the Croydon area had 1,206 red (imminent) air raid warnings, and the then Borough of Croydon was the most afflicted borough in the London area during the 'flying bomb' era. Coulsdon and Purley came tenth in this league. The railways suffered their share, notably at West Croydon and Norwood Yard.

The Nunhead – Crystal Palace (High Level) line was closed again on 22nd May 1944 but re-opened on 4th March 1946, a year in which passenger journeys soared to 398 million on the S.R. In November it was announced that all S.R. lines east of Portsmouth were to be electrified, but little resulted for many years.

Upon Nationalisation on 1st January 1948 all lines in the Borough became part of British Railways, Southern Region. Passenger journey figures for that Region showed a slight decrease during that year – to 374 million. The number of passengers arriving at their London termini in the busiest hour had, however, reached 141,000.

In 1951 census figures for Croydon showed a population of 249,870, and it was established that 33% of the working population of Coulsdon and Purley travelled to work in Central London.

In the same year the withdrawal of passenger services from the West Croydon – Wimbledon line was proposed. It was, however, decided that as freight traffic was still needed little savings would result as most of the track, signalling and staff would still be required.

The 'covered way' on the Quarry line at Cane Hill, Coulsdon had its top removed during 1954, turning it into a brick lined cutting. High chain link fencing was provided on either side of the cutting to deter the hospital patients and a high sided footbridge was provided to take a footpath in the hospital grounds across the cutting.

The Nunhead – Crystal Palace (High Level) line was finally closed on 20th September 1954 – the first Southern suburban electrified line to have suffered this fate.

Coincidental with the resignalling of the Brighton line north of Coulsdon in the early 1950s the main lines were retitled 'through' lines.

On 13th June 1955 Addiscombe (Croydon) station was shortened in name to Addiscombe.

During 1956 the number of passengers arriving at the Southern Region London termini in the busiest hour had risen to 171,000, and in 1957 the number of passenger journeys on that Region overall was ten million more than those of any other Region, and also exceeded the total number of passenger journeys on all Class 1 railways in the U.S.A. put together! Locally, 32,000 season tickets were sold at Purley during that year. Consequently trains were becoming seriously overcrowded and several stations had their platforms lengthened to accommodate longer trains either in connection with 10-car suburban services on the Mid Kent and Tattenham Corner/Caterham routes, or in readiness for the influx of traffic yet to come from Gatwick Airport when it re-opened as a major airport in 1958.

Bomb damage at West Croydon station, 23rd June 1944.

The brick-lined cutting (formerly the 'covered way') at Coulsdon, viewed from the footbridge.   *Author*

Above: Devastation caused by German air-raids on 9th October 1940.

Below: Wagons turned into matchwood by bomb damage, Norwood Yard, 23rd June 1944.

Right: Bomb damaged signals at West Croydon.

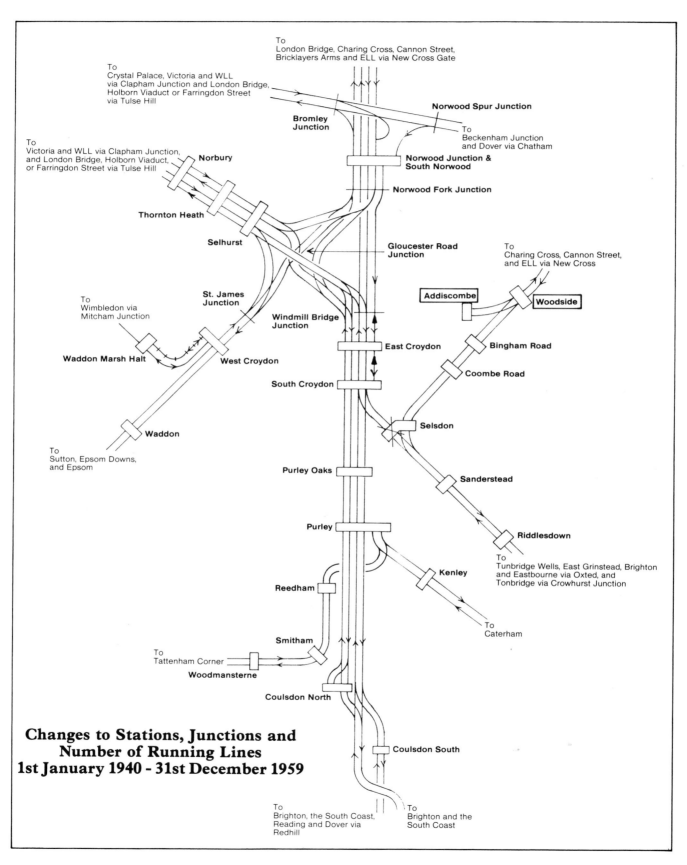

To
London Bridge, Charing Cross, Cannon Street,
Bricklayers Arms and ELL via New Cross Gate

To
Crystal Palace, Victoria and WLL
via Clapham Junction and London Bridge,
Holborn Viaduct or Farringdon Street
via Tulse Hill

Norwood Spur Junction

Bromley Junction

To
Beckenham Junction
and Dover via Chatham

To
Victoria and WLL via Clapham Junction,
and London Bridge, Holborn Viaduct,
or Farringdon Street via Tulse Hill

Norbury

**Norwood Junction &
South Norwood**

Thornton Heath

Norwood Fork Junction

Selhurst

**Gloucester Road
Junction**

To
Charing Cross, Cannon Street,
and ELL via New Cross

**St. James
Junction**

Addiscombe

Woodside

To
Wimbledon via
Mitcham Junction

**Windmill Bridge
Junction**

Bingham Road

Waddon Marsh Halt

West Croydon

East Croydon

Coombe Road

South Croydon

Waddon

Selsdon

To
Sutton, Epsom Downs,
and Epsom

Sanderstead

Purley Oaks

Purley

Riddlesdown

To
Tunbridge Wells, East Grinstead, Brighton
and Eastbourne via Oxted, and
Tonbridge via Crowhurst Junction

Kenley

Reedham

To
Caterham

Smitham

To
Tattenham Corner

Woodmansterne

Coulsdon North

Changes to Stations, Junctions and
Number of Running Lines
1st January 1940 - 31st December 1959

Coulsdon South

To
Brighton, the South Coast,
Reading and Dover via
Redhill

To
Brighton and the
South Coast

1st January 1960 - 31st December 1979

The population of Croydon was 252,501 in 1961 whilst Coulsdon's figure was 23,863. During the 1950s commuter traffic generally had increased by 4.8% and in the case of Surrey by 8.1%.

A proposal to rebuild East Croydon station under a development which was to include office accommodation was announced during that year. This would have been in keeping with the rest of the town where office blocks were springing up, completely changing the character of the centre.

During the Autumn of 1962 the iron girder bridge taking the Quarry line over the Redhill line near the Borough boundary at Hooley was replaced in concrete.

B.R. proposed the closure of the Woodside – Selsdon line on 4th March 1963 and after the customary protests and considerations it was given a three year reprieve in December which was destined to last for over 19 years!

In 1965 B.R. Southern Region passenger journeys were down to 351 million.

Through running facilities between B.R. and the East London line were severed on 1st April 1966, and on 30th October the Norwood Spur line was taken out of use, although the track remained in situ for another 6 years.

The Channel Tunnel proposals next hit the headlines. Several alternative routes had been considered and it was announced that the route was to be from a terminus in the Kensington area taking a course just to the east side of the West London line and the Brighton line to Balham, where it would enter a tunnel to emerge in the vicinity of Coombe Road, and then run to the east side of the Oxted line to Sanderstead where it would cross to the west side. It would continue on that side until it crossed the Redhill – Tonbridge line near Crowhurst Junction whereupon it would turn eastwards to run to the south of, and parallel to, that line. Much concern was expressed by residents near the proposed route who feared that the value of their properties would drop.

The term 'Halt' was discontinued as from 5th May 1969, whilst another B.R. policy was to reduce the number of stations named after two places.

In December another programme of electrification was announced. All the remaining lines on the Southern Region were to be converted. This only involved the Oxted line within the Borough, but a combination of a lack of support from local authorities, who expressed the fear that suburban development would result, spoiling their environment, and shortage of B.R. finances meant that, yet again, it came to nothing.

Passenger journeys on B.R. Southern Region had increased to 356 million in 1970.

As Coulsdon and Purley Urban District Council combined with the old Borough of Croydon to form the London Borough of Croydon, separate figures of population were not published in the 1971 census. The combined figure was 333,670 of which 32,890 used the train daily to and from their place of work.

The Cross London link via Farringdon Street was closed on 3rd May 1971.

During that year the West Croydon – Wimbledon line was again proposed for the withdrawal of passenger services and after three years of consideration it was reprieved in July 1974.

B.R. Southern Region passenger journeys had dropped to 306 million in 1975, the year in which the Channel Tunnel scheme was abandoned.

The goods line between West Croydon and Waddon Marsh was closed on 1st February 1976.

There was speculation around this time that the London Underground system might be extended to serve the 'rail starved' eastern extremities of the Borough, but this came to nothing.

Selsdon station when Oxted trains still called, showing buildings on all four platforms and connecting footbridge.   *Lens of Sutton*

Selsdon station as rationalised. Small buildings on Mid-Kent platforms only and overbridge demolished. In latter days even these buildings were taken away, leaving only a small booking hut on the 'down' Mid-Kent platform.   *Lens of Sutton*

Renewal of the bridge carrying the 'quarry line' over the Redhill line south of Coulsdon, autumn 1962.   *Author*

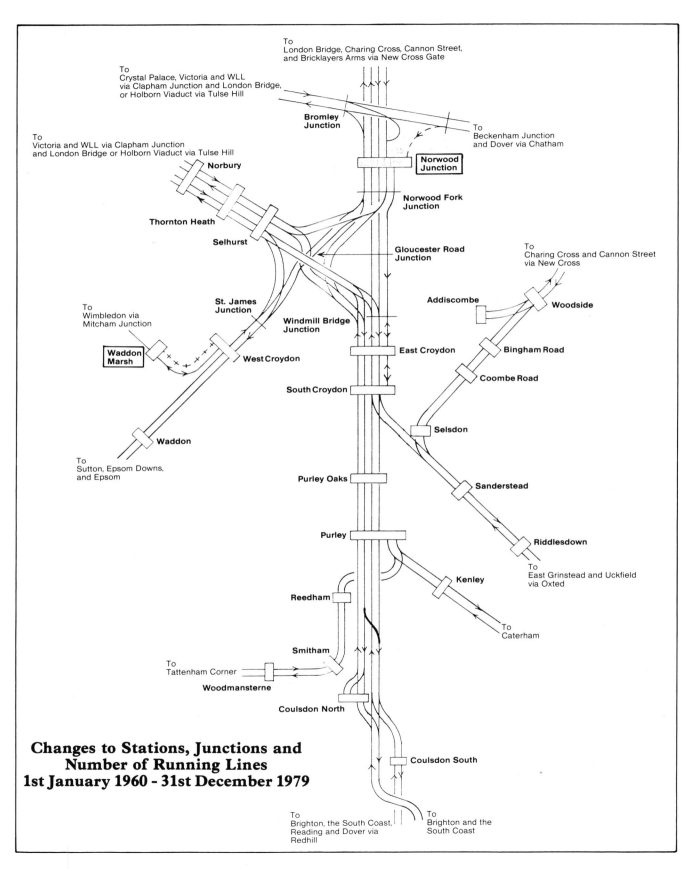

To
London Bridge, Charing Cross, Cannon Street,
and Bricklayers Arms via New Cross Gate

To
Crystal Palace, Victoria and WLL
via Clapham Junction and London Bridge,
or Holborn Viaduct via Tulse Hill

Bromley Junction

To
Beckenham Junction
and Dover via Chatham

Norwood Junction

To
Victoria and WLL via Clapham Junction
and London Bridge or Holborn Viaduct via Tulse Hill

Norbury

Norwood Fork Junction

Thornton Heath

Selhurst

Gloucester Road Junction

To
Charing Cross and Cannon Street
via New Cross

Addiscombe

Woodside

To
Wimbledon via
Mitcham Junction

St. James Junction

Windmill Bridge Junction

Waddon Marsh

West Croydon

East Croydon

Bingham Road

Coombe Road

South Croydon

Selsdon

Waddon

To
Sutton, Epsom Downs,
and Epsom

Purley Oaks

Sanderstead

Riddlesdown

Purley

Kenley

To
East Grinstead and Uckfield
via Oxted

Reedham

To
Caterham

Smitham

To
Tattenham Corner

Woodmansterne

Coulsdon North

Coulsdon South

Changes to Stations, Junctions and Number of Running Lines
1st January 1960 - 31st December 1979

To
Brighton, the South Coast,
Reading and Dover via
Redhill

To
Brighton and the
South Coast

1st January 1980 To Date

During the Winter of 1980/1 Coulsdon North station and the Woodside – Selsdon route, including the stations at Bingham Road, Coombe Road and Selsdon, were proposed for closure. All the stations involved were served by peak hour trains on Mondays to Fridays only. There were the usual protests but consent was given in the case of Coulsdon North on 9th June 1981. Alternative turnround facilities would, however, be provided at the adjacent Smitham station as part of the conditions of closure, under the Brighton line Re-Signalling Scheme (see Chapter Three), by October 1983 when the closure would take place. Until that time Coulsdon had four stations – Coulsdon North, Coulsdon South, Smitham and Woodmansterne – a luxury which probably no other place of its size in the world enjoyed. It was rather remarkable that this 'extravagance' had lasted so long, bearing in mind that all these stations were only heavily used at commuter peak hours, and many towns twice its size have no station at all following railway economies.

Early in 1981 another line closure was put forward. This was the short spur between Norwood Fork Junction and Selhurst, which was only being used by a handful of passenger trains on Mondays to Fridays.

On 29th August Bricklayers Arms was completely closed to commercial traffic, the tracks to and from Bricklayers Arms Junction were retained as sidings for railway departmental use, until finally being severed late in 1984.

In September it was announced that plans for the new East Croydon station development had finally fallen through, B.R. would eventually modernise the station buildings itself, but finance would not be available for several years.

The population of Croydon showed its first decrease – to 316,557 in 1981.

The direct 'local' lines between Windmill Bridge Junction and Norwood Fork Junction (avoiding Gloucester Road Junction) did not require consent for closure as there was the alternative route via Gloucester Road Junction. It was taken out of use early in 1982, being removed (except for a portion temporarily retained as a siding) on 11th April, to make way for the extensive earthworks associated with the major remodelling of the track layouts in the area under the Brighton Line Re-Signalling Scheme. The work is described in more detail in Chapter Three.

Consent was given to the closure of the Norwood Fork Junction – Selhurst spur early in 1982 and it was closed to passenger services from 16th May, although it was retained for a period for other purposes, including the unloading of trains of material for the remodelling work, in particular the colliery waste used for the building of new embankments.

Another large scale development of the East Croydon station site was announced in March 1982. It was said to be only in the early stages of investigation, but should it be progressed it would be one of the largest office blocks in the town – no mean thing in a town which in the previous 25 years had developed into one of the principle centres of offices in the country, with many huge office blocks, giving the town a 'Manhattan' skyline. During September Croydon Council's plans sub-committee accepted the proposal. It was revealed that there would be a new station frontage leading to a large concourse with improved booking hall, which would be linked to bus services and a possible restaurant. There would be 624,000 sq. ft. of office accommodation and 13,000 sq. ft. of recreational facilities. If all went well the work would be completed in 1989.

In the nicest possible way no-one could honestly suggest that the Woodside – Selsdon line had ever been an economical success. It is doubtful if it showed a profit throughout its 98 years

existence. For much of that time one or two coach trains had proved sufficient and although ten coach electric trains were run in the 1950s and 1960s this was to cater for the numbers using the trains north of Woodside. The line had, after all, been without a passenger service from 1917 to 1935 when motoring was not so prevalent, without apparent inconvenience. As South Croydon, East Croydon or Addiscombe stations are within walking distance of the stations on the route they tended to draw passengers away, as they generally had more frequent and/or faster services. Passenger counts taken during 1980 revealed that Bingham Road was used by 116 passengers on an average day, whilst Coombe Road and Selsdon dealt with 50 and 36 respectively, a grand total of 202! Not surprisingly consent for closure was given on 9th September 1982, albeit with a stipulation that B.R. must not do anything after closure which would prejudice the route being considered for an alternative form of transport, pending a special investigation.

In November the Greater London Council indicated that Croydon Council had acted illegally in accepting the East Croydon station development proposal. They should have obtained a G.L.C. directive. They would take the matter to the High Court. However, early in 1983 they changed their minds and withdrew their objection.

During the winter of 1982/3 the platforms at Smitham, Reedham and Purley Oaks were lengthened to accommodate the trains which would be diverted to and from Smitham when Coulsdon North closed.

The platform extensions at Smitham 1982/3 ready to accommodate additional and longer trains upon closure of the adjacent Coulsdon North station.   *Author*

The lightly used Bromley Junction – Beckenham Junction line was converted to a single line from a point just outside the Borough to Beckenham Junction on 9th January 1983, and the Norwood Fork Junction – Selhurst spur was finally put out of use on 14th February, the track being removed subsequently to make room for the remodelled layout.

The Woodside – Selsdon line closed after the last service on Friday 13th May and Coulsdon North after the last train on Friday 30th September.

It took only until July 1983 for the investigators to announce their findings on the future of the former line. They found it unsuitable for a road – not unexpectedly bearing in mind that it passed through tunnels. The future of the trackbed was given consideration, various different possibilities being proposed. It seems likely that it will become park or common land.

Stock to form semi-fast train to Victoria passes the shunting box and remains of the locomotive depot (left) as it leaves the carriage sidings en route to platform 1, Coulsdon North, 1st July 1983.
John Scrace

A new flyover at Gloucester Road Junction was brought into use on 1st October whereupon the 'local' lines between Windmill Bridge Junction and Gloucester Road Junction were taken out of use.

Work soon started on realignment of tracks at the former site of Coulsdon North to permit increased speeds, the connections between the former 'through' lines and the Quarry line being removed, Stoats Nest Junction ½ mile nearer London now being the confluence point of the Redhill and Quarry lines into the four lines northwards which had now been transposed from 'through' and 'local' to 'slow' and 'fast' respectively.

Upon the new layout being completed for the Gloucester Road area the emergency spur was taken out of use on 8th April 1984.

At around this time another station development was announced. This time it was West Croydon that was to have a large scale development with associated office complex. It was only in its early stages of consideration.

Not so, a modernised and extended Maintenance and Repair Depot at Selhurst, work on which had commenced early in the year; Completion is scheduled for 1986.

The Channel Tunnel was again under consideration but whether or not it will affect the Borough this time remains to be seen.

Approval to the electrification of the Oxted line to East Grinstead, thus completing the electrification of all the Borough's routes, was given on 13th May 1985. Completion is due in 1987.

On 28th June the re-opening and electrification of the former route via Farringdon Street (now Farringdon) was announced. This would permit through dual voltage trains between the northern and southern suburbs, including Croydon, by 1988.

Apart from these and the development of East Croydon station which, it appears from an announcement in February 1985, will be somewhat scaled down and financed by B.R. again owing to lack of interest by developers, it cannot be envisaged that there will be many alterations in the near future – the re-signalling schemes have reviewed the requirements of the whole area and carried out what was considered necessary to cater for present day requirements.

Stopping train from Victoria arriving in platform 2 at Coulsdon North, 13th September 1979. *John Scrace*

Left: Elmers End – Addiscombe train at Woodside, 13th May 1983.   *John Scrace*

Right: Elmers End – Sanderstead train at Coombe Road, 6th May 1983, seven days before the station's closure.   *John Scrace*

Below: East Croydon station, viewed from Essex House, the former Divisional Managers office. In the station is class 47 No. 47510 *Fair Rosamund* with the 10.23 Manchester – Brighton train, 25th April 1984.   *John Scrace*

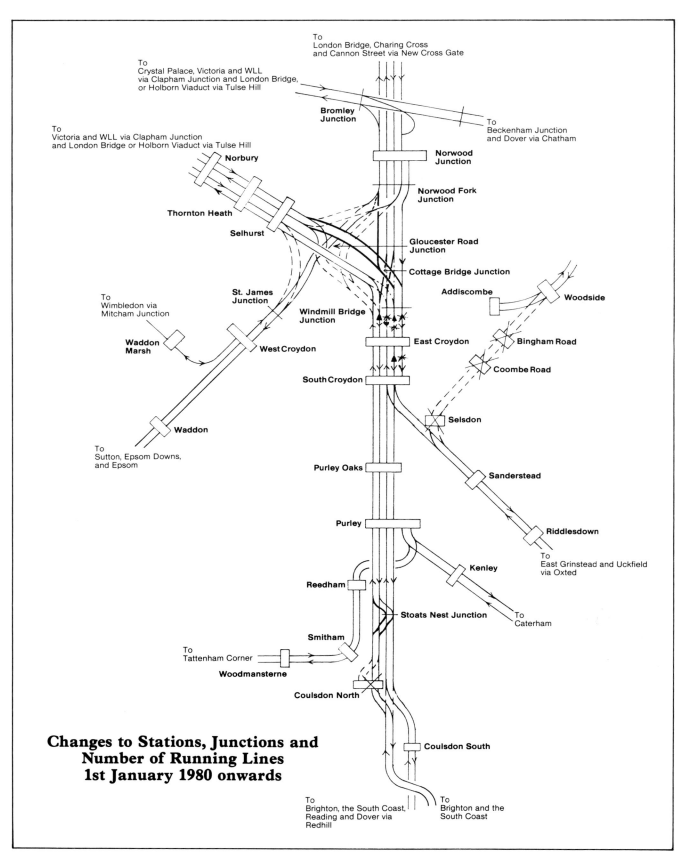

To
London Bridge, Charing Cross
and Cannon Street via New Cross Gate

To
Crystal Palace, Victoria and WLL
via Clapham Junction and London Bridge,
or Holborn Viaduct via Tulse Hill

Bromley
Junction

To
Beckenham Junction
and Dover via Chatham

Norwood
Junction

To
Victoria and WLL via Clapham Junction
and London Bridge or Holborn Viaduct via Tulse Hill

Norbury

Norwood Fork
Junction

Thornton Heath

Selhurst

Gloucester Road
Junction

Cottage Bridge Junction

St. James
Junction

Addiscombe

Woodside

To
Wimbledon via
Mitcham Junction

Windmill Bridge
Junction

Bingham Road

Waddon
Marsh

West Croydon

East Croydon

Coombe Road

South Croydon

Selsdon

Waddon

Purley Oaks

Sanderstead

To
Sutton, Epsom Downs,
and Epsom

Riddlesdown

Purley

To
East Grinstead and Uckfield
via Oxted

Reedham

Kenley

Stoats Nest Junction

To
Caterham

Smitham

To
Tattenham Corner

Woodmansterne

Coulsdon North

Coulsdon South

**Changes to Stations, Junctions and
Number of Running Lines
1st January 1980 onwards**

To
Brighton, the South Coast,
Reading and Dover via
Redhill

To
Brighton and the
South Coast

Part One - **19th Century Passenger Services**

The train service at the opening of the London & Croydon Railway in 1839 consisted of twelve trains each way on weekdays – hourly from 08.20 to 11.20 and from 14.20 to 21.20. They left both London Bridge (referred to in early timetables as Tooley Street) and Croydon (later West Croydon) at the same time and took 35 minutes. On Sundays there were eleven at 09.20, 10.20, then the customary church interval, and hourly from 13.20 to 21.20.

A locomotive depot was provided at Croydon to the north west of the 'up' platform against the wall.

The London & Brighton Railway started with 4 trains between London Bridge and Haywards Heath on weekdays and 2 on Sundays plus one between London Bridge and Horley and one between London Bridge and Croydon (later East Croydon). When Brighton was reached 6 trains were provided to and from London Bridge on weekdays plus 2 between London Bridge and Croydon. Two of the Brighton services were withdrawn from 1st December 1841 until early 1842. On Sundays there were 3 Brighton trains and one to Croydon.

The fastest took 2¼ hours between London Bridge and Brighton (average speed 22.5 mph). This, however, compared favourably with the 6 hours taken by the horse carriages, as did the fares charged.

Examples of the fares at this time are:-

London Bridge To	Single	
	1st Class	**2nd Class**
Jolly Sailor	1/9 (9p)	1/3 (6p)
Croydon	2/- (10p)	1/6 (7½p)
Godstone Road	2/6 (12½p)	2/- (10p)
Stoats Nest	3/- (15p)	2/6 (12½p)
Brighton	14/6 (72½p)	9/6 (45½p)

A Day Return from London Bridge to Brighton was £1 First Class and 15/- (75p) Second Class. A Third Class Single fare of 7/- (35p) applied, but only on the 21.00 goods train!

The fare by horse carriage was 21/- (£1.05) inside, 12/- (60p) outside.

With the advantages in cost and speed and the fact that the majority of people had never been to the seaside to sample the benefits to health which had been popularised, it is not surprising that the railway soon attracted considerable traffic.

The first excursion train ran on Easter Monday 8th April 1844 at 12/- (60p) First Class, 8/- (40p) Second Class and 5/- (25p) Third Class, for the return journey. Various periodicals of the time give its load as 35 carriages and 4 locomotives, 38 carriages and 4 locomotives, and 45 carriages and 4 locomotives. In the first two cases no alteration in load en route are mentioned, and in the first case the journey time was quoted 'as 3 hours and 50 minutes and the number of passengers for the whole day is quoted as upwards of 7,500. In the case of the third it was reported that 6 more carriages and a locomotive had been attached at both New Cross and Croydon making a total of 57 carriages and 6 locomotives into Brighton. In this case an overall time of 4½ hours is quoted! Whichever, if any, is right it is obvious that it was a success.

During 1844 there were 7 London Bridge – Brighton trains (one omitting the Croydon stop) and 3 London Bridge – Croydon services in the L & B timetable, plus 6 S.E.R. trains between London Bridge and Dover. The L & C were running 21 trains – 14 to and from Bricklayers Arms and 7 to and from London Bridge.

Fares had been reduced on the L & C (using Bricklayers Arms, avoiding tolls).

Bricklayers Arms To	**1st**	**2nd**	**3rd**
Croydon/Jolly Sailor (single)	1/3 (6p)	1/- (5p)	9d (4p)
Croydon/Jolly Sailor (return)	2/- (10p)	1/6 (7½p)	1/- (5p)

The single fare between London Bridge and Croydon was 2/3 (11p) First Class and 1/9 (9p) Second Class, a considerable difference.

The London Bridge – Brighton fares had been reduced, except on expresses, the single fare now now being 12/- (60p) First Class, 8/- (40p) Second Class and 5/- (25p) Third Class. Season tickets had been introduced, First Class only, at £14 monthly, £24 for two months and £100 per year. These were reduced in 1845 to £12, £25 and £50 respectively.

The timetables indicated that Post Horses could be had at London Bridge and Brighton stations at the following rates:- From London Bridge to any part of London (including the Post Boy) 10/6 (52½p), from Brighton. From Brighton station to any part of Brighton 5/- (25p) or any part of Kemp Town or Hove 6/- (30p), all expenses paid.

Whilst some of the fares and rates aforementioned appear to be cheap it must be remembered that the average weekly wage of an unskilled worker was 10/- (50p).

The early locomotives were of the 4 or 6-wheeled type with 0-4-0, 2-2-0, 2-2-2 or 0-4-2 wheel formation (the first number indicating the number of small leading wheels, the second the number of larger driving wheels and the third the number of small trailing wheels). Some had wooden lagging sometimes painted green or alternate red and green stripes. Some L & B locomotives had highly polished brasswork including their numbers on a vermilion background in a gilded plate on the footplate side. Others were painted Indian Red on their underframes and wheel splashers.

Carriages were small 4-wheeled vehicles, the First Class resembling horse carriages, the Second Class were usually roofed but not closed in, whilst the Third Class resembled open wagons with plank seats. The S.E.R. when giving evidence to the Commission of Railways boasted 'We give Third Class passengers seats and give them sides 4ft. high'.

In 1845 the Dover service had increased to 8, 3 of which were expresses. The fastest took 151 minutes (average speed 36.3 mph). The L & B trains were now taking 1½ to 2½ hours between London Bridge and Brighton, except for the 06.25 Parliamentary train which took 3 hours and 25 minutes. (Parliamentary trains were obligatory by Act of Parliament for the benefit of the poor. At least one train a day had to be run at 1d a mile fare, with a minimum average overall speed of 12 mph).

An express at 17.00 from London Bridge was introduced. This starting time for the principal business express continued for about 130 years unchanged, although gradually speeded up and/or provided with additional stops.

On 1st January 1847 an express at 08.45 from Brighton was introduced. This was the counterpart of the 17.00 from London Bridge and also ran for a similarly long period, albeit with a few changes in stopping places and overall time and minor variations in starting time.

By October 1851 suburban services were increasing. For example on the London Bridge – West Croydon – Epsom line there were 22 trains each way on weekdays. Half of these, however, only ran between London Bridge and West Croydon.

Writers of the 1850s described the South Eastern Railway's three classes of carriages as 'padded saloons with six compartments', 'large roomy carriages with high wooden sides and extremely narrow doorways' and 'breezy open trucks used by the navvies'.

The London Bridge – Brighton service had increased to 12 trains by 1853.

From 1st December 1855, rather surprisingly considering the state of the relationship between the L.B. & S.C.R. and S.E.R. at the time, tickets on the London Bridge – Reigate route were made interchangeable on the trains of the two companies.

In August 1856 the Brighton service was 13 trains, plus a Mondays only excursion. The return excursion fare London Bridge to Brighton was First Class 7/6 (37½p), Second Class 5/6 (27½p) and Third Class 3/6 (17½p).

The journey time of the 17.00 train from London Bridge to Brighton was reduced to 70 minutes in 1858.

By this time London Bridge station was dealing with 167 trains on weekdays and 13.5 million passengers per year. 15 trains per day went to Dover or Margate via East Croydon and Redhill, 14 to Brighton and the South Coast via Croydon, 24 to Croydon or Epsom and 25 to Crystal Palace.

In March 1859 there were 5 expresses and 9 other passenger trains to Brighton, including one from Pimlico. The overall time had, however, been slowed to 80 minutes.

The ordinary London – Brighton fares were reduced in 1860 to:-
First Class express 12/- (60p), Second Class express 7/6 (37½p), First Class ordinary 9/6 (47½p), Second Class ordinary 7/- (35p), First Class yearly season £40, and Second Class yearly season £35.

In 1862 the London Bridge – West Croydon – Epsom service was again improved and along with the Victoria service via Crystal Palace, West Croydon was well served.

The L.B. & S.C.R. were now collecting tickets on London bound trains at East Croydon, time being added to the schedules for the purpose, thus slowing down most overall journeys. The fastest train from Brighton to London was, nevertheless, reduced to 75 minutes.

Some express trains were now being hauled by 2-2-2 tender locomotives whilst the slower main line trains had 2-4-0 types. East/New Croydon – London trains were invariably provided with unusually ugly tank locomotives with two domes on the boiler, a safety valve being mounted on the second. These were known as 'Crystal Palace tanks'.

Some First Class carriages were now 6-wheeled, the remainder having three compartments holding three passengers each side. Third Class carriages with open sides were still in use on excursion trains.

With the opening of the West London line, London & North Western Railway services ran between Euston, Kensington (Addison Road) and New Croydon. Through carriages from Harrow were also attached for a time.

When Croydon (Addiscombe Road) opened it had a small 4-road locomotive shed and the two terminus lines continued on to a turntable. A service of 11 trains each way was provided on weekdays, none on Sundays. By the following March this number had increased to 16.

By the Summer of 1865, although there were still 14 trains between London and Brighton, most of them now had both London Bridge and Victoria portions which joined or separated

at East Croydon. The fastest overall timings were 65 minutes, accomplished by the 08.45 from Brighton and the 17.00 from London Bridge, now named the 'City Limited'.

The number of S.E.R. trains varied little with the opening of their new main line via Sevenoaks, but the principle expresses took the new route.

From 2nd October 1867 two Brighton trains in each direction ran to and from Cannon Street. These were the 08.45 and 09.45 'up' and the 16.00 and 17.00 'down', five minutes being added to the London end of their schedules.

The Mid Kent services now totalled 19 trains, splitting or combining Beckenham Junction and Croydon (Addiscombe Road) portions at New Beckenham.

From 1st January 1868 Central Croydon station was dealing with 12 'down' and 13 'up' London Bridge trains which took 38 minutes for the journey, plus 4 'down' and 3 'up' services via the West London line (hereafter referred to as the WLL) on weekdays. The Sunday service was one 'down' and two 'up' London Bridge services and three to and from Clapham Junction.

The London – Brighton fares were increased in 1869, the First Class now being 17/6 (87½p) and the Third Class 6/6 (32½p). There was, however, a 3/- (15p) excursion fare.

From 1st January 1869 the WLL services were reorganised. An L.B. & S.C.R. service ran between Kensington (Addison Road) and New or Central Croydon via Crystal Palace, two of the trains being semi-fast taking only 31 minutes, whilst the Euston service turned round at Crystal Palace and no longer entered the Borough.

Suburban services continued to expand.

The East London Railway (usually referred to as the East London line and hereafter shortened to ELL) was run by a committee of interested railway companies and had no trains of its own. It was worked from its opening from New Cross (L.B. & S.C.R.) to Wapping by the L.B. & S.C.R. with 23 trains in either direction, providing passengers from the Croydon area with connections to the East End.

West Croydon locomotive depot was enlarged prior to 1870 to accommodate the increasing number of locomotives. It now had a two road shed and a 46ft. turntable and provided locomotives for suburban passenger trains, local freight services and shunting.

By 1871 the Central Croydon – London Bridge service had decreased to three each way and there was one 'down' train from Victoria.

As from 1872 William Stroudley, the new locomotive engineer of the L.B. & S.C.R., introduced a new colour scheme for his passenger locomotives. Sometimes known as 'Scotch Green' but officially as 'Improved Engine Green', it was in reality a colour variously described as golden ochre – almost an orange ochre, mustard or yellow. The panelling was edged in dark green, lined out with a black band edged with red, yellow and black lines. The buffer beams were elaborately painted and lined out in several colours. The engine name was in gold leaf outlined with red, sea-green and black. Outside springs were yellow as were the centres of the wheels. Other parts were painted in claret and the cab roof was white. Surely the most colourful livery ever seen in this country. He also had a passion for naming his locomotives, even the small tanks.

Places within the L.B. & S.C.R. area, from large towns to tiny hamlets not necessarily possessing a station, featured largely among the names which were painted in large letters on the tank sides or on the wheel splashers of tender locomotives. Goods locomotives were painted olive green with a black band. Those fitted with the air brake had fine red lines on either side of the black band.

S.E.R. locomotives were dark green with red/brown underframes, and the L.C.D.R. locomotives were also dark green.

The S.E.R. carriages were flesh coloured above, brownish below. Invariably no two carriages on a train would be identical in size, height or contour and to ruin the appearance even further the guards vans had raised glazed roofs (popularly called 'Birdcages') in which the guard sat to view the signals. Most were small four-wheeled vehicles. The Third Class carriages were a bare rectangular box with hard wooden seats and half partitions, so low that upon sitting down one had to take care not to knock off the hat or bump heads with the person in the next compartment! Oil lamps giving poor illumination were provided – one to every four compartments. They often dripped oil on to passengers from time to time throughout the journey. On the credit side the First Class carriages were quite comfortable, and the S.E.R. were the first company to provide lavatories in trains.

The L.C.D.R.'s Third Class carriages were of the same poor standard as those of the S.E.R., only more so! There was a gradual improvement in evidence on the S.E.R. but not on the L.C.D.R.

The L.B. & S.C.R. carriages were similar but some of their First Class ones were superior. Their carriages were somewhat more regular in size and shape. They were decorated in varnished mahogany with gilt lines, soon to be changed to mahogany red. The roofs were white and the ends of guards brake vans were vermilion.

By 1874 most of the L.B. & S.C.R. main line expresses were provided with 2-2-2 locomotives.

The first Pullman car on the L.B. & S.C.R. was introduced on the 10.45 from Victoria to Brighton on 1st January 1875. It was named *Jupiter*.

The 'City Limited' was now, however, being regularly hauled by 2-4-0 tender locomotives Nos. 206 *Carisbrooke* or 207 *Freshwater*.

From 1st May 1875 a service was introduced between Willesden Junction (London & North Western Railway) and New Croydon via the WLL.

At about this time the L.C.D.R. changed their locomotive colour scheme to medium green with black bands and red and white lines. Underframes were black.

In 1876, upon the ELL being extended to Bishopsgate Junction – thus providing a through link with Liverpool Street (Great Eastern Railway), the L.B. & S.C.R. started a through service between that station and Croydon. During 1877 this was extended to and from Brighton. The S.E.R. also provided some trains on the ELL from their New Cross station. Passengers from the Croydon (Addiscombe Road) line would thus have been able to travel via the ELL by changing at New Cross, and from 1st April 1880 through trains were provided – interestingly between S.E.R. and Great Eastern Railway stations, via a joint line, yet hauled by L.B. & S.C.R. locomotives!

By this time the usual power on short distance services between West Croydon and Wimbledon, Crystal Palace and Epsom Downs was 0-6-0 tank locomotives, popularly known as 'Terriers' and 2-4-0 tank locomotives were in use on the Norwood Junction – Beckenham Junction services.

The first all 'Pullman' train, known as the 'Pullman Limited' ran between Victoria and Brighton from 1st December 1881. Apart from one coach which had been used to test the equipment since October this was also the first train to be electrically lit, the power provided by batteries. This train was withdrawn for a period, then reinstated, during 1882.

During that year the 08.45 from Brighton commenced 'slipping' a Victoria portion at East Croydon. Under the slip coach arrangement special apparatus was provided to permit a train to be split into two portions without stopping. Provided all signals were clear for the train the guard of the rear portion would operate the apparatus at a given point. The front portion would continue through the station non-stop, whilst the rear portion would gradually decrease speed until being brought to a stand in the station by the guard operating the brake. If the signals were not clear the slip would not be made and the train would have to stop in the station and be split in the conventional way. This system had previously been used for 'down' trains at Caterham Junction between January 1861 and January 1879.

The famous 'Gladstone' class 0-4-2 locomotives were introduced in 1882. This class, and some of the other 0-4-2 tender locomotives on the L.B. & S.C.R., were unusual for express types in not having small leading wheels. They were, however, highly successful and were utilised on the principle expresses. The S.E.R. were still using the 2-2-2 and 2-4-0s on their expresses,

'Gladstone' class 0-4-2 No. 187 *Philip Rose* at East Croydon on a 'down' train.
Pamlin Prints

although 4-4-0 types were coming into favour. The 2-2-2 type were known as the 'Mail' engines as the Dover Mail train was one of their regular duties. They had 7ft. driving wheels and were cabless. S.E.R. locomotives were now being painted black, with red lining on passenger classes, and their carriages were rich dark crimson lake with white roofs. Moreover, they were becoming more uniform in size and shape.

In 1883 belt-driven dynamo lighting was introduced on the L.B. & S.C.R., a method later adopted nationally.

During that year the Liverpool Street – Brighton service was withdrawn.

The S.E.R. services over the ELL were diverted to and from St. Mary's (Whitechapel) when that station opened on 3rd March 1884 until 6th October of the same year when these, too, were taken off upon the Metropolitan and District Railways providing the ELL services. The Great Eastern Railway had been working all the freight trains.

Croydon (Addiscombe Road) was now dealing with 25 arrival and departures on weekdays and 4 on Sundays.

Upon the opening of the Oxted line there was a service of 4 L.B. & S.C.R. and 4 S.E.R. trains, the latter running only between London Bridge and Oxted at first, two being extended to Edenbridge (SER) and one to Tonbridge from 1st August 1884. By 1885 the L.B. & S.C.R. service had increased to 5 East Grinstead trains, one of which continued through to Tunbridge Wells, and 3 trains between London and Oxted. The Tunbridge Wells train did not call at East Croydon.

As from 1st February 1886 the Great Eastern Railway, who had previously run only non-passenger trains over the ELL, revived the service between Liverpool Street and New or Central Croydon. There were 7 trains which took 50 minutes. This company also operated all ELL trains which served their Liverpool Street terminus.

From 1st June of the same year there were five London & North Western trains between Central Croydon and Willesden Low Level via WLL. These were an extension of New Croydon services which had been running since 1st May 1885. They called at all stations except Wormwood Scrubs and took 55 minutes.

During the 'eighties most carriages were still six-wheeled but some non-corridor bogie First Class coaches had been introduced.

Three Pullman cars marshalled together with brake/ luggage/lighting vans were brought into use by the L.B. & S.C.R. in 1888. One car was called 'Prince' and was referred to as a buffet, although it had no bar! Another named 'Princess' was known as the 'Ladies Car', although male escorts were permitted – provided they did not smoke! The third, 'Albert Victor', was a smoking car. These were the first vehicles gangwayed through closed vestibules in Great Britain, and lavatories were provided. They were painted dark greenish brown with gold leaf decorations and the roofs were red oxide.

In 1889 the number of Brighton expresses had increased to 15 in each direction.

Upon the final closure of Central Croydon station, its services, including those to and from Willesden and Liverpool Street, again reverted to using New Croydon as their turnround point.

The S.E.R. had some good bogie coaches by now and their six-wheeled carriages were as good as any. They also had Pullman cars and other luxury types of coaches, including a 'Continental Club train' on their Folkestone and Dover expresses which occasionally ran via the Borough in the event of a blockage on their main line.

By 1893 the London – Brighton service had increased to 28 'down' and 24 'up', and soon afterwards the L.B. & S.C.R. began to conform with the majority of British main line companies by using 4-4-0 locomotives on express trains.

From 1896 yellow lines were added to the red lines on S.E.R. locomotives and polished brass casings were provided on safety valve settings. Goods locomotives were generally black, although some were dark green with black bands and white lining.

L.C.D.R. locomotives at this time were black with a broad grey band, the outer edge having a thin vermilion line, the inner edge a yellow line. The monogram of the Company's initials was in shaded gold. Goods locomotives were black without the grey band. Buffer beams were vermilion with the numbers in bold shaded gilt numerals.

The first advertised London to Brighton in one hour service was on 2nd October 1898.

A three-road locomotive shed with 50ft. turntable was opened by the S.E.R. at Purley in 1898. Situated between the main line and the Kingswood branch, it provided locomotives for their local passenger and freight services, such as Purley - Caterham, Purley - Kingswood (and later Tattenham Corner), Woodside - Selsdon Road and Elmers End - Hayes. On the Caterham and Tattenham Corner lines 2-4-0 and 0-4-4 tank locomotives were usually utilised.

Croydon (Addiscombe Road) locomotive shed had disappeared by the time the remodelling of the station was completed in 1899. The turntable beyond the platform ends had gone too, one being provided in a siding behind the signal box on the 'up' side of the line north of the station.

The 'City Limited' was at this time usually hauled by 4-4-0 tender locomotive No. 213 *Bessemer*.

From 1899 twelve-wheeled Pullman cars appeared on the Brighton expresses. Some were fitted with movable chairs.

There were now six Oxted line trains to Tunbridge Wells (L.B. & S.C.R.) via the direct route.

With the quadrupling of the lines the L.B. & S.C.R. extended their suburban services from South Croydon to Stoats Nest from 5th November 1899. The majority of passengers between London Bridge and East Croydon or Purley, however, continued to use the faster S.E.R. services.

Upon the amalgamation of the S.E.R. and L.C.D.R. in 1899 a red and teak livery was adopted for coaching stock.

Part Two - **20th Century Passenger Services**

During 1900 the L.B. & S.C.R. opened a locomotive depot at Stoats Nest. It had a two-road shed and 55ft. turntable and was principally provided to cater for their suburban services and local freight workings. However, some main line work was covered by its locomotives and men.

Harry Wainwright, the S.E.C.R.'s locomotive engineer from 1900, introduced a new livery for his locomotives – light green with broad bands of even lighter green edged with yellow and red. The copper or brass dome castings, chimney caps, the beading around the wheel splashers, the covering surrounding the firebox in the cab, the cladding band at the smokebox and where the smokebox joined the boiler barrel were all highly polished. The letters S.E. & C.R. were in gold, shaded with red, on the tender or tank sides. S.E.C.R. locomotives in this livery and L.B. & S.C.R. ones in 'Improved Engine Green' would have been running simultaneously on the lines through East Croydon. It is sad that colour photography could not have captured a picture with both depicted side by side!

Trains on the West Croydon – Wimbledon line were still being operated with 'Terrier' locomotives, whilst the carriages were four and six wheeled with Open Third Class. There were about 10 trains either way on the Purley – Tattenham Corner line on normal weekdays but on Derby Day 1901 excursions from Margate, Dover, Hastings and the Reading line brought 2,283 passengers. There were also specials from London and East Croydon. A total of fifty special trains in all were run conveying between 14,000 and 15,000 racegoers. The S.E.C.R. service over the Oxted line at this stage was 6 trains from Cannon Street (including a 16.57 fast to Oxted) and 4 from London Bridge. The majority went through to Edenbridge (S.E.C.R.) or Tonbridge via Crowhurst Junctions. There were 3 'up' trains via Crowhurst

Junction to Charing Cross, including an 'express' from Dover Town which ran via the Mid Kent line, but did not call at Sanderstead.

Some high speed running was tried out with the 'Pullman Limited' which, on 21st December 1901, reached Brighton from Victoria in just under 50 minutes behind 4-4-0 No. 70 *Holyrood*. On Christmas Day No. 68 *Marlborough* took 51 minutes.

Eventually a special record attempt was made on 26th July 1903 when a test train of 3 Pullman cars and one van, hauled again by *Holyrood* ran from Victoria to Brighton in 48 minutes and 41 seconds and returned in 50 minutes and 20 seconds. The former record still stands, at least officially, until the present day between these two stations.

In March 1904 D. Earle Marsh, the new locomotive engineer of the L.B. & S.C.R., limited the naming of locomotives and discontinued the use of 'Improved Engine Green' livery. His livery was dark green, lined out in red and white. An experimental livery of umber brown was tried out. This had black bands with orange and yellow lining, or edged with a darker umber band with black lines with a gilt line each side. Yellow later replaced the gilt. Monograms of the Company's initials or its coat of arms were on the wheel splashers of express locomotives. Others had LBSCR in gilt on the tender or the tank sides. This was later reduced to LBSC. Goods locomotives were black, lined in red. All buffer beams were vermilion with the engine number in gilt, later yellow.

4-4-2 locomotives were now being used on main line expresses on the L.B. & S.C.R. whilst the 'Terrier' 0-6-0 tank locomotives and 0-4-2 tanks worked the majority of their suburban services.

L.B. & S.C.R. 0-4-2 tank No. B625 at West Croydon, 5th December 1926. Note the overhead wires.   *H.C. Casserley*

Steam railmotor arriving at Coombe Lane.   *Lens of Sutton*

By now there were 7 trains from London Bridge to Tonbridge via Oxted and the Crowhurst Junctions, whilst the service between London Bridge and Victoria via Norwood Junction and Selhurst ran 11 times a day.

June 1904 saw the start of through services between Brighton, the Midlands and the North of England via the WLL. At first this consisted of Liverpool, Manchester and Birmingham coaches attached to or detached from Euston services at Willesden Junction. From 1st March 1905 the service became an independent through working.

More bogie coaches were being introduced by this time.

On 31st July 1905 the District line proper was electrified and in consequence that Company, but not the Metropolitan, withdrew its steam trains from the ELL. The L.B. & S.C.R. increased theirs to compensate.

The Mid Kent service had increased to 31 trains – 3 to Beckenham Junction, one to Croydon (Addiscombe Road) and 27 which split at New Beckenham into portions for both destinations. At Elmers End there were 19 connecting trains to Hayes and at Woodside 10 to Selsdon Road. A similar number of trains ran in the opposite direction.

A S.E.C.R. Kitson steam railmotor No. 16 made its appearance on the Woodside – Selsdon Road line in 1906. The S.E.C.R. and L.B. & S.C.R. worked this joint line on an alternate year basis, the L.B. & S.C.R. train usually consisting of a 'Terrier' and one coach, based on Stoats Nest depot.

By October 1906 there were 62 through trains to the South Coast from Victoria or London Bridge, 28 of which were for Brighton, 19 for Eastbourne, 2 for Newhaven and 13 for destinations via Horsham.

In December the Metropolitan Railway withdrew their services from the ELL, whereupon the S.E.C.R. commenced to run a limited service between their New Cross station and Whitechapel.

During 1906 and 1907 only a service was run between Paddington, on the Great Western Railway and Brighton via the WLL.

More tank locomotives were appearing on L.B. & S.C.R. main line expresses, and for the 'City Limited' special coaches were provided. These were very roomy, had superior seats and some basket chairs which were not fixed. These coaches were gangwayed to one another and to the Pullman cars.

The L.B. & S.C.R. had a tendency to be grandiose with their principal trains – Royal train locomotives had a crown affixed at the front of the chimney and a huge Royal coat of arms mounted on the front buffer beam. Bunting was also draped around the locomotive giving it a somewhat carnival appearance. Similar arrangements were made for visiting dignitaries with flags and/or boards of welcome indicating the purpose of the visit in place of the coat of arms. Sometimes the locomotive would be specially renamed for the occasion. Even the locomotive working the Annual Station Masters and Inspectors Excursion would be similarly decorated.

The 'Pullman Limited' was renamed the 'Southern Belle' from 1st November 1908 and the through service between Brighton and the Midlands and the North of England became the 'Sunny South Express' in 1909.

By now there were 12 trains each way on the West Croydon – Wimbledon line.

From 1910 the 'Southern Belle' was speeded up to reach Brighton in the hour on Sundays.

The Kitson steam railmotor on the Woodside – Selsdon Road service was replaced by a Beyer Peacock steam railcar during that year.

More eight-wheeled coaches were now appearing, including S.E.C.R. 'Birdcage' sets. Most of that Company's suburban trains were now worked by 0-4-4 tank locomotives. The L.B. & S.C.R. suburban trains were provided with 0-6-0 'Terriers' or

0-4-2 tanks, although 0-6-2 and 4-4-2 tanks were taking over the heavier peak hour trains.

4-4-2 tank locomotives had also been put to work on the 'Sunny South Express'. Through locomotive working between Brighton and Rugby had been introduced and L.B. & S.C.R. No. 23, with No. 26 in reserve, were used alternately with London & North Western Railway No. 7 *Titan*, a 4-4-0 tender locomotive. The trials had been instigated by the latter company to show the capabilities of *Titan*, but much to its surprise it was the tanks which came off best. With the bunker loaded to capacity with about 3¼ tons of coal they would run from Brighton to Rugby and back again without recoaling – averaging only 27lbs. of coal per mile, always managing the 90½ miles between East Croydon and Rugby without taking water, and timekeeping was exemplary.

Croydon (Addiscombe Road) now had 30 arrivals and departures on weekdays and 14 on Sundays.

From 31st December 1911 regular through passenger services between the ELL and places south of New Cross (L.B. & S.C.R.) were withdrawn, although the route was still available for occasional special trains.

The number of London – Brighton trains had increased to 33 by the summer of 1912, there were 46 trains to and from Coulsdon & Smitham Downs (the former Stoats Nest) and 16 on the West Croydon – Wimbledon line in the weekday service. Between 08.00 and 09.00 there were 14 L.B. & S.C.R. trains from East/New Croydon to London, 6 from West Croydon, 8 from Purley, 3 from Waddon, 6 from Thornton Heath, 3 from Norbury and 5 from Norwood Junction.

The new A.C. overhead electric trains were painted in umber livery, a colour soon to be extended to L.B. & S.C.R. steam trains as well.

Up to this time the majority of freight trains had been hauled by 0-6-0 tender and 0-6-0 and 0-6-2 tank locomotives, and whilst this continued, 2-6-0 tender locomotives were taking over some of the heavier ones.

The ELL was electrified between the New Cross stations and Shoreditch from 31st March 1913 whereupon the Metropolitan Railway again provided all the passenger services over the line. These continued beyond Shoreditch to South Kensington via Baker Street, and later to Hammersmith, no doubt providing useful connectional facilities for passengers to and from the Croydon area changing at the New Cross stations.

With the comparatively short journeys covered by their trains, the L.B. & S.C.R. made considerable use of tank locomotives which, if required, could run to and fro without turning. With the main line trains becoming increasingly heavier large 4-6-2 and 4-6-4 tank locomotives were introduced in the years immediately prior to the First World War. These often worked the heaviest expresses and the 'Southern Belle'. Return excursion fares London – Brighton were 8/6 (42½p) First Class and 5/9 (29p) Second Class.

S.E.C.R. passenger services on Mondays to Fridays immediately prior to the First World War included 36 'down' and 37 'up' trains serving East Croydon, Coulsdon & Cane Hill had 19 'down' and 18 'up', the Caterham line 28 'down' and 26 'up' and the Tadworth branch 23 'down' and 20 'up'. There were 10 trains from Norwood Junction to Beckenham Junction, via the Norwood Spur line, and 9 in the opposite direction, all one class only, and 12 each way between Crystal Palace and Beckenham Junction, one of which continued through to Orpington, whilst one in the opposite direction started up from Bickley. The Oxted line had 13 'down' and 12 'up' trains, two in either direction running via the Mid Kent line. An unusual working was an 08.00 from London Bridge to Oxted via East Croydon which ran non-stop to Selsdon Road in 20 minutes, calling only at that station and Upper Warlingham, and terminating at Oxted at 08.39. It returned at 08.57 via the Mid Kent line, running non-stop between Sanderstead and New Beckenham. There were 37 arrivals at Addiscombe Road and 39 departures, including semi-fast services, the 'Flyer' being the 07.20 from Addiscombe Road to Cannon Street calling only at Woodside & South Norwood (07.24) then non-stop to London Bridge (07.42), arriving at Cannon Street at 07.46. Large 0-6-4 tank locomotives were being introduced on this line. On the Woodside – Selsdon Road section there were 20 'down' and 19 'up' passenger trains. Two each way were the through Oxted services, the remainder the steam rail cars. (In the case of East Croydon, the Oxted line and the main line to Coulsdon, there would, of course, have been L.B. & S.C.R. services as well.)

There were two passenger trains in either direction between Charing Cross and the Reading and Tonbridge lines via East Croydon and Redhill Junction which also conveyed horse and carriage traffic to and from the intermediate stations. A fascinating feature of their timings was that whilst shunting would have to be performed at each station where a horse box and/or carriage truck had to be attached or detached, no extra time was allowed. For example the 'up' services left Coulsdon & Cane Hill at 12.17 and 21.03, Purley at 12.21 and 21.08 and East Croydon

A rare view of the 'Sunny South Express' at Selhurst, in this instance with an L.B. & S.C.R. class 'B2' or 'B3' in charge.
R.C. Riley Collection

'Down' train approaching East Croydon. A tank locomotive stands in Hall & Co's siding. *Lens of Sutton*

Right: 'Up' train in East Croydon Main, hauled by an 0-6-2 tank locomotive. *H.C. Casserley*

Below: A 'down' train composed of former S.E.C.R. locomotive class 'L1' No. A789 and stock passing L.B. & S.C.R. signals at Windmill Bridge Junction. Note the 'Birdcage' coach behind the locomotive. 3rd October 1926. *H.C. Casserley*

at 12.29 and 21.15. Either the shunting was exceedingly swift or the train ran progressively later on busy days.

S.E.C.R. fares at this time included:-

	First Class	Second Class	Third Class
From London Bridge to East Croydon Return	2/6 (12½p)	1/9 (8½p)	1/3 (6p)
From London Bridge to Coulsdon & Cane Hill Return	3/10 (19p)	2/9 (13½p)	2/2 (11p)
From London Bridge to Purley Return	3/6 (17½p)	2/6 (12½p)	1/9 (8½p)
To London (Special Reduced Fares on specified trains on Wednesdays only)			
From Smitham, Reedham Halt or Kenley	2/3 (11p)	2/- (10p)	1/6 (7½p)
From Purley	2/1 (10½p)	1/9 (8½p)	1/6 (7½p)
From Coombe Lane	1/6 (7½p)	1/5 (7p)	1/1 (5½p)

Workmens return tickets to London Bridge on trains arriving there before 08.00 were available from Woodside 4d (1½p), East Croydon or Croydon (Addiscombe Road) 5d (2½p), Purley 7d (3p) and Coulsdon & Cane Hill 8d (3½p), among other places. There was also a workmans return ticket from East Croydon to Coulsdon & Cane Hill for 5d (2½p).

Friendly and other societies were offered party prices (return tickets for single fare plus a third) for trips to certain country spots within the Borough:- Coulsdon & Cane Hill, Kenley (for Riddlesdown), Woodside or Coombe Lane (for Shirley Hills), Selsdon Road and Sanderstead.

A Sunday excursion to Boulogne cost 16/6 (82½p) First Class, 10/- (50p) Third Class from East Croydon.

An afternoon excursion to Margate leaving East Croydon at 12.30, arriving at Margate at 14.40, returning at 20.15 with an arrival back at East Croydon at 22.29 was available for 2/6 (12½p) Third Class.

Examples of Day Return fares from East Croydon or Purley were:-

	First Class	Second Class	Third Class
Aldershot	5/4 (27p)	4/3 (21p)	3/9 (19p)
Ramsgate Town	14/- (70p)	9/3 (46p)	7/6 (37½p)
Tunbridge Wells	4/8 (23p)	3/6 (17½p)	3/3 (16p)

Drastic cuts in services were made during the First World War. The number of London – Brighton trains was cut to 26, whilst the 'Sunny South Express' and the Woodside – Selsdon Road, Norwood Junction – Beckenham Junction and Crystal Palace – Beckenham Junction services were withdrawn. A grey livery was also used for locomotives as a wartime economy.

By the end of the war the West Croydon – Wimbledon service was being operated with a two coach push and pull set hauled by an 0-4-2 tank locomotive.

After the war no Sunday service was provided by the S.E.C.R. on the Oxted line neither did they resume their withdrawn services. Despite the absence of a regular passenger service, the Woodside – Selsdon Road line remained open for other traffic – freight trains, light locomotives to and from Purley locomotive depot, excursions and the seasonal hop pickers trains. Families, mainly from the East End and South London would emigrate to the Kentish farms where they would live in primitive huts for three or four weeks during the hop picking season. For the majority this was their only 'holiday' – they could afford no other and, moreover, they could be earning money at the same time. Over 30,000 people would be conveyed, chiefly from London Bridge, in trains usually consisting of ancient non-corridor coaches with vans containing their belongings to various Kentish stations. At weekends similar trains would run to convey their relatives and friends down to the farms to visit them. Many of these trains would be routed via the Mid Kent line, Woodside, Oxted and Crowhurst Junctions.

After the war one of the L.B. & S.C.R.'s 4-6-4 tank locomotives was named *Remembrance*. It was painted grey with black bands and white lining and lettering. Under the name on each tank was a bronze plaque inscribed 'In grateful remembrance of the 532 men of the L.B. & S.C.R. who gave their lives for their country, 1914 - 1919.'

From July 1921 the Metropolitan Railway managed the East London Railway. As mentioned before they already provided the entire passenger service.

In December 1921 the 'Sunny South Express' re-started as a portion to and from Euston services at Willesden Junction, and as a separate train again from 15th March 1922.

L.B. & S.C.R. services to London were building up as the trend to live 'in the country' became more popular. There were now 14 trains from East Croydon, 8 from West Croydon, 7 from Purley, 3 from Waddon, 11 from Thornton Heath and 8 from Norbury between 08.00 and 09.00 on Mondays to Fridays. The Oxted line had 24 'down' and 21 'up' L.B. & S.C.R. services on weekdays. Both this line's totals and the figures for East Croydon and Purley above would be increased by S.E.C.R. trains.

By the Summer of 1923 the London – Brighton service had reached 31 'down' and 28 'up' trains, with additional services on Mondays and Saturdays. On Sundays there were 14 'down' and 16 'up'. The 'Southern Belle' had been restored to its 60 minute schedule after having been slowed down during the war.

To the end of their separate existence the L.B. & S.C.R. expresses were formed of miscellaneous bogie coaches with Pullmans scattered in the formation. There were still six-wheeled coaches on some main line trains, whilst some suburban trains were still utilising four-wheeled carriages dating from the 1890s! Even the early suburban D.C. third rail electric trains were rebuilds of wooden steam coaches.

In 1924 the London – Brighton service was remodelled – no less than 9 'down' and 6 'up' trains being scheduled to complete their journeys in the hour.

The Southern Railway adopted olive green with yellow lines and wording for their locomotives and coaches, electric and steam. There were still slip coaches off certain 'up' trains at East Croydon.

From 1925 the 'Sunny South Express' additionally conveyed through coaches to and from the former Midland Railway route.

During that year the East London line became part of the Southern Railway but the Metropolitan Railway continued to provide the passenger services.

Upon the extension of D.C. electrification to Coulsdon North and Sutton a service was provided every 20 minutes on Mondays to Fridays, except between 11.00 and 13.00 and after 21.00 when it was half hourly. On Saturdays it was every 20 minutes until 18.00 then half hourly, whilst on Sundays the half hourly service sufficed all day, supplemented by one train hourly from Victoria to both East Croydon and West Croydon via Crystal Palace.

The Addiscombe (Croydon) electric services were one to Cannon Street and one to Charing Cross each hour off peak, with 4 to Cannon Street and 2 to Charing Cross in the peak hours.

Purley locomotive depot was closed on 29th May 1928. The shed building remains to this day, having been converted to offices,

'Remembrance' class 4–6–4 No. B331 heads an 'up' train at East Croydon.   *H.C. Casserley*

'Down' train approaching South Croydon, 13th May 1931 with class 'I1' No. B595. Note also the station nameboard and lamp standards of the period.   *H.C. Casserley*

which over the subsequent years have been utilised as the District Engineers Headquarters, a Permanent Way Training School and for the examination of collected tickets.

Coulsdon (originally Stoats Nest) locomotive depot also closed during 1928. The majority of the shed has been demolished, but a small portion, to the south of Platform 2 remained, until the closure of Coulsdon North station, being used by carriage cleaning staff.

From 17th June 1928 there were 3 trains an hour during the peaks and at least half-hourly off peak services on most suburban routes. Services between London Bridge and Coulsdon North, however, ran only in the peak hours. Owing to the density of traffic on the Charing Cross and Cannon Street lines at London Bridge the Tattenham Corner/Caterham services could not be accommodated in peak hours and had to turn round in London Bridge terminus, but ran through, principally to Charing Cross, at other times.

By this time the London – Brighton service had increased to 34 in the 'down' direction and 30 in the 'up' still with additional trains on Saturdays and Mondays.

The 'Sunny South Express' now conveyed a portion for Leeds and Bradford.

The former locomotive depot at Purley pictured in 1983. The legend 'S.E.R.' cast in the masonry remains on the end of the roof. At the other end the year of building (1898) is similarly retained.
Author

Above: Coulsdon & Smitham Downs in 1920. The picture shows, left to right, the locomotive depot, South signal box and locomotive and carriage sidings. The goods yard was further to the right. Class 'E4' 0-4-4T No. B492 is visible on the right.
R.C. Riley Collection

Right: Coulsdon North station on the left of the elegant gas light, with the locomotive depot on the right. The date is 12th February 1928, just before closure of the depot. *H.C. Casserley*

Side destination boards were introduced upon the electrification of the Tattenham Corner/Caterham service in 1928, to indicate to passengers which portion to join, owing to the trains splitting at Purley. These square boards were attached between the leading drivers cab and guards van and indicated the principle stations only, an example being LONDON BRIDGE, EAST CROYDON, PURLEY, TADWORTH BRANCH. These boards were gradually extended to other suburban services, whether or not they divided en route, and certain main line trains.

During 1929 the superseded overhead A.C. electric trains were converted to D.C. third rail. Some motor coaches were converted to freight brake vans, distinguishable by long verandahs at either end. Some were to remain in revenue earning traffic and latterly on engineers trains well into the 1970s.

From 6th July 1930 the Victoria – Coulsdon North service on Sundays was diverted to Tattenham Corner, Coulsdon North station being closed on the Sabbath, passengers using the adjacent Smitham station.

The electric trains provided on the West Croydon – Wimbledon line were two-car units, consisting of former A.C. overhead electric First Class trailer coaches, converted as necessary. These coaches had been withdrawn from the Crystal Palace lines when there was found to be little demand for First Class travel in that area. They ran for a while on steam commuter services before being converted to D.C. They still had a 'pit' in the roofs, which formerly held the overhead pantograph, giving them a distinctive appearance.

Above: 'On shed' at West Croydon on 17th April 1927 are Nos. B266 and B581.
H.C. Casserley

The service ran every 20 minutes in peak hours, half-hourly off peak. In the case of the former, timetabling paths over the single line sections for these trains which had short turnround times at either end of the journey, had to fit in between other services at Mitcham Junction, and also cross one another where facilities existed, were so critical that the rare quoting of ¼ minutes as station timings in the Staff Working Timetables were resorted to.

By this time the number of trains via the Crowhurst Junctions was reduced to one 'down' and two 'up'.

'Schools' class 4-4-0 and 'King Arthur' class 4-6-0 tender locomotives were now in use on the principle services on the Brighton main line, the displaced locomotives being generally demoted to the Oxted line.

Upon the electrification of the Brighton line new main line electric trains were provided in various units of 2, 4, or 6 cars, the latter including a Pullman car. The fastest timing was still one hour, the density of traffic provided precluding any speeding up. For a start instead of 7 expresses *a day* from London to Brighton there were 6 trains, including a non-stop, 2 semi-fasts and a Worthing semi-fast *every hour*, even off peak, which had to intermingle, over the same number of lines as before, with the stopping services, steam passenger trains to other destinations and parcels and freight services. There were additional trains in the peak periods and at summer weekends and a heavy excursion programme during which periods non-passenger trains were not run.

London Transport was formed and provided the regular ELL passenger trains from 1st July 1933 and under its various titles of London Passenger Transport Board, London Transport Executive and London Regional Transport, has continued to do so for over 50 years, in contrast to the many companies previously involved.

On 29th June 1934 the 'Southern Belle', now electric, was renamed the 'Brighton Belle' and the 'City Limited' lost its title. The latters special coaches were remodelled and converted into electric trains, one motor coach – on 6-car Pullman unit No. 3041 – lasting until the unit was withdrawn in the 1960s. It was distinguishable in that its body sides were straighter than the others.

From 4th July 1935 electric services were extended to and from Eastbourne, Ore (Hastings), Newhaven and Seaford, further reducing the number of steam trains on the main line, but again increasing the number of trains overall. In connection with this, additional 6-car units were provided. These included Pantry cars instead of Pullmans. Many 12-car main line trains henceforth were composed of one 6-car unit of each type.

When the Woodside – Selsdon line re-opened it was given a service of three electric trains an hour in the peak periods and two off peak, the majority to and from Cannon Street.

During 1935 West Croydon locomotive depot, which had lost its turntable some years before, was closed and replaced by a new depot with five shed roads and a 65ft. turntable at Norwood Junction, in the space between the main lines and the 'down' line from Bromley Junction.

During 1936 the last 6-wheeled coaches were run in ordinary services, although they did appear for a few more years on hop picker specials.

An example of the single fares at this time is London to Brighton 9/6 (47½p) First Class, 6/3 (31p) Third Class. It must be borne in mind when comparing such fares that an unskilled workers wage was around £2. 10s. 0d. (£2.50) per week.

Left: West Croydon locomotive depot on 24th May 1926 with Nos. B266 and B270 on the left.
H.C. Casserley

52

The Newhaven boat train passing East Croydon hauled by a former L.B. & S.C.R. 4-4-2 'Atlantic' locomotive.   *Pamlin Prints*

L.B. & S.C.R. and S.E.C.R. mixed traffic locomotives, the 4-4-2s, 4-4-0 'Schools' and 4-6-0 'King Arthur' types were still in use on steam main line trains. London, Midland & Scottish and London & North Eastern Railway locomotives, too, would work through to the South Coast with holiday and excursion services.

In 1937 a relief train to the 15.15 Charing Cross to Hastings, via Sevenoaks, service was introduced. This ran via the Mid Kent line and Crowhurst Junctions.

The West Coast routes via Horsham and via Worthing to Littlehampton, Bognor Regis and Portsmouth were electrified from 3rd July 1938, further reducing the number of steam passenger trains.

The number of weekday trains from London to Brighton was now 68 and there were 29 Oxted trains. On the Woodside – Selsdon/Sanderstead line there were 40 'down' and 39 'up' trains, whilst Addiscombe (Croydon) dealt with 45 arrivals and departures. The same number of trains ran between Crystal Palace and Beckenham Junction. Between 08.00 and 09.00 East Croydon now had 27 trains to London, Purley had 15, West Croydon 12, whilst Waddon could boast 9.

The electric suburban services, with the odd exceptions, had, up to now, consisted of journeys between the London termini and the extremities of the suburban system, or a station short thereof, by the most direct or a reasonably direct route, interlinked like a spiders web by other services.

Those passing within the Borough boundaries in either direction were:-
Victoria - Epsom Downs via Thornton Heath and West Croydon.
London Bridge - Epsom Downs via Forest Hill and West Croydon.
Victoria - West Croydon via Crystal Palace and Norwood Junction.
Victoria - Beckenham Junction via Crystal Palace.

Victoria - Coulsdon North via Thornton Heath and East Croydon.
London Bridge - Coulsdon North via Forest Hill and East Croydon (peak hours).
Charing Cross/Cannon Street - Tattenham Corner/Caterham via Forest Hill and East Croydon.
Charing Cross/Cannon Street - Addiscombe (Croydon) via St. Johns and Elmers End.
Charing Cross/Cannon Street - Sanderstead via St. Johns and Elmers End linked by the following:-
West Croydon - Wimbledon via Waddon Marsh and Mitcham.
West Croydon - Holborn Viaduct via Sutton, St. Helier, Wimbledon, Tulse Hill and Herne Hill.
London Bridge - London Bridge via Forest Hill, Norwood Junction, Thornton Heath, Streatham and Peckham Rye.
The latter service along, with another which did not serve the Borough, – London Bridge - Forest Hill, Crystal Palace, Tulse Hill, Peckham Rye - London Bridge (and in the opposite direction) were popularly referred to as 'roundabouts' or 'rounders'.

The West Croydon - Holborn Viaduct service was usually combined with the Victoria - West Croydon via Crystal Palace and Norwood Junction service resulting in an extremely circuitous route between the two London termini – but 2 miles apart. Stopping at all stations en route meant that the overall journey time was around 1¾ hours! Even more interestingly between Streatham Hill and West Norwood such trains passed across the bridge over the Streatham line within sight of Tulse Hill station nearly an hour before or after calling at that station when travelling on the line below!

Main line electric trains ran between Victoria and London Bridge and places outside the suburban area, mainly the South Coast, via East Croydon. Some were fast, others semi-fast or 'all stations' (south of Purley) and generally each type of service ran hourly off peak. Steam services ran principally on the Oxted line

Former London & South Western Railway suburban electric train approaching Coulsdon North on the then 'down' local line. The through lines are on the right, and the Tattenham Corner lines, parallel at this point, can be seen on the left, below the houses. *Author*

to Brighton, Eastbourne, East Grinstead and Tunbridge Wells West etc., albeit not to a regular interval pattern.

The standard off peak main line electric service was:-
3 trains Victoria - Brighton - one non-stop, one semi-fast and one 'all stations'.
2 trains London Bridge - Brighton - one semi-fast and one 'all stations'.
1 train Victoria - Littlehampton via Worthing.
1 train Victoria - Ore (Hastings) via Eastbourne.
1 train Victoria - Portsmouth/Bognor Regis via Three Bridges and Horsham (certain hours only).

Most services, suburban and main line, were considerably increased at peak hours, a far larger percentage using London Bridge (the city gents' station) as the London terminus than at off peak times, and with different destinations or starting points and intermediate stops. Additional regular coastal services ran during the summer months.

The Second World War resulted in reductions. From 11th September 1939 most suburban services were cut to half hourly in the peak hours and hourly off peak, whilst some services were suspended. This proved inadequate, particularly in the peak hours, and a normal weekday service was resumed a week later. Emergency passenger service cuts from 16th October 1939 included the Crystal Palace – Beckenham Junction service becoming a shuttle between those two stations, Addiscombe (Croydon) being served during weekday peak hours only, and the Mid Kent service to and from Sanderstead becoming hourly during off peak periods and running only until 19.00 (15.00 on Saturdays) and not at all on Sundays. Various other main line and suburban services also experienced cuts.

Diesel shunting engines, among the first to be introduced, were operating in Norwood Yard during 1939.

Trains nationally were slowed down as a wartime pre-caution. This resulted in the Borough being party to the fastest

start to stop run in England for a while during the Spring of 1940 – Three Bridges to East Croydon at an average speed of 54.3 mph, until this, too, was slowed down.

Malachite green was adopted during 1940 for coaching stock, whilst most locomotives were painted black as a wartime measure.

Between May 27th and June 4th 1940 there were no trains serving Coulsdon South and the line to Redhill to allow the latter station to be solely used by Dunkirk evacuation trains.

From 1941 the electric services on the East London line no longer went beyond Shoreditch or Whitechapel.

1942 saw the introduction of electric locomotives. These first appeared on trial runs with 14 coaches. They were later used on freight and parcels workings and after the war on Newhaven boat trains and Royal trains.

The 3 and 6-car suburban trains were proving inadequate; for the remainder of the decade efforts were made to rectify the situation. At first two 3-car units would be run with two trailer coaches inserted between them. Other units were split up and reformed into 4-car units, all wooden bodied, whilst some had one larger steel coach inserted. Some all steel bodied 4-car units were eventually introduced, albeit many utilising parts from withdrawn wooden units.

The Brighton – London via Oxted line was a favourite trial and testing ground for locomotives leaving Brighton Works. On 21st June 1945 the first of the new streamlined 'West Country' class 4-6-2 locomotives being built there put in an appearance over this route. They were later to be stationed at Brighton Depot from where they were used on this route and also main line locomotive hauled workings.

From 1st October Coulsdon North was re-opened on Sundays.

For Derby Day 1946 34 trains were run to Tattenham Corner between 09.00 and 12.00.

Former L.M.S.R. 2-6-4 tank locomotive No. 42100 on a Victoria –
Brighton (via Oxted and Uckfield) train just south of Sanderstead,
30th August 1955.   *S.C. Nash*

More suburban services were reinstated from 7th October 1946, including the return of through working between Victoria and Beckenham Junction via Crystal Palace.

Train services were seriously affected by chalk falls on both the Redhill and Quarry lines in the vicinity of Hooley, simultaneously from 13th to 17th January 1947.

Full pre-war services were generally restored on all lines by 27th October 1948, although some suburban services were still subject to change, particularly the Addiscombe (Croydon) and Sanderstead via Mid Kent line routes, and the line between Crystal Palace and Beckenham Junction. Being some of the lightest used lines they were always the first to be considered whenever reductions or other economies were to be made.

From about this time former London, Midland & Scottish 2-6-4 tank locomotives were used for a period, mainly on the Oxted line. Some of these were painted black with huge white lettering 'BRITISH RAILWAYS' on the tank sides and large numbers on the coal bunker. On that line too, special trains, some with Pullman cars, were being run for Lingfield Steeplechases and special trains were also run to and from Edenbridge Town for the spectacular Guy Fawkes celebrations held in that town in the post war era, which attracted crowds from a wide area. Former London, Midland & Scottish Railway 2-6-2 tank locomotives had joined their 2-6-4 sisters on Oxted trains until B.R. Standard 2-6-4 tank locomotives, built at Brighton, gradually took over from them and the older L.B. & S.C.R., S.E.C.R. and S.R. types, the more veteran of which were scrapped. L.B. & S.C.R. 0-4-2 tank locomotive No. 32253 for example, built as No. 253 *Pelham* in 1882, had ventured regularly to East Croydon to work the rear portion of the 18.10 from Victoria commuter train,

A similar locomotive, No. 42097 passing Selsdon with a Tunbridge Wells to Victoria (via Ashurst) train on 21st April 1951. A Mid-Kent line electric train is in the background.   *S.C. Nash*

'Down' London Bridge to Tunbridge Wells West (via Ashurst) train passing Selsdon, hauled by ex-S.E.C.R. 'D' class 4-4-0 No. 31586, 28th August 1951. *R.C. Riley*

'Down' Oxted line train from Victoria passing over the local lines from Windmill Bridge Junction to Norwood Fork Junction (uplifted 1982). Gloucester Road Junction signal box (superseded in 1954) is on the left. Between the two, in the background, Selhurst Depot and Gloucester Road electrical switch cabin are visible. 'I3' class No. 32028 is in charge of the train, 21st April 1951. *S.C. Nash*

which divided there, until 1949, others dating back to the 1890s taking over until their turn came to be superseded.

After experiments with various colours B.R. decided to paint their express passenger locomotives royal blue with black and white lining, other passenger types green with black and orange lining, the remainder black. Locomotive hauled passenger vehicles were to be carmine (crimson) lake, corridor coaches having cream upper panels. Electric trains were to continue to be green. However, the royal blue was soon dropped in favour of green.

A Government call to save fuel resulted in the weekday evenings, Saturday afternoon and Sunday services between Crystal Palace and Beckenham Junction being withdrawn from 5th February to 22nd March 1951.

Electric locomotives had now appeared on a regular basis, mainly being used on the Newhaven boat train and main line freight services. An experimental diesel locomotive No. 10800 was also being tried out on Brighton – London services via Oxted, introducing a new form of traction to the Borough's passenger trains.

During the 1950s some new 2 and 4-car suburban electric multiple units were introduced. These had automatic couplers and an advanced electro-pneumatic braking system supplementing the air brake. Like main line units they used numerical headcodes. The older units continued to use letters until they were withdrawn, two headcodes applying to each route for several years.

Numerous assorted steam and diesel locomotives, many from other regions, also passed through the Borough to and from tests being carried out south of Three Bridges to test wear on rail ends.

Train travel was enjoying a boom time. Several reasons were attributable – a tendency to enjoy life after six years of war and subsequent years of continuing restrictions, few families had a car and, if they had, petrol was limited if not rationed, working class people were enjoying better pay and conditions allowing them more leisure time in which to go out and enabling them to afford to go on holiday. As yet there was little television to keep them at home and, moreover, fares were being held low.

Suburban and seaside traffic was at a particularly high level. There were for example 51 'down' trains on Mondays to Fridays on the Tattenham Corner line. Notwithstanding this 29 additional trains were run between 09.00 and 13.00 on Derby Day 1953, 25 return trains running between 17.00 and 19.00.

A very full excursion programme was serving the South Coast resorts and relief services were run to many of the normal trains, particularly on Saturdays. In the case of excursion trains for day trips to the coast experience had shown that if they all started from the London termini they would, on sunny days, be full and standing room only upon departure. It became the practice for some to be run empty to a suburban station to start up as a passenger train from there, usually calling at several more suburban stations – thence non-stop to the resort. This gave passengers from such stations a chance of a seat.

The converted A.C. electric units working the West Croydon – Wimbledon line were withdrawn in 1954, being replaced by new 2-car units.

Regular interval off peak services were introduced on the Oxted line with the Summer service in 1955. The one and only regular service booked via the Crowhurst Junctions – the 07.26 from Edenbridge to London Bridge – was withdrawn at the same time.

From 20th June 1955 10-car trains were provided during peak hours on the London Bridge – Tattenham Corner/Caterham services in an attempt to ease the overcrowding problem.

An example of the popularity of day trips to the coast can be obtained from the figures for August Bank Holiday Monday 1956 when there were 59 advertised trains from the London termini or suburban stations to the South Coast between 09.00 and 11.59 and 82 trains returning between 18.00 and 21.59.

The Brighton Works shunting locomotive – former L.B. & S.C.R. 'Terrier' 0-6-0 tank, built in June 1878 – resplendent in Stroudley's 'Improved Engine Green' livery, came up to the Borough to work the special Centenary trains over the Purley – Caterham line on 6th August 1956. The stock was a S.E.C.R. 'Birdcage' three coach set, thus suitably recognising the involvement of both companies in the early days.

Locomotive hauled trains were still headed by various types from vintage L.B. & S.C.R. and S.E.C.R. classes, through S.R. examples, and up to the latest B.R. Standard locomotives. London Midland and Eastern Region classes also appeared regularly on inter-regional services.

Some platform lengthening took place at several of the Borough's stations during the 1950s to cater for longer trains which were provided to cater for the increasing number of passengers. When Addiscombe platforms were lengthened to take 10-car trains, which were provided in peak hours on the Mid Kent lines from 4th March 1957, No. 1 platform line had to be re-routed to pass behind the signal box and No. 3 platform was abandoned.

Main line diesel locomotives were beginning to appear in greater numbers during the closing years of the 1950s, one of the first services to be regularly diesel hauled being the 14.42 from Margate to Cannon Street via Redhill and East Croydon. The livery sported by these locomotives was olive and dark green.

Services in 1958 included 29 trains each way on the Oxted line, Addiscombe dealt with 52 arrivals and 53 departures, the Woodside – Selsdon line had 37 each way, and the West Croydon – Wimbledon 40. The Victoria – West Croydon via Crystal Palace service consisted of 43 'down' and 44 'up', the Victoria – Beckenham Junction via Crystal Palace having 41 each way. There were 53 from Victoria via Thornton Heath to West Croydon/Epsom Downs and 51 in the other direction, the London Bridge – West Croydon/Epsom Downs service providing another 49 'down' and 50 'up'. Coulsdon North had 47 arrivals from Victoria and 15 from London Bridge and 47 departures to Victoria, 17 to London Bridge. The Tattenham Corner service was 54 'down', 52 'up', whilst the London Bridge – London Bridge 'Roundabout' service via Forest Hill, Norwood Junction, Thornton Heath, Streatham and Peckham Rye consisted of 42 trains, with 44 the other way round. Coulsdon South was served by 41 'down' and 38 'up' trains. The S.E.R. origin of this station and the tendency of 'city gents' to use London Bridge was still very much in evidence at that station – there being no direct train to Victoria between 07.08 and 10.09!

The Mid Kent services on the Addiscombe and Selsdon lines had, ever since the outbreak of the Second World War, varied considerably. Various timetable permutations involving through trains to and from London, shuttle services to and from Elmers End, the hours at which trains were provided and frequency of services had been experienced, often differing considerably on Mondays to Fridays, Saturdays and Sundays. The Crystal Palace – Beckenham Junction line had seen similar variations in train service patterns, too. Other routes had remained fairly constant up to this time.

Significant changes in traffic flows were, however, taking place. One was an increase in main line passenger travel consequent upon the establishment of a new town at Crawley in Sussex and the re-opening of Gatwick as a major international airport. To cater for these the existing Bognor Regis/Horsham –

Victoria – Tunbridge Wells West (via Oxted) train arriving at East Croydon in the early 1950s. This photograph depicts a locomotive of S.E.C.R. origin but carrying its B.R. number (31509). The upper quadrant signal (left), shunting signals and warning notice (foreground) are S.R., whilst the remaining signals and North signal box are L.B. & S.C.R.   *Lens of Sutton*

'Up' 'pick-up' freight train takes the Mid-Kent line at Selsdon en route to the sidings which were connected to that line, 30th August 1955. The locomotive is a former L.B. & S.C.R. 'C2X' class 0-6-0 No. 32445.   *R.C. Riley*

Three Bridges services were extended to Victoria and back, attaching a portion at Gatwick Airport on the 'up' journey and dropping it off on the way back, as from 9th June 1958, adding more trains to this busy main line.

Until this time peak hour services had run until early afternoon on Saturdays, but the five day working week was now firmly established so off peak services were provided all day on Saturdays from 14th June 1958.

There was also a notable reduction in off peak travel on certain lines, particularly in the suburban area and services were consequently reduced, the Tattenham Corner/Caterham line being one of the first affected, a 30 minute interval service being provided off peak instead of a 20 minute one from 15th September 1958. Others were to follow suit.

The 2.31pm West Croydon – Wimbledon train composed of converted 'A.C.' overhead unit No. 1810 leaves the industrial surroundings of Waddon Marsh on 23rd October 1954.   *J.J. Smith*

Some fares at this time were:-

	SINGLE FARES	
	First Class	**Second Class**
East Croydon – Victoria/ London Bridge	2/9 (13½p)	1/10 (9p)
East Croydon – Charing Cross	3/3 (16p)	2/2 (11p)
Thornton Heath Heath – Victoria		1/6 (7½p)
Thornton Heath – London Bridge		1/10 (9p)
Norwood Junction – Charing Cross/Victoria		1/10 (9p)
Norwood Junction – London Bridge		1/6 (7½p)
Coulsdon North or Kenley – Victoria/London Bridge		2/6 (12½p)
Coulsdon South – Victoria – London Bridge	4/- (20p)	2/8 (13p)
Addiscombe – Charing Cross		2/2 (11p)
Addiscombe – Cannon Street		2/- (10p)
Waddon Marsh – Victoria via Mitcham Junction		1/10 (9p)
Waddon Marsh – London Bridge via Mitcham Junction		2/2 (11p)
Waddon Marsh – Waterloo via Wimbledon		2/2 (11p)
Waddon Marsh – Victoria/ London Bridge via West Croydon		2/- (10p)
London – Brighton	12/9 (63½p)	8/6 (42½p)

Against these prices it must be borne in mind that an unskilled worker was earning less than £10 per week.

The Woodside – Selsdon service was altered to run only during peak hours on Mondays to Fridays and until mid afternoon on Saturdays from 2nd November 1959.

A stranger in the camp! Former L.S.W.R. 0-4-4T class 'M7' No. 30054 heads a 'down' Oxted line train through Selsdon on 30th August 1955.
R.C. Riley

1960 - 1978

This was a period of considerable changes. Steam trains and Pullman cars disappeared, the mechanised maintenance of track was introduced which required long weekend possessions of the line, particularly affecting Sunday travel where cancellation or diversion of services or alternative bus services were often necessary, whilst the Beeching Report discouraged occasional travel, as did the increases in fares.

Travelling habits through the period changed dramatically, increasing for much of the time in respect of peak hour travel, and all day long with the growth of Gatwick Airport, but generally decreasing so far as occasional travel, South Coast holidays and day trips were concerned. Some of this could be attributed to increased car ownership, the trend towards continental and air holidays and coach travel, and television having lessened the need for an outing to find entertainment.

The majority of Summer only, excursion and inter-regional services were withdrawn during the 1960s as the number of passengers dropped.

Changes to train services and workings were numerous, frequent and of such complexity that to list them all would be superfluous. These eighteen years will, therefore, be dealt with collectively, grouped under various headings.

WEEKDAYS – Main Line

At the start of the period holiday traffic was still heavy. For example on Saturday 11th August 1960, in addition to a full main line service with relief trains, excursions and special trains, there were the regular inter-regional Summer services from Manchester, Sheffield and Birmingham to the South Coast, and it was found necessary to provide relief trains from Stoke-on-Trent and Leicester.

During the early 1960s, owing to the work of electrifying the line between Sevenoaks and Dover, trains from the Sevenoaks route were frequently diverted via East Croydon and Redhill. This provided much variety in trains and locomotives including three named services – the 'Golden Arrow', the 'Night Ferry' and the 'Man of Kent'.

Upon the completion of this work in 1962 most through services via Redhill to and from places beyond Tonbridge were either cut back to turn round at that station, or were withdrawn. From 18th June 1962 the Portsmouth/Bognor Regis express services which had been running via the main line were altered to run via Mitcham Junction, Sutton and Dorking, giving that route an hourly service.

A hangover from S.E.C.R. days, the 17.25 from London Bridge to Reading and Tunbridge Wells West (latterly Tonbridge) steam passenger train via Redhill, was withdrawn from 18th February 1963, being replaced by a London Bridge to Reigate electric train with connecting services to Reading and Tonbridge at Redhill. For many years this train had maintained tradition by running non-stop to Coulsdon South – the first 'pure' S.E.C.R. station! The corresponding 'up' service, from Reading only, was also withdrawn. The 'up' service had for its last few years called at East Croydon.

An unusual service ran on Saturday evenings from 28th March 1963 between Victoria and Brighton, returning in the early hours of Sunday morning. This was the 'Regency Belle' organised by Charter Tours Ltd. in conjunction with the Brighton artistic set. The train was formed of refurbished Pullman cars with specially elaborate interior decorations, steam hauled by a West Country Class 4-6-2 locomotive in 'Royal' condition. There were Bunny Girl-type hostesses and a meal en route. Upon arrival at Brighton coaches conveyed the participants

to an hotel for dancing, gaming etc. – all in on a package fare. The venture was a great success on the first night but in subsequent weeks the numbers dwindled rapidly and it was discontinued after only four weeks.

The electric Pullman and Pantry 6-car units were superseded by new 4-car units in the mid 1960s. Some of the non Pullman or Pantry coaches were reformed into 6-car units and were in use as such for a few more years. The 'Brighton Belle', however, continued to operate until 1st May 1972 when it, too, was discontinued, except for a few commemorative trips shortly afterwards.

The 'down' 'Brighton Belle', unit No. 3053, passing East Croydon on 4th February 1972. *John Scrace*

The overall time of non-stop trains from Victoria to Brighton was reduced to 55 minutes on 10th July 1967.

The building of an L.C.C. overspill estate at Merstham and the rapid growth of places such as Burgess Hill and several other Sussex villages resulted in additional passenger traffic, including commuters to and from East Croydon and London. Additional peak hour trains were squeezed into the timetable, and extra stops were made by established services to serve these places. The pattern generally was for different trains to call at each of these stations to spread the load and to avoid turning the faster trains into 'all stations' services. This resulted in some unusual stopping sequences such as non-stop from East Croydon to Merstham, Balcombe or Wivelsfield.

To serve the ever growing Gatwick Airport traffic additional trains between Victoria and Gatwick Airport, over and above the Bognor Regis/Horsham services were introduced gradually during the 1960s and early 1970s, some initially running only during the summer months, or at night, or only weekends, until eventually two an hour were run in either direction during the daytime off peak hours, and one per hour at night, daily all the year round. Some of the night services were extended through to and from Brighton from 4th October 1974.

The growing importance of Croydon as a business and shopping centre was also recognised, some trains formerly running fast through East Croydon being altered to call at that station.

Oxted Line

From 18th June 1962 diesel multiple units and diesel locomotive hauled passenger trains were introduced on the Oxted line, reducing the number of steam trains running within the Borough.

A 7-coach train composed of converted electric stock – Set 900, later 701, was used on certain Oxted line services for a period

Stock to form an East Croydon – East Grinstead train behind B.R. standard 2-6-4T No. 80139 on 11th May 1960.　*John Scrace*

Diverted 'down' 'Golden Arrow' approaching South Croydon hauled by 'Battle of Britain' class pacific No. 34085 *501 Squadron*, 31st January 1960.　*S.C. Nash*

'Hop-Pickers' train on 10th September 1949 passing over the viaduct across a quarry south of Riddlesdown. It is composed entirely of former S.E.C.R. vehicles – an 0-6-0 freight locomotive, No. 31270, and 'Birdcage' stock, both dating from the early part of the century.   *Pamlin Prints*

from September 1963. This presented a strange sight on this non-electrified route as the drivers cabs were not removed.

Machines in the hopfields and the fact that many 'hoppers' now possessed a car meant that the 'Hoppers Specials' were no longer required.

Steam services on the Oxted line ceased from 6th January 1964 and from the same day through trains to and from Brighton via this route were discontinued.

There was a proposal to convert certain displaced 6-car main line electric units into push and pull sets, but only one – Set 601 – was so converted, being used on the Oxted line from 17th January 1966 for a short period, either hauled or propelled by a diesel locomotive.

Suburban

During the period under review off peak economies had become a first priority. Most services which had run more frequently than every 30 minutes were reduced to that interval.

Another economy was the withdrawal of platform staff at several stations. In connection with this as from 6th September 1965 the Tattenham Corner/Caterham services which attached or divided at Purley were altered, the Tattenham Corner portion now being at the London end of the combined trains between Purley and London. Booking offices on the Tattenham Corner branch were closed for the last few trains at night, on Saturday afternoons and all day on Sundays, tickets being sold by conductors on the trains. From 5th May 1969 this was extended to all trains except for the peak hours on Mondays to Fridays.

During off peak hours both the Tattenham Corner and Caterham lines were served by shuttle services to and from Purley from time to time, necessitiating changing at Purley into the service which ran through.

Other notable changes were:-

WEEKDAYS

Routes via East Croydon

Coulsdon North off peak services turned round at East Croydon, Coulsdon North station being open only during peak hours on Mondays to Fridays from 4th May 1970. This resulted in South Croydon and Purley Oaks being served only by Tattenham Corner/Caterham services off peak. Purley was, of course, also served by the stopping main line services.

Routes via West Croydon

Off peak services on the Epsom Downs branch were reduced from 10th September 1962, only the Victoria via West Croydon service going through, the London Bridge via West Croydon service turning round at Sutton. This was later changed, the Epsom Downs branch being served only by a service to and from London Bridge via Mitcham Junction, the Victoria via West Croydon services turning round at Sutton and the London Bridge via Forest Hill service at West Croydon. The latter was in practice usually combined with the West Croydon - Holborn Viaduct services (instead of the Victoria via Crystal Palace services as hitherto, this service now turning round at West Croydon). The time taken for the overall journey between London Bridge and Holborn Viaduct via the circuitous route was again around 1¾ hours, between two London termini only a mile apart! From 7th May 1973 things were again modified, the London Bridge via Mitcham Junction services turning round at Sutton, the Victoria via West Croydon services being extended to and from Epsom Downs again.

From 14th June 1964 Holborn Viaduct station was closed on Saturday afternoons, the West Croydon services turning round at Blackfriars. This applied all day on Saturdays from 4th May 1970 until 8th October 1976 when the entire line between Holborn Viaduct and Herne Hill (exclusive) lost its Saturday service, the trains being diverted to and from Victoria via Sutton, Wimbledon, Tooting and Balham.

The West Croydon – Wimbledon line lost its late evening services on Mondays to Fridays and its entire evening service on Saturdays from 7th November 1966.

'Roundabout' services and Crystal Palace – Beckenham Junction line

The London Bridge - Peckham Rye - Tulse Hill - Crystal Palace - Forest Hill - London Bridge (and in the opposite direction) service was altered to run only between London Bridge and Crystal Palace via Peckham Rye and Tulse Hill (and return) during off peak hours from 17th June 1963.

From 10th July 1967 the two 'Roundabout' services were combined to run from London Bridge to London Bridge via Peckham Rye, Tulse Hill, Streatham, Thornton Heath, Norwood Junction, Crystal Palace, Tulse Hill and Peckham Rye (and in the opposite direction). This new service was withdrawn on Saturdays from 9th October 1976.

The Crystal Palace – Beckenham Junction line was still subject to changes; these included a shuttle service between the two stations on Saturdays from 9th October 1976.

Mid Kent Lines

Variations in services continued as before, the principle changes being the reduction of the services. The Woodside – Selsdon line lost its Saturday service entirely from 2nd February 1967. Both this line and the Addiscombe branch suffered gradual reductions in the number of through trains to London, shuttles to and from Elmers End being provided in lieu. From April 1976 both lines were served only by shuttles (except for the odd Addiscombe services).

Peak Hours

During the period 1960 - 1978 the peak hour services on some lines were increased, but on others were reduced to take account of changing traffic flows.

SUNDAYS

Main line

The principle changes during the period were much in line with those applying to off peak weekday services, except for the London Bridge - Brighton or Three Bridges stopping services which were re-routed via Peckham Rye, Tulse Hill and Crystal

Palace to replace withdrawn suburban services (see later) from 9th July 1967 until 10th October 1976 when they, too, were withdrawn.

From 2nd May 1977 certain former non-stop Victoria - Brighton trains made an additional stop at East Croydon.

Suburban

The Crystal Palace - Beckenham Junction line continued with its variations in service, sometimes with through services to and from Victoria and at other times having a shuttle service between the two places. At the start of the period it had the novelty of a through service to and from London Bridge, brought about by the London Bridge - Peckham Rye - Tulse Hill - Crystal Palace - Forest Hill - London Bridge 'Roundabout' service, ceasing to run over the portion between Crystal Palace and London Bridge via Forest Hill (and in the opposite direction). As the Beckenham Junction line was served by a shuttle service at the time the two services were combined until 13th June 1960 when through services between Victoria and Beckenham Junction were resumed, whereupon the London Bridge service turned round at Crystal Palace. The latter was altered from 7th September 1964 to run only between Tulse Hill and Crystal Palace until being withdrawn along with the London Bridge - Tulse Hill - Streatham - Thornton Heath - Norwood Junction - Forest Hill - London Bridge (and in the opposite direction) 'Roundabout' service from 9th July 1967, when the London Bridge main line service was re-routed via Tulse Hill and Crystal Palace to compensate. Upon the main line service itself being discontinued from 9th October 1976 the London Bridge - Tulse Hill - Streatham - Thornton Heath - Norwood Junction - Forest Hill - London Bridge (and in the opposite direction) service was resurrected and a new service between London Bridge and East Croydon via Tulse Hill, Streatham and Thornton Heath was introduced. Both ran hourly.

The Victoria - Coulsdon North services ran only between Victoria and East Croydon from 6th September 1965.

Hourly services only were provided on the Tattenham Corner line from 7th September 1964. The Caterham line, however, continued to be served half hourly. After a few years it was reduced to hourly, alternate trains running only between Charing Cross and Purley. From 1st May 1977 the latter turned round at East Croydon instead, but an additional shuttle service, alternating with the through Charing Cross trains, was provided from Purley, giving the Caterham line two trains an hour again, albeit not with an even half hourly interval.

Holborn Viaduct station was closed on Sundays from 15th June 1964, the West Croydon services turning round at Blackfriars until the entire line between Holborn Viaduct and Herne Hill (exclusive) lost its Sunday service from 9th October 1976, the trains being diverted to and from Victoria as on Saturdays.

The West Croydon - Wimbledon line lost its Sunday service from 7th September 1964 and the Epsom Downs branch from 5th May 1969, the latters Victoria services via West Croydon turning round at Sutton.

GENERAL

Norwood Junction locomotive depot was closed in January 1964, a Diesel Depot in Norwood 'up' Yard taking over its function.

At about this time dark blue livery was adopted for all coaching stock and locomotives, corridor coaches having wide pale grey upper panels.

Electro-Diesel locomotives, which could run on either electric or diesel power, were introduced in the late 1960s, gradually replacing the electric ones.

Examples of singles fares in 1966 were:-

	First Class	Second Class
East Croydon – Victoria/London Bridge	4/2 (21p)	2/9 (13½p)
East Croydon – Charing Cross	4/11 (24½p)	3/3 (16p)
West Croydon – Victoria/London Bridge		2/9 (13½p)
West Croydon – Charing Cross		3/3 (16p)
Coulsdon North/Kenley – Victoria/London Bridge		3/9 (18½p)
Coulsdon South – Victoria/London Bridge	6/- (30p)	4/- (20p)
Thornton Heath – Victoria		2/3 (11p)
Thornton Heath – London Bridge		2/9 (13½p)
Addiscombe – Charing Cross		3/3 (16p)
London – Brighton	£1.0s.9d (£1.03½p)	14/- (70p)

The 1978 timetable

Until 1978 any revision of the services in the Croydon area, however extensive, was in reality only a further adaptation of the timetables which had applied since pre-Second World War times. In fact many services which had escaped the changes were still running at the same times, or very slightly modified.

B.R. Southern Region eventually decided that the time-tables had been soled and heeled too many times and introduced a completely new timetable, particularly on the Central Division which largely covered Croydon, as from 8th May 1978. The majority of services bore little resemblance to those hitherto. Even those which bore some similarity invariably ran at different minutes past the hour. So different were the nature of the new services and the routes they took that the numerical headcodes had to be completely revised.

One of the aims of the new timetable was to provide as many stations in the Central Division as possible with direct services to and from Gatwick Airport and either East or West Croydon. Where this was not possible a reduction in the number of changes of train was attempted. All regular passenger trains now called at East Croydon.

So far as the main line off peak services were concerned the principle changes included the discontinuance of the self-contained Victoria - Gatwick Airport services, these being replaced by half hourly services between Victoria and Brighton, which ran semi-fast between Victoria and Gatwick Airport, where a portion was detached on the 'down' and attached on the 'up' journey, but stopped at all stations between Gatwick Airport and Brighton. Between the latter stations these replaced the former Victoria and London Bridge stopping services which turned round at Three Bridges, the London Bridge trains running via Tulse Hill and Crystal Palace, giving stations on that route through trains to and from Gatwick Airport. The Victoria - Portsmouth/Bognor expresses, formerly via Mitcham Junction and Epsom, were re-routed via East Croydon, stopping at Gatwick Airport to pick up passengers on the 'down' and to detrain on the 'up' journey only. The Victoria - Ore and Victoria - Littlehampton via Worthing services called at Gatwick Airport for the same purposes, as did a Victoria - Brighton semi-fast service which had a different stopping pattern.

The half hourly Victoria - Bognor Regis/Horsham services still detached a portion at Gatwick Airport on the 'down' and attached on the 'up' journey, along with the aforementioned

Brighton trains providing four detachments and attachments per hour. These were the four services an hour which were publicised on Gatwick Airport advertisements but, in fact, if the all stations services and trains which called only to set down or pick up passengers from and to places south of Gatwick Airport were taken into account, there were now ten trains an hour to and from London serving the station!

The units which formed the portions detached and attached at Gatwick Airport (and under normal working generally remained on such services) soon appeared painted with the legend 'Rapid City Link London - Gatwick' in large white lettering on the sides of the coaches and with a 'ribbon' bearing the same words along the roofsides.

The principle changes in the Monday to Friday suburban services were:-

The withdrawal of the off peak 'Roundabout' services and curtailments of the peak hour ones.

Services were provided between London Bridge and East Croydon via Tulse Hill and Crystal Palace, alternate trains being the London Bridge - Three Bridges main line stopping service and a London Bridge - East Croydon suburban train.

Considerable changes were made to peak hour services, among them the provision of a 15 minute interval service on the Tattenham Corner/Caterham - London Bridge service, whilst the West Croydon line services included trains via Epsom and London Bridge trains via Crystal Palace and Tulse Hill. The West Croydon - Holborn Viaduct service now ran during off peak hours only and took the direct route via Thornton Heath, Streatham and Herne Hill. In the peak hours it ran instead to and from London Bridge via Thornton Heath, Streatham and

Peckham Rye. With other trains taking the direct route via Forest Hill there were services between West Croydon and London Bridge via three routes.

On Saturdays and Sundays the off peak main line and suburban services were somewhat similar. However, with the Holborn Viaduct line closed the West Croydon services, whilst still taking the direct route via Thornton Heath and Streatham, ran to and from London Bridge on Saturdays and did not run on Sundays. The London Bridge - West Croydon service was extended to run via Sutton, St. Helier, Wimbledon, Tooting and Peckham Rye to and from London Bridge, providing another 'Roundabout' variation in either direction. As there was no London Bridge - Three Bridges service via Tulse Hill and Crystal Palace on Sundays, trains were provided between London Bridge and East Croydon running alternate half hours via Tulse Hill and Crystal Palace or Tulse Hill, Streatham and Thornton Heath respectively. On Sundays the Crystal Palace - Beckenham Junction line was served by a shuttle service between Streatham Hill and Beckenham Junction.

1979 - 1984

From 14th May 1979 the above shuttle service was extended to and from Clapham Junction.

Inter-Regional passenger services were also re-introduced with locomotive hauled trains daily in either direction between Brighton and Manchester (Piccadilly) via the WLL. These were provided principally to give holiday-makers from the Midlands and North through trains to and from Gatwick Airport and Brighton, avoiding the need to cross London with their luggage. They took a circuitous route to serve various centres of

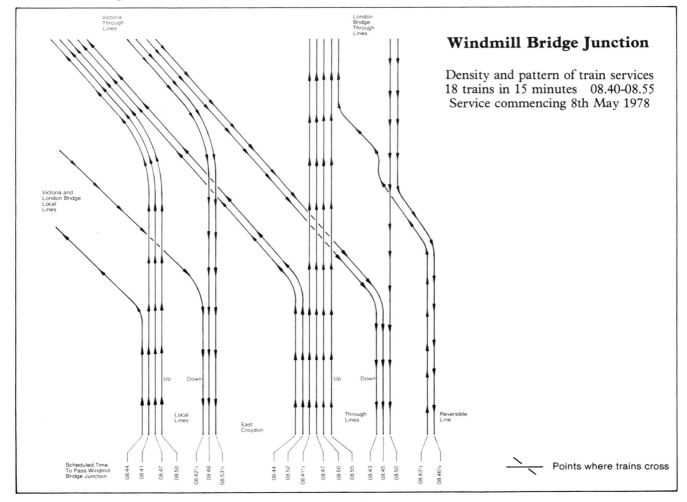

Windmill Bridge Junction

Density and pattern of train services
18 trains in 15 minutes   08.40-08.55
Service commencing 8th May 1978

Points where trains cross

population to give them similar facilities. Calling at East Croydon they also provided through facilities to and from these towns for the Borough's residents. They were non-stop between East Croydon and Reading, the other stops being Oxford, Banbury, Leamington Spa, Coventry, Birmingham (International) and (New St), Wolverhampton, Stafford, Crewe, Wilmslow, Stoke-on-Trent and Stockport. Not all of these stations were served by all the trains, various routes being taken, and some were served only on Saturdays and Sundays.

During 1980 non corridor trains began to appear painted with the wide grey band round the window area. Suburban electric trains so painted were also fitted with fluorescent lighting and a public address system enabling the guard to make announcements when necessary.

The service commencing 10th May 1980 brought a few changes, principally on the main line on Saturdays and Sundays, the Three Bridges stopping services being extended to and from Brighton, calling at all stations south of Three Bridges, in place of the Victoria semi-fast to Gatwick Airport then 'all stations' service which now ran only between Victoria and Gatwick Airport calling only at Clapham Junction.

At this time, even making allowance for the odd train cancellations, more than 1,400 passenger trains alone were run daily on Mondays to Fridays within the Borough's boundaries, around 1,000 of them passing through the multiple junction complex between East and West Croydon, Selhurst and Norwood Junction. Over 700 served East Croydon whilst West Croydon dealt with around 350.

In the peak hour, 08.00-08.59, the number of passenger trains leaving stations in the Borough in the direction of London was:- East Croydon 39, Norwood Junction 13, West Croydon 12, Purley 10, South Croydon, Selhurst, Thornton Heath and Norbury 9, Waddon 8, Purley Oaks, Woodside and Sanderstead 6, (two of the latter changing at Elmers End) Waddon Marsh 5 (changing at West Croydon or Mitcham Jct.), Coulsdon South, Reedham, Kenley and Riddlesdown 4, Coulsdon North, Smitham, Woodmansterne, Addiscombe, Bingham Road, Coombe Road and Selsdon 3 (the last four stations requiring a change at Elmers End).

There were consequently 178 alternative possibilities for catching a train from a Borough of Croydon station to a London terminus during that hour! There was at least one train (and sometimes several) advertised to leave at least one of the stations within the Borough on every minute within that hour with the exception of 08.08 and 08.38, the most popular times being 08.33 and 08.39 when six trains left Woodside, Riddlesdown, Thornton Heath and East Croydon (3 trains) and Coombe Road, South Croydon, Thornton Heath, Waddon Marsh and East Croydon (2 trains) respectively.

A further example of the facilities which the Borough's residents were enjoying could be obtained by considering Coulsdon in isolation. Although a small part of the Borough it had four stations - Coulsdon North, Coulsdon South, Smitham and Woodmansterne - served by 21, 39, 38 and 38 'up' trains respectively on Mondays to Fridays. Compare this with the entire COUNTY of Northamptonshire, served by only five stations - Northampton, Wellingborough, Kettering, Long Buckby and Kings Sutton. The 'up' service from these stations consisted of 23, 18, 21,19 and 10 trains respectively, despite the fact that the first three places each have a far greater population than Coulsdon. Moreover, there are several towns throughout Great Britain with a population higher than Coulsdon which have no station at all.

Another indication of the service provided was the fact that there were through services between East or West Croydon and more than 170 stations serving London, Gatwick Airport, the South Coast from Hastings to Portsmouth, the Midlands and the North of England, and the stations along these routes. The majority were served hourly or more frequently, although a few were served by only one or two specific trains.

Alterations to services henceforth consisted mainly of reductions for one reason or another. A glance at the timetable commencing 1st June 1981 reveals that economies had been made to poorly patronised services, particularly evening and weekend suburban trains. During the evening on Mondays to Fridays the Victoria - Beckenham Junction via Crystal Palace and London Bridge - Sutton via Forest Hill and West Croydon services were withdrawn. The Victoria - West Croydon via Crystal Palace service was altered to run via Thornton Heath, the Victoria - Epsom Downs trains running instead via Crystal Palace. The Caterham services ran only to and from London Bridge instead of Charing Cross, and made additional stops to cover the withdrawn Sutton service.

Somewhat similar arrangements applied on Saturday evenings and Sundays but as the London Bridge service via Forest Hill continued beyond Sutton as a 'roundabout' service on those days, that part of their journey was covered by extending the London Bridge - West Croydon via Streatham and Thornton Heath service on Saturday evenings and the Victoria - Sutton via Thornton Heath and West Croydon on Sundays, providing two more 'roundabout'/interlinking variations.

On the main line the most significant changes were to the off peak stopping services. The majority were now run between London Bridge and Redhill (instead of Three Bridges) on Mondays to Fridays and Brighton on Saturdays, via Tulse Hill and Crystal Palace, the increased frequency doing away with the need for the alternating London Bridge -East Croydon suburban service via that route. On Sundays, however, they were routed between London Bridge and Brighton via Forest Hill and Redhill.

Epsom Downs signal box was destroyed by fire during the night of 16th/17th November 1981. It was due to be superseded by the Victoria Signalling Centre in October 1982 (see Chapter Three) so renewal could not be justified. The temporary signalling arrangements provided, permitted only a shuttle service over a single line to and from Sutton, connecting with Victoria and London Bridge via West Croydon services which had to turn round at Sutton.

The major civil engineering and resignalling work being carried out in the East Croydon area in connection with the Brighton line resignalling scheme (see Chapter Three) taking place simultaneously with the building of a massive new airline terminal on a raft above the platforms at Victoria, led to further cuts and alterations from 5th October 1981. In connection with the former there was a need to thin out the density of peak hour services in the East Croydon area. Among the reductions were all three Mondays to Fridays morning peak services to London Bridge which called at Coulsdon South, resulting in that station having no direct train to London Bridge before 09.20. Twenty three years earlier it had no Victoria peak hour services!

With the work at Victoria, a couple of platforms were out of use at any one time throughout the period and consequently fewer trains could be dealt with. Several suburban services turned round at Clapham Junction and some main line services, including practically all Oxted line trains, ran to and from London Bridge instead, peak hour commuters on that line having the opposite plight to that of their Coulsdon South colleagues. Other services were altered, diverted, or made additional stops in lieu of the withdrawn services.

Similar diversions applied at weekends and several changes were made to other services. A major change on Saturdays was the introduction of yet another variation in main line stopping services. These now ran between Charing Cross and Redhill via

Left:
The 07.30 Manchester – Brighton train leaving East Croydon with class 47 No. 47534 on 15th April 1983.
John Scrace

Below: Pride of the line. A 'down' 'Gatwick Express' approaching South Croydon on 2nd June 1984. The locomotive is ED No. 73121 named *Croydon 1883-1983* in commemoration of the centenary of the granting of Borough status.
David Brown

Forest Hill and stopped additionally at certain suburban stations, taking the place of the Caterham services north of Purley. Alternate trains stopped at either South Croydon or Purley Oaks, thus reducing the frequency of services at those stations. Passengers to and from the Caterham and Tattenham Corner lines had to change at Purley, shuttle services being run on both branches. The route formerly taken between London Bridge and Norwood Junction via Tulse Hill and Crystal Palace was covered by a new suburban service. In the evening, when the Charing Cross - Redhill service was reduced to hourly, alternative Caterham services ran through to and from London Bridge.

Another alteration was to the Victoria - Portsmouth via East Croydon service on Saturdays. This no longer conveyed a portion for Bognor Regis, a separate train running via Mitcham Junction. Instead it was combined with the Victoria - Horsham service north of Gatwick Airport, running separately south thereof. Certain fast and semi-fast Brighton services were altered or withdrawn on both Saturdays and Sundays.

The train service commencing 17th May 1982 had few changes except for those in connection with the closure to passengers of the direct route between Selhurst and Norwood Junction. Coulsdon South commuters did, however, gain one morning peak train to London Bridge; the 07.11 from Bognor Regis calling additionally.

From August a suburban 4-car unit (No.4732) appeared in Southern Railway green livery. This was the last of the air-braked-only type to be overhauled prior to their withdrawal and was so painted to celebrate the event with the intention that it be used for enthusiasts specials and possibly for eventual preservation. It was also used on ordinary services, often coupled to, and contrasting with, a blue or blue and grey unit.

From 4th October through working was resumed on the Epsom Downs branch and some alterations were made to services as necessary to take account of the revised layout and working arrangements in the East Croydon area consequent upon the resignalling work.

The timetable commencing 16th May 1983 deleted the services on the Woodside - Selsdon line, now closed, and the Brighton - Manchester services were rescheduled, one southbound one starting only from Wolverhampton. Otherwise there were few changes.

On 16th July 1983, to celebrate 50 years of electric traction on the Brighton main line, a special record run was attempted from London Bridge to Brighton. It had been alleged that 47 minutes 44 seconds in the 'down' and 46 minutes 43 seconds had been achieved during trials prior to public electric services, but these were never made official. The special covered the journey in 41 minutes 38 seconds, thus definitely and officially setting up a new record from London to Brighton, albeit from London Bridge. The record of 1904 still stands, at least officially, from Victoria.

The pre-1951 suburban electric multiple units were scheduled for withdrawal with the revision of timetables from 1st October 1983, but in practice some continued to run for a few more weeks. Coulsdon North services were withdrawn from the same date, the station having closed, additional services being run to and from London and nearby Smitham to compensate. There were other minor changes.

The effect of the various cut backs meant that the feature on which the success of the Southern electric system had been built - frequent standard interval off peak services, fairly similar seven days a week and easy to remember, often making the need for reference to a timetable unnecessary - had gradually been

An Elmers End – Sanderstead train calls at Bingham Road on 6th May 1983.

John Scrace

eroded by the requirements of economical working and the engineering restrictions, until it had now gone 'right out of the window'. Five distinct suburban off peak patterns applied - Monday to Friday middle of the day, Monday to Friday evening, Saturday until late evening, Saturday late evening and Sundays - all with different services. Main line services, too, differed on Mondays to Fridays, Saturdays and Sundays.

With 4 million air passengers a year using Gatwick Airport station and with the prospect of considerable increases it was considered necessary to segregate airport passengers from others. Many of the former, being foreigners and/or unused to rail travel, had become something of a nuisance to ordinary passengers, often cramming themselves and their considerable baggage into any London service, including the stopping trains, instead of keeping to the services with Gatwick portions.

The answer was to provide frequent non-stop services of a distinctive type with clear directions to passengers, and so far as possible keeping to their own platforms, between Victoria and Gatwick Airport.

New trains composed of air conditioned stock resplendent in the latest 'Inter-City Executive' livery of dark grey upper and light grey lower panels with a red stripe along the side, worked on the 'push-pull' system, with an electro-diesel locomotive at the southern end, were provided. During the early part of 1984 these made trial and press runs, some even as additional passenger trains for public use.

During the same period, whilst the track layout at South Croydon was being remodelled in connection with the Brighton Line Re-signalling (See Chapter Three), opportunity was taken to install conductor rails between South Croydon and Selsdon where they could link up with those remaining from the now disused electrified route between Woodside and Sanderstead. There was speculation as to the reason, some thinking that an electrified service might be forthcoming between Sanderstead and the Brighton main line, but this seems unlikely for there is no crossover provided at Sanderstead under the re-signalling. It is probably only installed in readiness for future electrification to East Grinstead. Nevertheless a trial run was made over the section on 28th March 1984 to test the equipment.

The introduction of the 'Gatwick Express', as it had become officially titled, was on 14th June 1984 running every 15 minutes non-stop in either direction between Victoria and Gatwick Airport for most of the day taking 30 minutes.

Understandably these trains could not be slotted into the existing extensive timetable without revisions. Coinciding with the near completion of the re-signalling of the Brighton line throughout, the associated remodelling and realignment of tracks having reduced the need for so many permanent speed restrictions, and the increase in electrical power to 750 volts, some speeding up of trains was possible.

A completely new timetable was introduced. The Victoria - Brighton fast service now took only 53 minutes, including the stop at East Croydon.

Certain services which had been withdrawn in recent years were re-introduced, others, such as the Oxted line trains, which had been diverted to and from London Bridge, reverted to Victoria, (as did those turning round at Clapham Junction) and Coulsdon South regained more London Bridge commuter services. The West Croydon - Wimbledon line, however, had its services reduced to half hourly in the peak hours.

Certain off peak economies were made too. These included the absence of Victoria -East Croydon stopping services (other

Since 1962 the Oxted line services have been basically covered by diesel multiple units, but there are insufficient to cover all peak hour services and a few locomotive hauled trains are used to supplement them. A London Bridge to East Grinstead train is pictured approaching Sanderstead behind Class 33 No. 33059 on 6th May 1983.

John Scrace

services covering the stations between Streatham Common and Selhurst except on Sundays when the only link with East Croydon was provided by a main line service calling only at Thornton Heath), shuttle services on the Tattenham Corner line on Mondays to Fridays, and a half hourly service instead of a 20 minute one on the Addiscombe line. There was an increase in the number of trains between East Croydon and Charing Cross. In addition to the two Caterham services there was one from Reigate as well, each hour. On Sundays the main line stopping services were half hourly instead of hourly, alternately serving Brighton and Littlehampton or Horsham. Several suburban stations outside the Borough lost their service altogether.

Another economy feature introduced with this timetable was that of a 20 minute interval service serving a route up to a given point whence two trains would serve one destination/ starting point and the third another, thus giving the former uneven intervals of 20 and 40 minutes between trains. This applied for example on the Victoria - Crystal Palace line, two serving West Croydon and one Beckenham Junction, also between Charing Cross and Purley, two serving Caterham and one Reigate. On other routes a half hourly service covered the heavier used London end and then divided to give an hourly service on two lines e.g. Victoria - Sutton via West Croydon, thence alternately to Epsom or Epsom Downs.

Additional Inter-Regional services were also introduced giving several trains a day direct between East Croydon and the Midlands and North, and adding Derby, Burton-on-Trent, Tamworth, Macclesfield, Leeds, Hull, Wakefield (Westgate), Doncaster, Sheffield, Liverpool (Lime Street) and Runcorn to the list of stations served by through trains.

The alterations were far too elaborate to itemise. The off peak services in either direction within the Borough are, however, listed below to contrast with those applying prior to 1960:-

Surburban

Mondays to Fridays - Middle of the day

Victoria and Epsom Downs via Thornton Heath and West Croydon.
Victoria and Epsom via Thornton Heath and West Croydon.
Victoria and Holborn Viaduct via Thornton Heath, West Croydon, Sutton, St. Helier, Wimbledon, Tooting and Herne Hill.
Victoria and West Croydon via Crystal Palace.
Victoria and Beckenham Junction via Crystal Palace.
London Bridge and East Croydon via Tulse Hill, Streatham and Thornton Heath.
London Bridge and East Croydon via Tulse Hill and Crystal Palace.
London Bridge and Holborn Viaduct via Forest Hill, West Croydon, Sutton, St. Helier, Wimbledon, Tooting and Herne Hill.
Charing Cross and Caterham via Forest Hill.
Purley and Tattenham Corner.
West Croydon and Wimbledon via Waddon Marsh and Mitcham Junction.
Elmers End and Addiscombe.

Mondays to Fridays - Late evening

Victoria and Epsom Downs via Thornton Heath and West Croydon.
Victoria and Blackfriars via Thornton Heath, West Croydon, Sutton, St. Helier, Wimbledon, Tooting and Herne Hill.
Victoria and West Croydon via Crystal Palace.

London Bridge and East Croydon via Tulse Hill, Streatham and Thornton Heath.
London Bridge and Epsom via Forest Hill and West Croydon.
Charing Cross and Caterham via Forest Hill.
Purley and Tattenham Corner.
Elmers End and Addiscombe.

Saturdays until the evening

Victoria and Epsom Downs via Thornton Heath and West Croydon.
Victoria and Epsom via Thornton Heath and West Croydon.
Victoria and London Bridge via Thornton Heath, West Croydon, Sutton, St. Helier, Wimbledon, Tooting and Peckham Rye.
Victoria and West Croydon via Crystal Palace.
Victoria and Beckenham Junction via Crystal Palace.
London Bridge and East Croydon via Tulse Hill, Streatham and Thornton Heath.
London Bridge and East Croydon via Tulse Hill and Crystal Palace.
London Bridge and London Bridge via Forest Hill, West Croydon, Sutton, St. Helier, Wimbledon, Tooting and Peckham Rye.
Charing Cross and Caterham via Forest Hill.
Purley and Tattenham Corner.
West Croydon and Wimbledon.
Elmers End and Addiscombe.

Saturday evening

Victoria and Epsom Downs via Thornton Heath and West Croydon.
Victoria and London Bridge via Thornton Heath, West Croydon, Sutton, St. Helier, Wimbledon, Tooting and Peckham Rye.
Victoria and West Croydon via Crystal Palace.
London Bridge and East Croydon via Tulse Hill, Streatham and Thornton Heath.
London Bridge and Epsom via Forest Hill and West Croydon.
Charing Cross and Caterham via Forest Hill.
Purley and Tattenham Corner.
Elmers End and Addiscombe.

Sundays

Victoria and Wimbledon via Thornton Heath, West Croydon, Sutton and St. Helier.
Victoria and West Croydon via Crystal Palace.
Victoria and Epsom via Crystal Palace and West Croydon.
London Bridge and East Croydon via Forest Hill.
Charing Cross and Caterham.
Purley and Tattenham Corner.

Main Line (all via East Croydon)

Weekdays

Victoria and Gatwick Airport (Gatwick Expresses).
Victoria and Brighton (calling only East Croydon)(not late evenings).
Victoria and Brighton Semi-fast via Quarry line.
Victoria and Brighton Semi-fast via Redhill.
Victoria and Portsmouth/Littlehampton via Worthing.
Victoria and Bognor Regis via Horsham.
Victoria and Horsham.
Victoria and Hastings or Ore.
Victoria-Oxted line.
Charing Cross-Reigate via Forest Hill.
London Bridge and Redhill via Tulse Hill, Streatham and Thornton Heath (middle of the day).
London Bridge and Redhill via Tulse Hill and Crystal Palace (evenings).

Sundays

Victoria and Gatwick Airport (Gatwick Expresses).
Victoria and Brighton Semi-fast via Quarry line.
Victoria and Brighton Stopping via Redhill.
Victoria and Hastings.
Victoria and Bognor via Horsham.
Victoria and Littlehampton or Horsham Stopping via Redhill.
Victoria and Portsmouth/Littlehampton via Worthing.
Victoria and Oxted line.

Unfortunately to timetable the Gatwick Expresses with their non stop timings it was necessary for other Victoria services to be bunched together following the express, leaving a gap ahead of the next express, and a small reduction in the number of ordinary trains. This lead to overcrowding, particularly on the first train of a bunch which had accumulated more passengers at East Croydon because of the gap. Those obliged to stand saw little comfort in watching the Gatwick Expresses passing through, often lightly loaded - an unavoidable feature when dealing with air traffic which fluctuates according to season, time of day, weather conditions, aircraft schedules and time-keeping, and which was also intentional to allow for the future anticipated growth in traffic. Before the end of the year, figures were published showing that more than twice as many passengers travelled between Victoria and Gatwick Airport than between any other two stations on the entire Inter-City network, and despite its relatively short distance, reflected in its fares, it came third in the amount of revenue taken!

Minor train service alterations were made from 1st October 1984 including the resumption of Victoria - Brighton express services during the late evening. In May 1985 alterations included off peak re-routings; the Victoria-Epsom via Thornton Heath and West Croydon taking the St. Helier route, the London Bridge service via West Croydon going instead to Epsom. The Sunday main line service called at Selhurst instead of Thornton Heath.

Examples of fares in 1985 are:-

SINGLE FARE TO LONDON FROM	First Class	Second Class
East Croydon	£2.10p	£1.40p
West Croydon, Waddon Marsh or Addiscombe		£1.40p
Norwood Junction	£1.80p	£1.20p
Riddlesdown	£2.60p	£1.70p
Coulsdon South	£2.70p	£1.80p
Kenley		£1.80p
Brighton	£9.10p	£6.00p

In some cases, however, a Day Return costs little more than a single ticket. Brighton for example can be visited for the day from London for £6.60 Second Class. For shorter distances the comparison is not so close, an East Croydon Day Return being £1.90 Second Class.

The popular belief is that rail fares have increased out of all proportion to income and the price of other commodities. This is not the case. Using the unskilled worker referred to throughout this section of the book, it is revealing to compare how long he had to work to provide the money to pay for ordinary Second Class tickets for himself, his wife and two children say from London to Brighton and back for a holiday. In 1841 nearly 6 weeks of his earnings would be needed (or over 7 weeks by horse carriage (outside)). In 1860 over 4 weeks pay would be used up. The reduction continued so that in 1936 by Third Class (Second having been abolished) nearly 4 days pay would suffice. The decrease continued largely as a result of fares being held low until in 1966 he would only need to use up about 1½ days earnings. At 1985 levels he still requires less than 2 days pay - up in comparison but still considerably less in proportion to pre-Second World War figures. Ordinary fares have increased to around 20 times their pre-war prices.

Many other everyday commodities have increased much more - particularly the cost of buying a house within the Borough, and there cannot be many occupations where pay has gone up less. Other types of tickets, which have concessions which fluctuate according to marketing demands, have, of course, increased by more or less than this amount. One of the biggest percentage increases has been that in respect of Season Tickets, made more noticeable by the fact that most commuters use them only 5 days a week nowadays. The scrapping of Workmens Tickets also resulted in a considerable increase in fares for those who had formerly used them.

Reduced off peak demand has made the Borough's railways gradually more commuter orientated. Almost half its stations have been affected by periods of train service withdrawal. Selsdon, Coombe Road, Bingham Road and Coulsdon North had only peak hour services long before their final closure. Waddon Marsh and the Crystal Palace - Beckenham Junction line have lost their Saturday evening and Sunday services, whilst Woodside and Addiscombe see no Sunday trains. Kenley and Purley Oaks are not served on Sundays although trains pass through, whilst Smitham and Sanderstead have known periods of Sunday closure in the past. Several stations have also had severe reductions in their off peak services. Even peak hour travelling has reduced, but to a lesser degree, and this is related to the comparable reduction in the number of trains run.

Despite this there are still around 1,200 passenger trains alone scheduled daily on Mondays to Fridays within the Borough, over 560 serving East Croydon and 235 West Croydon, with 148 possibilities of catching a train to a London terminus between 08.00 and 08.59, with nearly 180 stations served by direct services to and from East or West Croydon.

With such intensive services the whole timetable is like a huge jig-saw puzzle - if everything fits in its correct place all is well and the running of trains is a joy to watch. However, the slightest failure or incident causing delay to one train will result in delay to several following trains. All the delayed trains will then approach the next junction late and will conflict with the 'on time' trains on the other unaffected line. Trains on one line or the other will have to wait, resulting in further delays - so tight are the schedules - hence the delays 'snowball', particularly in the peak hours.

What are the prospects for the future? With new electric main line and suburban trains being introduced, a new maintenance, servicing and repair depot being developed at Selhurst to look after them, the electrification of the Oxted line and the Farringdon route, re-opened, (the latter giving through services between Croydon and the North London suburbs), the possibility of a more frequent cross London service via the WLL being considered, and the probability of new stations at East and West Croydon. The only cloud on the horizon is the continuing need for economies forced upon B.R. by the Government, and in the event of the more extreme options of the Serpell Report being applied, this would severely reduce the facilities presently enjoyed by the Borough's rail travellers.

Part Three - **Other Traffic**

The conveyance of considerable numbers of passengers has been the principle task for the railways in the Borough for most of their existence. Other traffic, however, has to be catered for.

FREIGHT

Once the conveyance of freight became established, shunting/marshalling yards were set up in various places, Norwood Yard, the selected site within the Borough, being provided during the 1870s and extended during the 1880s. In conjunction with this two goods loops were laid alongside the 'up' main line between Windmill Bridge Junction and Norwood Fork Junction about 1881 into which freight trains could be recessed awaiting acceptance into Norwood 'up' Yard. A third was added around the turn of the century. These became known as the 'Teetotallers Sidings', given the name by train crews who,when hoping to dispose of their train in the Yard, booked off and reached a pub before closing time, were thwarted by being held there! The third loop ceased to have an entrance at the Windmill Bridge Junction end soon after the First World War, becoming a siding from Norwood Fork Junction only. It was abolished after the Second World War. The second loop was put out of use on 17th April 1971, eventually being removed, the third remaining in use until 1982.

Other yards in the vicinity were at Bricklayers Arms/ Willow Walk, New Cross (Gate), Battersea and Redhill. Freight trains were run direct between these and other more distant yards, including those on the railways north of the Thames via the West London, East London or Farringdon Street routes, according to the nature of the regular traffic.

Many stations had their own small yards, usually with goods shed and crane, to serve the general traders and invariably the local coal merchants. 'Pick up' freight trains serving several stations were run from the larger shunting/marshalling yards conveying any traffic which had accumulated from the various incoming services, invariably including a general wagon of parcels carried at the cheaper freight train rates plus any empty wagons that had been ordered for outgoing traffic, and returning with surplus empty wagons and any loaded traffic which had emanated from the local traders. Upon arrival back at the shunting/marshalling yard these were forwarded on the appropriate service to another yard, thence from yard to yard as necessary until probably finishing their journeys on another 'pick up' service. Most 'pick up' trips were run in the early morning following the arrival of the bulk of the traffic from other yards during the night hours, returning after the morning passenger peak period. Over 20 such return trips were run daily from Norwood Yard.

The position of the Yards at Norwood - the 'down' yard stretching from Norwood Junction station to Windmill Bridge Junction and the 'up' yard from Norwood Fork Junction and near Selhurst to Norwood Junction - made for good working arrange-

View from Norwood Fork Junction signal box. From the left can be seen Norwood 'Down' Yard, the East Croydon – London Bridge main lines, the three 'Teetotaller' sidings, and the cottages which gave their name to Cottage Bridge Junction. In the foreground are the 'down' local lines to East and West Croydon.

A freight train at South Croydon c.1920 hauled by L.B. & S.C.R. 'C2' class No. 536.

Pamlin Prints

ments. Generally speaking the 'down' yard dealt with south-bound traffic and the 'up' yard with northbound traffic. To assist with this, freight trains from Battersea or the West London line were normally booked to run via Crystal Palace giving a 'down' side arrival at Norwood Yard. This served another purpose, the return northbound service would be in the 'up' yard so by running this via Thornton Heath the need for the steam locomotive to be turned was avoided. One awkward working was in respect of 'down' freight trains for the West Croydon direction. The line towards West Croydon from Norwood Junction is on a rising embankment to gain the flyover, so such trains had to propel from the 'down' yard back into Norwood Junction station and then charge up the rising gradient, sometimes failing in the attempt!

Some firms possessed private sidings served by rail. At East Croydon and Coulsdon North Messrs Hall & Co. provided their own locomotives to shunt their traffic - six different locomotives having been recorded over the years. The layout at their Coulsdon North depot was extensive. The site of these former sidings is rapidly disappearing under factory and warehouse development but it is still possible to see a re-inforced embankment which carried them in Ullswater Crescent, near Coulsdon South station.

Private locomotives, steam, diesel and electric have featured in the Gas and Electricity Power station private siding complexes at Waddon Marsh. Many other firms also had private sidings there, mostly connected to the goods siding between Waddon Marsh and Beddington Lane.

Half a mile to the west of Waddon station there was a private siding off the 'down' line serving the National Aircraft Factory from May 1918 until 1924, whilst on the 'up' Tattenham Corner line, one near the present site of Woodmansterne station

served Clock House Farm until 28th August 1926 and another nearer Purley, and controlled from Purley East signal box, served Reedham Orphanage.

At Norwood Junction there were private sidings leading from the 'down' shunting yard, the keys of which were kept in the Goods Foreman's Office.

At Selsdon a private siding leading from the 'up' Oxted line until the 1960s, was served with Continental Ferry wagons in the latter stages. After the goods yard at that station was closed new private sidings for unloading paraffin into storage tanks were installed. Similarly, at Purley part of the former goods yard was taken over to accommodate inwards trainloads of aggregate and coal.

Hall's chain loco (No. 9) at East Croydon 25th March 1933.

Pamlin Prints

Another Norwood Yard to Lewes freight train passing South Croydon in the late 1950s, hauled by former L.B. & S.C.R. 'K' class 2-6-0 No. 32341.
Author

The same service a few weeks later, now hauled by a relatively new class 71 electric locomotive.
Author

A revolution took place during the 1960s and 1970s. It had long been appreciated that the conveyance of odd wagon load traffic, with all its associated shunting and the need to run the 'pick up' trains, was highly uneconomical. As common carriers by law, however, the railways were obliged to carry it. A combination of the revoking of this obligation and the increasing popularity of road transport, which, now that petrol rationing had ceased, was able to provide point-to-point convenience at lower costs, meant that there was a sharp decrease in such traffic and many yards and sidings were no longer required and could be closed and removed. Not only did this cut the losses which had occurred from carrying uneconomical traffic (which could now be refused) allowing the remaining traffic to be concentrated in fewer places, but it also reduced the costs of maintaining and renewing the track, points and signals and the number of staff

required at many of the stations, and in some cases also released valuable land which could be sold.

Coulsdon South had been an early casualty, losing its freight facilities as early as 1st October 1931, the Southern Railway no doubt realising that there was no call for goods traffic to be dealt with at this station as well as at Coulsdon North and Smitham, particularly now that competition was over.

Other stations in the Borough ceased to deal with general freight traffic as follows:- Kenley 3rd April 1961, Sanderstead 20th May 1961, Smitham 7th May 1962, Woodside 30th September 1963, Addiscombe 17th June 1968, Thornton Heath, Waddon, Selsdon and Coulsdon North 7th October 1968, Purley 6th January 1969 and East Croydon 7th May 1973. Norwood Junction, no doubt due to its connecting with the 'up' yard from whence it could be served, survived until January 1982.

A 'down' freight train, hauled by former L.B. & S.C.R. 0-6-2T No. 32416, approaching West Croydon en route to Waddon Marsh, 8th June 1957.
J.J. Smith

Maunsell 2-6-0 No. 1825 throws out black smoke over the splendid gantry of signals as it approaches East Croydon with a Norwood Yard to Lewes freight on 5th October 1952.
J.J. Smith

During the period of decline attempts were made to run more profitable express freight trains with guaranteed next day arrival for the traffic. They were given names - 'The Midlands Merseyman' conveying traffic for the Midlands and North West from 6th January 1964 and the 'North East Trader' taking traffic for the north east from November 1965. Both started from Brighton and called at East Croydon. They attracted some traffic but did not really catch on.

The traffic best served by rail and the most profitable is full load traffic - complete trainloads between two places on a regular basis, often requiring only one locomotive and train crew to make the return journey with loaded and empty trains, and this became the policy. Examples that have already been so dealt with include aircraft fuel from Ripple Lane (Dagenham) and Stanlow (Cheshire) to Salfords (for Gatwick Airport), paraffin from the Isle of Grain (near Gravesend) to Selsdon, oil from the Isle of Grain to various power stations, oil from Fawley (Southampton) to Waddon Marsh, aggregate from Westbury (Wilts) to Ardingly and from Cliffe (near Gravesend) to Purley and Crawley, sand from Redhill to Ravenhead (Lancs) and breakfast cereals from Trafford Park (Manchester) to Crawley.

As a result of this policy the remarshalling of freight trains is rapidly becoming a thing of the past and little shunting is now performed even in Norwood Yard, which is a shadow of its former self, the majority of the sidings having been taken up.

PARCELS

Over the years miscellaneous parcels and mail forwarded by passenger trains have been conveyed in the guards van or in vans attached or detached to or from locomotive hauled trains. There were also some electric multiple unit trains which served as mail trains on a regular basis, the mail bags being loaded in the passenger compartments as well as the guards vans. Where possible trains which would otherwise be running as empty stock movements were utilised for the purpose.

There has, however, always been a need for several complete parcels van trains where the traffic is consistently heavy.

Among these have been the Dover night mail trains, which for many years included a travelling post office sorting coach in their formation. It was possible to post a letter, albeit at a slightly higher postal charge, into a letter box on the side of the sorting coach whilst either the 'down' or 'up' mail trains were in the platforms at East Croydon in the very early hours of the morning and it would almost certainly be delivered in Kent or London

(whichever direction the train was heading) by the first post the same day! Only the 'down' train still runs via East Croydon, minus the sorting coach.

Newspaper trains from London Bridge to Brighton and Bexhill daily, also to Chichester on Sundays, are run early in the morning. They were altered to run, along with the Dover mail, from Victoria instead of London Bridge when the resignalling work was taking place at the latter station in the 1970s, but reverted to London Bridge when the Victoria airline raft platform closures commenced.

A train from Angmering, and latterly Chichester, to Victoria has for many years conveyed market traffic.

Two services which ran until the 1960s were an early morning fish train from London Bridge to Brighton, attaching vehicles from the East Coast fishing ports which had arrived via the ELL at New Cross Gate, and a service from Willesden Junction to East Croydon via Crystal Palace and return. The latter was a 'hangover' from the days of separate railway companies. It was obliged to run to ensure the retention of running powers obtained by the London and North Western Railway and continued by the London, Midland and Scottish Railway, and often consisted of no more than a tank locomotive and a guards van conveying perhaps one or two parcels. Because of this it was known to the staff as 'Nuts and Bolts'. It was, in fact, shown in the staff Working Timetables as a Horse Box train, but particularly in the latter years such a vehicle would be unlikely. Should there be one, or a truck of cattle requiring transfer across London, this train was a means of conveying it.

There are also other general parcels and mail van trains between London and the coast, and in recent years with a reduction in the number of stations dealing with parcels traffic, there has been a tendency for through trains to distant destinations via circuitous routes, serving the principal towns en route and avoiding the need to tranship across London. Such an example was one either way between Bricklayers Arms and Didcot via East Croydon, Redhill and Reading.

EMPTY STOCK TRAINS

Quite a number of empty trains are run within the Borough. This is of necessity, the travelling habits being that a considerably greater number of passengers travel in one direction than the other, particularly in the peak hours.

At the start of suburban passenger services several empty trains will leave Selhurst Depot where they have been serviced during the night heading for various suburban locations to start up the service. After the morning peak, several trains which are now surplus to requirements will run to Selhurst Depot from terminating points, usually the London termini. They will be serviced and in mid afternoon will again run empty, usually to a London terminus, to form an evening peak service. After the evening peak some more trains will run empty to Selhurst Depot, whilst others will follow around midnight as the services finish.

Careful programming of the trains is designed so that different trains arrive at the Depot in each batch, thus rotating the servicing and maintenance.

The LMR 'Nuts and Bolts' train hauled by 2-6-4 No. 42367 in the former sidings between platforms 2 and 3 at East Croydon, awaiting its return to Willesden, 15th February 1962.   *S.C. Nash*

There is also some empty running in peak hours in the opposite direction to the passenger flow, by trains, having completed one early peak hour journey, returning to form a later one.

Trains taken out of service due to defects will also run empty to Selhurst Depot for attention, and if possible a replacement train will be run to take its place.

After completing a morning peak run to London a train of Oxted line diesel units runs to and from the Diesel Depot at St. Leonards (near Hastings) for servicing before forming an evening peak service.

MISCELLANEOUS

Over the years various assorted types of trains have run on the Borough's tracks.

Things of the past are circus and farm removal trains. In the case of the former the circus equipment, staff and animals would all travel from place to place in the same train, consisting of passenger coaches and covered vans. The farm removal would be a more unusual spectacle with the farm equipment, animals, the farmers family, and often his employees and their families too, along with their furniture, all on one train consisting of passenger coaches, horse boxes, cattle trucks, covered vans and flat wagons loaded with furniture containers, tractors, hayrakes, ploughs and carts, etc. These ran right up to B.R. days.

In the early 1950s the Household Cavalry Musical Ride passed through East Croydon en route between Windsor and Tunbridge Wells West via Oxted to appear at the Agricultural Show in the Royal Borough. Their train consisted of passenger coaches and horse boxes.

Travelling exhibition trains, usually consisting of converted passenger coaches containing the items already set out for display, and gaudily painted on the outside to advertise the wares, have been occasional visitors, invariably stopping for a few days in the remaining sidings behind East Croydon signal box, where the public were admitted.

The miscellaneous paraphernalia of the railway technical departments are often in the area. These have included diesel and steam cranes, used for track and bridge renewals and for re-railing derailed vehicles, and track relayers which take out and replace lengths of track in complete units. There are various 'On Track' machines such as tamping machines which lift the track and pack the ballast firmly beneath it, track lining machines which work on a 'magic eye' principle, seeking out and correcting defects in track alignment, levels and cant, rail grinding machines which grind the rail surfaces where necessary to smooth out uneven wear, track recording machines which run about like conventional trains but are fitted with sensitive apparatus which records deficiencies in the track on a graph, at the same time spilling a blob of paint to indicate the precise position of the spot requiring attention, and ballast cleaning machines which dig out the ballast from beneath themselves on to a built-in conveyor belt whence it is taken up to a vibrating sieve which separates small stones, dirt and rubbish from reusable ballast. The rejected matter falls on to another conveyor belt leading to a swivelling jib which allows it to be directed either into wagons on the adjacent line or on to the bank as desired. The re-usable ballast returns to the track below.

All these 'On Track' machines, as their name implies, perform their work to the track they are themselves running upon.

A converted electric multiple unit is used as a stores train, running between maintenance depots, including Selhurst.

There are also seasonal trains. In the autumn, on the Oxted line in particular, difficulties are experienced with fallen leaves on the rails. These become squashed and the sap is squeezed out. This, moulded with the leaves, and sometimes rain as well, forms a slippery solution on the rail surfaces causing adhesion problems for trains, both in running - the wheels spinning round - and when braking - the wheels sliding. This can cause considerable delay and excessive wear to the wheel tyres. To combat this a locomotive powered water cannon train is run. The vehicles are another converted electric multiple unit fitted with strong jets of water which are forced on to the rails to clear the solution. It is often necessary for the train to be run two or three times a day.

During the winter months ice forming on the electric conductor rails can result in difficulties for electric trains in obtaining power. Other converted electric multiple units therefore run, which spray a special de-icing fluid on to the conductor rails.

Weed killing spray trains are run, chiefly in the Spring. These deliver a weed killing solution to the tracks and their immediate surroundings.

Inspection Saloons are another occasional sight. These can either be attached to an ordinary train or be run separately, hauled or propelled by a locomotive. They convey the railway officers on tours of inspection. When used by the Civil Engineer they are invariably run separately, enabling scheduled stops to be made at pre-determined sites, often between stations, several engineering aspects being inspected in one trip. These are sometimes used for crew training, particularly to accustom them to changes during re-signalling.

Two or three times in an average year Royal trains pass through the Borough. A regular one is to Tattenham Corner on Derby Day. Others are usually in connection with Royal, Presidential or State Visits when Gatwick Airport is the arrival venue. Members of the Royal Family travel from Victoria to Gatwick Airport to meet the guests and the Royal train then conveys the combined ensemble to Victoria for the official welcoming ceremony. Rather than use the full Royal train for these short journeys, a 4-coach formation is used. Until 1977 this sometimes included an ancient Royal Saloon dating back to the early days of the century, with wooden bodywork and steam heating. As Southern Region locomotives were not fitted with the latter after steam trains ceased, diesel locomotives from other regions, which were fitted with steam generators, had to be specially allocated to work this train. A more modern collection of coaches is now provided and Southern Region locomotives, usually Electro-Diesels, can be used.

Despite the apparent monopoly of multiple unit trains within the Borough this chapter has shown that there is, indeed, quite a bit of variation and the traffic is not entirely devoid of interest.

Chapter Three

Signalling

When considering chapters on signalling and accidents a 'which came first, the chicken or the egg' situation arises, so interlinked are the two subjects.

Signalling had become necessary when the possibility of collisions was realised, accidents however continued, albeit at a declining rate as advances in signalling methods were made. Increasing speed and numbers of trains created new accident potential so signalling systems have been, and still are, constantly improved. As a result collisions are so infrequent that when one does occur it will make the headlines in the national press, and on radio and Television should there be even one injury or fatality, out of all proportion to the lesser coverage given to the daily collisions on the roads which kill thousands every year.

The deciding factor as to which to deal with first was the fact that most of the accidents were attributable to the misuse of signalling apparatus or the disregard of signals, so for the uninitiated the signalling must be explained first.

In the very early days trains were so infrequent that there was no need to keep them apart. Moreover, prior to the coming of the railways no-one had ever travelled faster than by horse and the consequence of a collision between vehicles at speed, particularly on a guided track where avoiding action by swerving cannot be taken, could not be envisaged.

The first 'signalling' was simply a wave from the policeman on the track setting the points by hand. This was soon improved upon by the introduction of flags and oil hand lamps.

The London and Greenwich Railway ran an intensive service and in consequence provided the first 'fixed' signals - red/orange discs mounted on posts. These showed full face to the driver of an approaching train to indicate 'Danger, Stop' and were rotated 90 degrees so that the edge only was shown to the driver to indicate 'Proceed'. The latter only indicated that the points were set, not that the line ahead was clear.

With the addition of the London and Croydon Railway services in 1839 the portion of line between London Bridge and Corbetts Lane was by far the most heavily trafficked line anywhere and it was realised that something better was required particularly to prevent collisions at converging points. At the Corbetts Lane Junction the first concentration of signals from one control point was installed. This consisted of a building resembling a lighthouse from which signals were exhibited to drivers after the policemen had set the points. The indications by day were with the rotating discs altered to mean 'full face to driver' - junction set for Croydon, 'edge on' - junction set for Greenwich. By night a powerful red reflected light was indicated in all directions if the route was set for Croydon and a similar white light if set for Greenwich. It will be realised that under this primitive method it was not possible to show 'Danger, Stop' in all directions at the same time and these signals could not be used to control the frequency of trains on the same route. They were really only junction route indicators, although of course they could only show one route set at a time and thus gave collision protection between the traffic of the two routes. The 'lighthouse' is sometimes referred to as the first signal box.

When the London and Brighton Railway came into being they provided similar rotating signals to those already in use except that they provided two discs, one on either side of the post and they controlled the spacing of trains.

With the addition of South Eastern Railway services known to be in the offing it is not surprising that new inventions in signalling were invariably introduced on the busiest railway - from London Bridge to Croydon. The first semaphore signal was tried out at New Cross in 1841 by the London and Croydon, followed in 1842 by a decision by both that Company and the London and Brighton to supersede the rotating discs with semaphores. The South Eastern Railway, being a later entrant, used semaphores from the start. These early semaphore signals gave three indications - arm horizontal, 'Stop' 45 degrees downwards, 'Caution', 90 degrees downwards into a slot in the post, 'Clear'.

'Time Interval' working was used. Under this system a signal indicated to a driver not only which way the points were set but also whether a prescribed period of time (according to locality) had elapsed since the previous train had passed. The driver still had to keep a good lookout for the train in front should it have broken down, slowed down or otherwise not kept its distance.

In 1843 the first installation with points and signals operated from the control point was introduced at Bricklayers Arms Junction. This, too, is also referred to as the first signal box and it certainly was more conventional than the Corbetts Lane lighthouse. The signals were operated by the feet in stirrups and the points by levers mounted alongside. The stirrups only were provided with simple interlocking to prevent them from conflicting with one another. The signals did not, however, prove that the points were properly set.

During the summer of 1844 a similar installation was provided at Brighton Junction near Croydon. The three junctions on probably the busiest railway in the world were now equipped with some form of signalling!

As train speeds increased it was found that drivers experienced difficulty in stopping in time upon sighting a signal at danger. It was considered that the solution was to provide another signal some distance on the approach side to give an advanced warning of the position of the signal ahead. These were originally called *distance* signals and later as *distant* signals. They either indicated 'Clear' if the signal ahead had been operated for the train to proceed, or 'Caution' if not. At first a train was required to stop at a signal at 'Caution' and then proceed slowly but this was later altered to require the driver only to slow down being prepared to stop at the signal ahead. They were introduced in 1846.

The L.B. & S.C.R. re-introduced the two disc rotating signals as distance signals to differentiate from the stop signals but the other companies provided identical signals, relying on the drivers knowledge of the route.

During the same year the S.E.R. introduced the electric telegraph, followed shortly afterwards by the L.B. & S.C.R. This supplemented the 'Time Interval' working by allowing messages to be passed.

At this stage at stations there was usually a signal for either direction on the same post midway along the platform and worked by the station clerk. At junctions signals usually sprouted from the roof of the signal box. The signals did not provide an indication of where a train should stop should they be at danger as is the case today, the driver was expected to use his discretion when stopping, and at junctions to stop short of the fouling point of other routes.

During the 1850s signal boxes were being provided more generally throughout the system, albeit with little or no inter-locking between signals, points etc. Collisions and near misses occurred and it was obvious that something more sophisticated was necessary. In 1851 the S.E.R. tried out single stroke bells between signals boxes on which code messages could be exchanged. The Electric Telegraph was also used, morse code messages relating to the running of trains being exchanged. In the following year they improved on this by introducing 'Block Working'. This was based on the portion of line between two signal boxes being regarded as a block section, upon which only one train at a time was permitted - no matter how long the first train might take to pass through the section. No longer were trains forwarded with a certain time interval behind the previous one, but with the certainty that the section was clear.

The L.B. & S.C.R. immediately went one better by installing primitive electrical instruments visually giving an indication of the state of the block section. These were installed between London Bridge and both stations at Croydon and simply indicated 'Train In' or 'Train Out'. Like most future types of block instruments they were named after the inventor - Bartholomew.

The railway companies were none too keen on providing improved signalling, (a) it was expensive, and (b) they considered that giving drivers an assurance that the block section was clear could result in their relaxing too much and not keeping a good lookout!

East Croydon was, nevertheless, resignalled, possibly as a result of the accident on 21st August 1854 (See Chapter Four).

At about this time another experiment was tried out at Bricklayers Arms Junction - simultaneous points and signals. With this system the operation of only one lever would alter the points and operate the relevant signal. This proved unsafe for should the points move ¾ over, the signal would show ¾ clear and should a driver accept that signal, a derailment would occur. As a result the junction was again resignalled, the new apparatus coming into use from 10th January 1858.

From about 1860 proper interlocking was adopted gener-ally and signalling began to be carried out in a more proper manner, signal boxes being provided at most stations and junctions situated between. From 1862 Tyers block instruments were installed on the busier lines of the L.B. & S.C.R. These instruments, working in conjunction with electrical single stroke bell codes between signal boxes, had indicators resembling two model semaphore signals, one white, one red (applicable to the line approaching and the opposite line going away respectively). The instruments had three bell keys - one used to accept a train (causing the small white arm at the accepting end and the small red arm at the signal box in rear to drop downwards to 45 degrees), one to acknowledge that the train had entered the section (causing the small arms to return to the horizontal position) and the third for sending any bell code which did not require the small arms to move. The main failing of Tyers instruments was that they indicated the same whether no train was signalled or there was a train in the section. An improvement worked on a similar principle was invented by Harper. This differed in having only two bell keys, any bell code requiring to be forwarded without moving the small arms having to be given on the bell key appropriate to the position of the white arm at the time. The main advantage over Tyers was that a rotary indicator at the acceptance end showed the three states of the block section - whether no train was signalled, a train was accepted, or a train was in the block section.

In 1864 Walkers instruments were invented on the S.E.R. These worked similarly and showed the three states of the block section but with only one bell key, the turning of the rotary indicator prior to giving the bell codes causing the arms to indicate appropriately upon the code being sent.

The train service density was increasing particularly on the main line and additional signal boxes were provided to increase the number of block sections and thus permit trains to run at more frequent intervals. One such box within the Borough was provided by 1865, being named Selsdon, although it was just south of South Croydon on the Brighton line.

Later in the decade Walker invented train describer instruments for use at the busiest places. These had clock faces on which the required descriptions were indicated in place of the hour numbers at both forwarding and receiving ends. There was one pointer hand to indicate the description of the train. At the forwarding end there were handles round the clock face opposite each description. To describe a train the handle applicable to the description previously sent had to be pushed back. This released the pointer hand which ticked round clockwise, one description at a time, by clockwork until the required handle for the train being described was pulled forward causing it to stop. The position of the pointer hand was electrically repeated at the receiving end thus advising the signalman there of the identity of the train. This was supplementary to the normal block signalling.

Interlocking between levers was installed on a greater scale during the 1870s. In 1872 the L.B. & S.C.R. decided to replace the double disc distant signals with semaphores. Signals generally whether stop or distant, were similar, painted red with a white band near the unpivoted end (except on the L.B. & S.C.R. where the band was black) and exhibiting a red light by night for either stop or caution, drivers route knowledge still being relied upon! The L.B. & S.C.R. thought up an idea to distinguish distant signals by day - cutting out a fishtail from the end of the arm. The first was installed at Norwood Junction in August 1872. The idea was such a success that it was adopted nationally.

All passenger lines on the S.E.R. and L.C.D.R. were controlled by block working by 1873 and by the end of 1874 the block system applied on all passenger lines of the L.B. & S.C.R. During 1877 the latter completed interlocking between all points and signals.

At first block working had consisted of messages between consecutive signal boxes when a train entered or left the section. On receipt of the latter another train could be signalled into the section. It was improved upon over the years until the eventual method of block working was as follows:- Provided that the bell signal had been received indicating that the previous train had left the section the signalman at the rear end (or entrance to) the section forwarded a coded bell signal to the signalman ahead requesting permission to signal an approaching train.

The signalman in advance had the control of the block section, with the power to accept or refuse the train. Normally he would accept provided that the block section and a specified distance (usually ¼ mile) beyond was clear and he would not be fouling or occupying it by shunting or passing a train over a junction, and his signals had been replaced to danger behind the previous train. Acceptance was by acknowledging the bell signal by repetition. If he was not in a position to accept he would not acknowledge. Not until he received the acknowledgement was the signalman in rear permitted to allow the train into the block section. When the train passed him he would forward another bell signal to indicate that the train had entered the section. Similarly when the train passed the signalman in advance he would forward another bell signal to advise the signalman in rear that the train had left the block section. This sequence was then repeated through consecutive block sections.

All bell signals, except a non-acceptance, were immediately acknowledged by repetition, thus ensuring that they were understood.

Under this system, with numerous bell codes available, both to describe the type of train and pass it through the section, also to cover emergency situations, it became possible to signal trains throughout a shift without speaking to the signalman at the signal box on either side, all messages being passed as coded bell signals, yet provide a safe method of working.

This method still applies today on lines where block working through block sections has not been superseded by more modern signalling methods.

The L.B. & S.C.R., however, had their own method of block working. Whilst the principles were the same, they acknowledged the 'Is Line Clear' bell signal (which they referred to as the 'Warning') even if the train was not accepted. An additional ring was given when accepting to lower the arm on the Tyers or Harpers instrument. The 'Warning' code was repeated to indicate that the train was entering the section. They also used a different code from other companies to indicate that the train had cleared the block section.

During the 1880s semaphore signals which dropped into slots on the post were being superseded by signal arms pivoted on the front of the post which moved downwards from horizontal to 45 degrees to indicate 'Clear'.

A much more advanced block instrument had now been invented and was being installed. This was Syke's Lock and Block. With all types of block instruments 'messages' applicable to the signalling of trains were exchanged between signal boxes by a system of bell codes. In the case of the older types of block instruments the actual bell codes being given either on the appropriate bell key or with the block instrument at the accepting end set to the correct position caused the indicators on the block instrument at the signal box in rear to alter.

With Sykes Lock and Block the bells and block instruments were separated, a plunger being provided to give an electrical release to the signal box in rear.

An elaborate combination of electrical currents, magnets, treadles on the rails and physical rodding between levers and block instruments ensured that once a train had been accepted it had to run completely through the block section, with all apparatus operated in a correct sequence, before the plunger could again be operated to accept another train.

The Sykes block instrument in its simplest form consisted of the plunger with an associated switch hook which could be placed over the plunger to prevent it being pushed, above which there was a glass-fronted indicator inside which were two moveable tablets. The bottom tablet, applicable to the block section approaching the signal box, could show either a blank indication or 'Train On', the top tablet, applicable to the block section ahead, could show either 'Locked' or 'Free'. On top of the instrument another glass-fronted indicator contained a miniature red signal arm. This also applied to the block section ahead.

The normal position of the Sykes block instrument when no trains were about was:-

Bottom tablet - blank, Switch hook - off the plunger, Top tablet - 'Locked', Miniature red signal arm - 45 degrees downwards.

Thornton Heath 12th August 1900. The 'Sunday Gang' are putting in a new cross-over line. Note the mixture of goods vehicles in the background and the well-to-do passengers looking on.

R.C. Riley Collection

The normal sequence of events to signal a train through a block section, say between 'A' and 'B' signal boxes (for simplicity both having only one 'stop' signal) was as follows:-

Provided the previous train had cleared the section when the train to be signalled reached a given point 'A' asked 'B' whether the line was clear for the train. (Should the previous train have still been in the section this was withheld until the message was received that it had cleared.)

'B', if ready to accept the train, pressed his plunger. (This altered his own bottom tablet to 'Train On', 'A's top tablet from 'Locked' to 'Free', raised 'A's miniature signal arm to horizontal, and released 'A's signal.

'A' operated his signal. (When 'A' operated the lever of the signal his top tablet returned to 'Locked'.)

'A' advised 'B' when the train entered the block section. On receipt of this 'B' placed his switch hook over his plunger.

When the train passed over a treadle on the rails beyond the signal 'A's top tablet once again changed to 'Free'. (This permitted 'A' to fully replace his signal lever, reverting his top tablet to 'Locked'). 'B' repeated the sequence to the signal box ahead. When he replaced his signal behind the train his bottom tablet changed from 'Train On' to blank.

He advised 'A' that the train was out of the section and took his switch hook off the plunger. This caused the miniature signal arm at 'A' lower to 45 degrees.

The apparatus for the block section 'A' to 'B' had now completed its proper sequence, had reverted to its original state and was available for the signalling of the next train.

Should this sequence not be fully carried out, e.g. the train terminate, or be shunted to a siding, or a treadle fail to operate, the apparatus remained locked up. Release keys had to be provided for use in such circumstances, strict caution and discipline being required by the signalman to ensure that the release key was only used when absolutely necessary and he had assured himself that he was in order to do so.

Refinements were introduced, such as additional Sykes apparatus between consecutive signals operated from the same signal box as well as for the block sections (thus locking each signal behind each train until the preceding train had passed the next signal and it had been replaced to danger) and points having to be set prior to the acceptance of a train from the signal box in rear, being locked in that position when the plunger was pushed.

Such additions, whilst in normal conditions provided considerable safeguards against signalmens errors, they unfortunately increased the number of occasions when it was necessary to use the release key, particularly at places where considerable shunting movements were carried out, each invariably not completing a full sequence of movement resulting in tablets or treadles not being actuated.

A facing point lock and simultaneously operated bar. The 'sliding bolt' is in the centre of the track and the end of the bar can be seen inside the top rail (left).

Consequently there were occasions, usually when a signalman was working under abnormal pressure, of the release key being irregularly used, resulting in more than one train being on a section of line at the same time, occasionally resulting in collisions.

In its complexity the Sykes block instrument and its associated refinements must have been every bit as revolutionary to the Victorian railwayman as electronic, computerised and micro-chip equipment is to the present day staff.

Other safeguards being introduced included various types of fouling bars on the inside of rails, depressed physically by a trains wheels flanges, and electrical treadles actuated by the passage of a train over them. These were invariably provided at places out of sight of the signalman or otherwise considered vulnerable. The operation and/or clearance of such equipment was electrically indicated in the signal box to give the signalman a visual reminder of the trains position, usually also being adapted to lock the levers of signals approaching them when the indicator showed the line to be occupied by a train.

Facing points (where trains diverge from one line to two in the normal direction of running) were being provided with locks, consisting of a sliding bolt in the centre of the track which passed through slots on the bar connecting the two point switches. If the points were not perfectly closed the slot applicable would not be in line with the bolt which would, consequently, not go in, and the lever could not complete its movement, preventing the signal from being operated. Some signals were also provided with detectors which worked on a similar principle. In this case the 'bolt' was provided beside the points, forming part of the signal wire route between signal lever and signal. The bar connecting the two point switches extended outside the rails to the 'bolt'. Both 'bolt' and bar had slots cut in them which had to be perfectly in line, thus proving the points to be perfectly set. If they were not, the 'bolt' and the wire beyond this point would not pull and thus the signal arm would not 'clear'.

Locks on facing points were often provided with a bar, operated simultaneously with the sliding bolt on the same lever. This horizontal bar, situated on the inside of a rail just below the wheel flanges of a train, lifted up and down again as the sliding bolt moved into or out of the slot. Should a signalman attempt to unlock the facing points whilst a train was passing he was prevented from doing so by the sheer weight of the train, the wheel flanges preventing the bar from lifting. The presence of trains on these bars was not indicated in the signal box, the trains wheel flanges only coming into contact with them in the event of a signalmans premature attempt to operate the lever. These levers were particularly heavy to operate (even without a train on the bar!) and required a certain technique and expertise in swinging the lever. This particularly applied where more than one lock and bar were worked from one lever, as was often the case, or if they were located some distance from the signal box. The longer distance points and signals worked manually by rod and wire were also heavy to operate, hernias being an accepted occupational hazard for signalmen.

There were physical limits to the distance such apparatus could be worked, in consequence a signal box had to be provided wherever points and/or signals were necessary if the nearest existing signal box was too far away. As signals were necessary at frequent intervals to cater for the intensive train services, particularly in the suburban area, and as most stations and junctions had points, signal boxes were numerous, some stations needing more than one.

The shunting signals of both the L.B. & S.C.R. and S.E.R. were in use. The former used a revolving type consisting of two discs set at 90 degrees to one another. The red disc, usually bearing a hand with pointing forefinger to indicate the position on the track the signal applied to, indicated 'Stop' when facing the driver. The signal revolved a quarter of a circle so that the green disc, usually with a white cross, faced the driver to indicate 'Proceed'. The latter, in early days, used a revolving type too, but with horizontal and 45 degree arms respectively, but later used a wide, stubby and thick cast iron semaphore arm which was cleared to 45 degrees in the lower quadrant by the simple means of the signal wire literally pulling the end of the arm downwards, and which returned to the horizontal 'Stop' position just as simply upon the wire being released, a heavy weight on the other end of the arm dropping by gravity.

The main running signals of both companies were also in evidence, varying in their appearance, principally as a result of the L.B. & S.C.R. signal arms being slightly tapered and the colour spectacles for the night indications being larger, particularly the green one. The S.E.R. signal arms often varied in length, and their colour spectacles were considerably smaller. Various subsiduary and repeater signals were provided where necessary.

S.E.C.R. lower quadrant signals at Woodside. The 'distant' signals are for Bingham Road Intermediate signals (left) and Addiscombe (right). The shunting signal is of the S.R. type.
Pamlin Prints

L.B. & S.C.R. lower quadrant signals at Selhurst Junction ('down' local line). The 'distant' signal on the left was controlled by Norwood Fork Junction, and the other two by Gloucester Road Junction – for trains to East or West Croydon respectively.
R.C. Riley Collection

L.B. & S.C.R. signals in 1918, (note the red 'distant' signals), the 'stop' signals were controlled from East Croydon South signal box. The 'distant' signals pointing to the left belong to East Croydon North signal box and those pointing to the right to South Croydon station signal box.

R.C. Riley Collection

L.B. & S.C.R. signal gantry. The 'stop' signals were controlled from South Croydon station signal box and the 'distant' signals from South Croydon Junction. The separate 'distant' signals apply to the Oxted line in conjunction with the 'stop' signal on the next post to the right. Photograph taken 11th September 1948.

Pamlin Prints

Within the Borough, block working, with the progressive introduction of Sykes Lock and Block apparatus on the principle lines and Harpers, Tyers or Walkers instruments elsewhere along with the treadles, locks, bars and signals that were in vogue in the 1880s, was to continue to be the method of signalling, albeit with minor improvements, for the next 50 - 100 years until eventually being superseded by more advanced systems.

Some signal boxes were, however, slightly relocated or rebuilt as a result of track layout alterations, or because extensions were required to the lever frames to accommodate the additional signals, points etc. being introduced. Selsdon signal box on the Brighton main line was superseded by a new box - called Purley Intermediate - 1,000 yards further south, on 29th January 1882.

On 23rd July 1885 West Croydon North signal box was replaced by a new box on the 'up' side of the line, and upon the opening of Coulsdon (S.E.R.) station on 1st October 1889 a signal box was provided there, at the south end of the 'down' platform.

During the 1890s the L.B. & S.C.R. conformed to the more general practice of a white band, instead of a black one, on red signal arms.

At about this time an intermediate signal box was provided on the 'up' side of the Oxted line, south of Riddlesdown Tunnel.

An unusual layout was provided from 17th March 1895. Gloucester Road Junction, which at that time was a simple double line junction of the East Croydon and West Croydon local lines to and from London Bridge, was altered physically so that the point switches were at Norwood Fork Junction and could be worked from the signal box there. The routes did not geographically separate there, the rails running interlaced to Gloucester Road to take their original courses. The advantage gained was the dispensing with Gloucester Road Junction signal box, an early example of the trend to reduce the number of signal boxes and signalmen that was to take place in future years, and still continued today. In this particular case it was probably an early part of the remodelling of the area which was to take place over the next eight years.

Until 21st March 1897 there had been two signal boxes just to the south of East Croydon, practically opposite one another. One was called Fairfield Junction and controlled the junction of the Central Croydon branch and the local lines, whilst the other, East Croydon South, controlled the remainder of the layout. From that date a new East Croydon South signal box was commissioned to take over the work of both boxes, Fairfield Junction and the old South boxes being abolished.

In conjunction with the revised layout, with a proper junction between the Brighton main line and the Kingswood and Caterham branches, from 31st October 1897 there were three signal boxes at Purley station, Purley North and Purley South at the respective ends of the 'up' main line (now No.3) platform - both L.B. & S.C.R. boxes, and Purley East, a S.E.R. box, situated in the 'V' of the junction of the Kingswood and Caterham lines, to deal with the trains serving those two branches only, plus the connection with the S.E.R.'s new locomotive depot between the Kingswood and Brighton lines. As Purley was an L.B. & S.C.R. station the east signal box came under the jurisdiction of the Kenley Station Master!

Along with the remodelling and enlarging of Croydon (Addiscombe Road) station in 1899 a new signal box replaced the old one.

Upon the Brighton line being quadrupled in 1899 Purley Intermediate signal box was superseded after a life of only 17 years, closing on 23rd July. A replacement box, 300 yards further south, was called Purley Oaks, being near the new station. It was brought into use in stages, being fully commissioned on the day of the opening of the new lines - 5th November. South Croydon Junction signal box was also relocated, from a position just to the south of the 'down main' platform into the 'V' between the 'main' and Oxted lines. New signal boxes were provided at Stoats Nest Central (80 levers), controlling the new terminus (the erstwhile Coulsdon North), Stoats Nest South (35 levers), at the junction on the Quarry line just south of the station, which also worked a connection between the 'down' Quarry line and the Carriage Sidings/Locomotive Depot, and Stoats Nest Shunting (36 levers) used for movements between the terminus and the sidings. The previous Stoats Nest signal box dating from 1874 was pulled down and a new box built. This was called Stoats Nest North, had 24 levers, and controlled only the original two main lines and the connections from them.

At about this time Electric Train Staff apparatus was installed on the West Croydon - Wimbledon line. This was an improvement on previous primitive methods of ensuring that only one train was allowed on to the single line at one time - even more essential than on double lines as a head-on collision could result. Under the new system instruments were provided at either end of each single line block section, containing 'staffs' (resembling batons) which were a drivers authority to allow his train on to the single line. The signalman requiring to run a train would withdraw one from his instrument upon an electrical release being given by the signalman at the further end of the single line block section. This release could only be given if all the 'staffs' provided were in the instruments at both ends of the section totalled together. As a 'staff' was withdrawn it passed through and turned a rotary mechanism. This interrupted an electrical circuit linking the instruments at both ends of the single line block section preventing another 'staff' being withdrawn until the one in use was returned to the instrument at either end, re-creating the electrical circuit. Safety and flexibility were achieved by this system, for all trains could enter the single line block section in possession of a 'staff' from whichever end was required next, so long as there was still at least one 'staff' still in the instrument at the end it was to enter, for if an uneven flow of traffic had occurred if there were, say, 16 'staffs' provided, whether there were 8 in each instrument or 15 in one and 1 in the other the electrical circuit was operative and a 'staff' could be withdrawn.

The similar appearance of both 'stop' and 'distant' signals by night was also being overcome. A new type of signal lamp case and other equipment for distant signals, known as Coligny Welch apparatus, was being introduced. The lamp and its case had an additional side glass through which the oil light shone into reflecting apparatus resulting in a white fishtailed light appearing to the right of the red or green indication.

On 3rd June 1901 a signal box was provided at Smitham prior to the opening of the station there, and at about the same time another called Asylum was introduced a matter of ¾ mile further down the Chipstead Valley line.

Upon the Streatham Junction - Windmill Bridge Junction line being quadrupled in 1903 another junction (to and from the new local lines) was required at Gloucester Road and as trains would require to run to and from both East and West Croydon the original Gloucester Road Junction was re-instated, albeit slightly further south, the interlacing being removed. A Gloucester Road Junction signal box was again provided, but as it controlled the junctions at Gloucester Road and St. James Junction as well, this allowed the signal box at the latter to be abolished. Thornton Heath and Selhurst Junction signal boxes had to be relocated to make room for the new local lines.

In the early days of the new century another signal box was introduced on the Quarry line. This was called Cane Hill

Intermediate, and being on the 'down' side just south of the covered way, it was within the Borough. Stoats Nest North signal box, which had been on the 'down' side behind the sidings, was abolished shortly afterwards, its work being added to the Central box. With the renaming of Stoats Nest station on 1st June 1911 the Central, South and Shunting boxes were prefixed Coulsdon until about 1918 when the full prefix of Coulsdon & Smitham Downs was used.

In view of the anticipated increased train services resulting from the impending electrification, new signal boxes, simply to shorten the block sections, were provided within the Borough at Norbury Manor (between Norbury and Thornton Heath) and Whitehorse Road (between Thornton Heath and Selhurst). They were erected in the Summer of 1914 but so far as can be established they were never used. The delay in the completion of the electrification due to the First World War appears to have given time for reconsideration, for when electrification eventually came the more extensive services were catered for without them.

West Croydon North signal box got in the way of the work associated with the overhead electrification so it was abolished on 16th May 1915, being replaced by a new signal box of the same name (later West Croydon 'A' and eventually West Croydon signal box). Due to lack of space it was positioned high up to be clear of the future overhead wires and their structures, which provided the signalman with a fine aerial view of the station area and the lines under his control.

Coulsdon North signal box, which started its 84 year existence as Stoats Nest Central and was in turn known as Coulsdon Central, Coulsdon & Smitham Downs Central, and Coulsdon North No. 1 before gaining its final name. (The back of Smitham signal box can be seen on the right). *Author*

Norwood Fork Junction signal box and flyover. It controlled both the high and low level lines.
Railway Magazine

THE INTRODUCTION OF THE TRACK CIRCUIT

Track circuits consist of a portion of railway line electrically wired up to take a small electric current through the rails so that when a train straddles the two rails a short circuit occurs, de-energising a relay. This cannot only be converted into a visual and/or audible indication of the presence of the train in the signal box, but also to hold the signal in rear at danger and/or lock the levers of points thus preventing the signalman from moving them prematurely in the route over which the train is running.

The first experimental one had been installed as early as 1876 but their use was slow in being adopted. The absolute reliability, so vital to rail safety, was doubted and it was not until the 1910s that they appeared in any numbers, replacing treadles in vulnerable places rather than as a general provision on a large scale. It was then realised that the biggest revolution in signalling practice was possible. By installing several track circuits over a continuous stretch of line each holding the signal in rear at danger it was possible to dispense with block sections and block instruments, consecutive trains being signalled to proceed purely upon the clearance of the relevant track circuit. Moreover, signals on lines where no points intervened could be made to work automatically, without any action by a signalman, purely upon the occupation and clearance of the track circuits.

Electric power was also being provided to operate signal arms and points at greater distances from the signal boxes than hitherto. Electric colour light signals were then developed. These gave a better indication of the state of the line ahead, each being able to display red, yellow and green (each signal in effect acting as a distant signal for the next) and provided they were evenly spaced a better flow of traffic was possible. Their powerful beams penetrated fog better than the old signal arms and oil lamps and thus permitted normal working during fog, dispensing with the need to provide fog-signalmen with detonators and flags or handlamps to assist the drivers in observing the signals, or two block sections having to be clear before a train was signalled in their absence.

During the latter part of the 1920s the lines in the Holborn Viaduct - Elephant & Castle and Charing Cross and Cannon Street - Hither Green area were re-signalled in this way. On the most intensive trafficked lines signals with an additional yellow aspect were introduced. This gave an extra indication - two yellows - giving the driver a preliminary warning that the next signal was at yellow, the closeness of the signals demanded by the train service otherwise giving insufficient distance for braking the train between the yellow and red signals.

With electric signals and points it was possible to miniaturise the lever frames as the signalman no longer had to use physical force.

Train describing was also modernised. Electric magazine-type describers were installed. The signalman pressed the relevant button applicable to the description required. At the

Bromley Junction signal box on 9th October 1920 looking in new condition.

signal box ahead the descriptions of approaching trains were indicated in rows of light bulbs, first, second and third trains being indicated should that many be approaching. Should four or more be described the indications would be stored up and appear as the preceding ones were removed.

With the track circuits being indicated 'clear' or 'occupied' on an illuminated diagram and automatic signals being provided where possible, each signalman was able to control a greater area and regulate the trains better. This permitted the number of signalmen and signal boxes to be reduced, and only the fact that at this time the electric points equipment would not allow control from more than about a mile from a signal box prevented even further reductions.

The new method of working was popularly referred to as colour light signalling for the obvious reason that the electric signals showing various colours was the most noticeable difference. Such signals can, and are, used in block working areas in lieu of semaphore signals so such a title is hardly correct. The new signalling system relying on track circuits instead of block instruments was officially termed 'signalling on lines where block apparatus is not provided', a lengthy title. It is today known as 'Track Circuit Block', a much more convenient description which will be quoted henceforth.

With the renaming of the stations following the grouping of the rival companies to form the Southern Railway, Coulsdon & Smitham Downs Central and South signal boxes became Coulsdon North Nos. 1 and 2 respectively, the S.E.C.R. Coulsdon signal box becoming Coulsdon South.

Also as a result of the grouping there was some standardisation of signalling equipment. As semaphore arms were renewed, Southern Railway standard metal arms were substituted for the old wooden ones. At first these were of the lower quadrant type - the arm pointing downwards to 45 degrees when cleared, but these were soon to be superseded by arms which moved 45 degrees upwards instead - known as upper quadrant. The S.R. also introduced disc type shunting signals, either mechanical or electrical - the latter being of the solenoid floodlit type - and miniature colour light shunting signals.

The arms of distant signals were changed during 1927 and 1928 from red to yellow with a black chevron near the unpivoted end, with a yellow light by night when at 'caution'.

Upon electrification of the Tattenham Corner and Caterham lines and the consequent closure of Purley locomotive depot Purley East signal box was abolished during October 1928, its remaining work being transferred to Purley South box.

With the considerable increase in train services upon electrification it was realised that the signalman at West Croydon South signal box would experience great difficulty in exchanging train staffs with drivers of the West Croydon - Wimbledon passenger trains using the bay platform on the 'up' side, his signal box being on the 'down' side three lines away. Not only would he have to cross these busy lines twice every 20 minutes for each Wimbledon train arriving and departing, but he would not be in the signal box during such times to perform the rest of his duties which were extensive - there being around 24 trains an hour to be dealt with in peak periods. To overcome the problem the Electric Train Staff instrument for the passenger single line was split. Whilst the signalman still controlled the bells, indicators and acceptance apparatus the portion of the instrument housing the train staffs was located separately in a small building on the bay platform. A porter would collect the train staff from the incoming driver, insert it into, and withdraw it from, the instrument under the signalman's authority, and hand it to the driver of the outgoing train. The Electric Train Staff instrument for the goods line was worked conventionally as such trains ran to and from the main lines and the signalman could cope himself. This method

generally worked satisfactorily, but it was necessary to ensure that the porter arranged to be in attendance on any occasion when a train required to run to or from the passenger single line and the main lines to deal with the train staff. His absence would result in the train being delayed on the main lines, with reaction on following main line services.

A new signal box - at the Wimbledon end of the new Halt island platform - was provided at Waddon Marsh upon electrification and the provision of the goods line. This superseded the old one which had been on the 'up' side of the line, by the level crossing which had now been closed.

East Croydon Central Shunting box was put out of use on 11th October 1931.

A signal box was provided at the Tattenham Corner end of the island platform at the new Woodmansterne station on 13th April 1932. It was one of four provided on the branch to increase the number of block sections, and thus permit a more frequent train service to be run on Epsom Race days only. The other three were outside the Borough. It replaced Asylum signal box which had been on the 'up' side of the line, and was put out of use on the same day.

Three-position S.R. Standard Block instruments were now being introduced. These were operated by turning a commutator which moved a pointer at the accepting end of the block section. It could be turned to indicate three positions - 'Normal', 'Line Clear' or 'Train on Line' on the bottom of two indicators. Such indications were repeated on the top indicator at the box in rear. By this means a signalman was provided with a clear indication of the state of every block section approaching or going away from his signal box. Over the next 40 years or so this type of instrument, or the similar but improved B.R. version, was installed as renewals became due to supersede the ancient Walkers, Tyers and Harpers instruments within the Borough. Sykes instruments were not usually superseded by the new instrument, tending to last until Track Circuit Block working was introduced. An exception was the Coulsdon - Redhill line where standard block instruments superseded Sykes' in the late 1970s.

The first Track Circuit Block scheme within the Borough was in the extreme south - from Coulsdon North No.2 signal box southwards to Balcombe Tunnel Junction via the Quarry line, commissioned on 5th June 1932 and extending onwards to reach Brighton on 16th October. This was, at the time, the longest stretch of track circuit block working in the country (36 route miles). It was installed with economy in mind. Except at Brighton where a miniature lever signal box with 225 levers was installed, and at Haywards Heath where a new manual lever signal box was provided, the new signalling was operated from the existing manual lever frames in the old signal boxes and whilst the main line running signals were electric colour lights most of the points, shunting signals and signals leading from branch lines on to the main lines remained manually operated by rod or wire. The lever handles of electrically operated signals or points were cut short to prevent the signalman from inadvertently exerting great pressure on such levers as had been necessary hitherto when they worked rods and wires. The magazine type train describers showing the first three trains approaching, as described earlier, were provided on the re-signalled lines.

Twenty-two signal boxes were dispensed with, only one - Cane Hill Intermediate - being within the Borough, whilst nine others now opened only when required for shunting, etc., their signals working automatically when they were switched out of circuit.

Another form of signalling made possible by track circuits and power worked signals was the use of intermediate block sections. By providing stop and distant signals at some intermediate point between two signal boxes it was possible to split a normal block section into two separate block sections, giving greater line capacity, without the need for an additional signal box. Usually the signalman in rear operated the intermediate signals and controlled the intermediate section, being track circuited from his last 'normal' signal to just beyond the intermediate stop signal. Only the portion of line from the intermediate signal to the signal box ahead utilised the block instrument. Upon a train clearing the track circuit the signalman could replace the intermediate signals and signal another train up to them.

Such a section was provided on the 'down' line at Bingham Road, controlled from Woodside, on 29th September 1935, ready for the re-opening of the line to passenger traffic the following day. Other changes were the abolition of the bay platform at Woodside, the 'special occasion' signalling at Coombe Road (formerly Coombe Lane) and Selsdon Road North signal box, the latters work having been added to Selsdon Road Junction (re-named Selsdon Junction) signal box from 22nd September 1935.

Some automatic signals were installed, providing track circuit block working, between Streatham Common South and Thornton Heath signal boxes from 16th February 1936, allowing Norbury signal box to be dispensed with.

The work of Coulsdon North No.2 and Coulsdon South station signal boxes was transferred to Coulsdon North No. 1, which resultantly became plain Coulsdon North, from 2nd May 1937. Track circuit block working was also introduced between Purley South and Coulsdon North on the 'down' lines only. On the 'up' main line an intermediate block section known as Orphanage had been provided by this time.

The gradual introduction of track circuit block signalling continued, mainly in the inner London suburban area outside the Borough boundaries, until the outbreak of the Second World War in 1939 put a stop to most modernisation plans.

Riddlesdown Tunnel Intermediate signal box was dispensed with from 19th June 1948, colour light intermediate signals,

worked from Sanderstead for the 'down' line and Upper Warlingham for the 'up' line being provided to compensate.

The North and South signal boxes at West Croydon were renamed 'A' and 'B' respectively on 2nd October 1949.

The next portion of track circuit block signalling involving the Borough was from the north end of Norwood Junction to Bricklayers Arms Junction, commissioned on 8th October 1950. New miniature lever signal boxes of modern and pleasing architectural design were provided at Forest Hill (47 levers), New Cross Gate (71 levers) and Bricklayers Arms Junction (55 levers), replacing eight manual signal boxes (none in the Borough) totalling 274 levers. Norwood Junction North manual signal box remained to transfer the signalling from one system to the other, whilst Penge West signal box, now only opened when required for shunting etc., being dispensed with after freight facilities were withdrawn from the goods yard there from 4th May 1964.

The existing track circuit block signalling between Streatham Common and Thornton Heath was modernised and extended to Selhurst on 5th October 1952, Thornton Heath signal box now being opened only as necessary for shunting and/or crossing movements between the main and local lines.

The rings were taken off the goods line signal arms between West Croydon and Waddon Marsh on 23rd February 1954. They had hitherto been provided to differentiate them from those of the passenger line, but such a system was not correct under B.R. standards.

On 21st March 1954 a very complicated conversion to track circuit block working was commissioned. Six signal boxes - Norwood Junction North, Norwood Junction South, Norwood Fork Junction, Gloucester Road Junction, Selhurst Junction and Windmill Bridge Junction - with a combined total of 390 manual levers - were made redundant, all their intensive work of running over 1,000 trains a day through the numerous junctions, plus movements to and from Norwood Shunting Yards, Locomotive Depot and Selhurst Carriage Depot being taken over by two new

The famous set of L.B. & S.C.R. signals at the north end of East Croydon station. The 'stop' signals were controlled from East Croydon North signal box, the 'distant' signals pointing to the left from Windmill Bridge Junction and those pointing to the right from East Croydon South signal boxes.   *S.C. Nash*

miniature lever signal boxes situated at Norwood Junction (107 levers) and Gloucester Road Junction (131 levers). In less than seven hours 160 old semaphore signals were removed, the new colour light signals, track circuiting and magazine train describers throughout were put into use and 110 sets of points were converted from manual rodding to electric motor operation. The main lines were re-named as 'through' lines. Also abolished were Tyers' double line block instruments adapted for bi-directional movements and shunting over goods loops and lines where either end was controlled in different signal boxes.

On 24th April 1954 the connection between the carriage sidings and the 'down' quarry line at Coulsdon North was removed.

The next stage of track circuit block working was to link up the new installation at Gloucester Road Junction with the original 1932 scheme at Coulsdon North, thus completing track circuit block working throughout between Victoria, London Bridge and Brighton via the quarry line.

This was commissioned on 8th May 1955. Three new miniature lever signal boxes were provided at East Croydon (103 levers), South Croydon (31 levers) and Purley (71 levers). The manual Coulsdon North box (80 levers) was retained. Seven signal boxes were abolished. These were East Croydon North, East Croydon South, South Croydon Station, South Croydon Junction, Purley Oaks, Purley North and Purley South.

Up to this time in the miniature lever signal boxes where block instruments were required to and from semaphore boxes on adjacent lines, these had been positioned on top of the otherwise neat 'console', resulting in an untidy effect. In the case of South Croydon (for the Oxted line) and Purley (for the Caterham and Tattenham Corner lines) miniaturised Sykes instruments were set into the 'console' panelling. The tablets and treadles of these instruments did not drop with a thud as did the normal type, and they were often referred to as 'Silent Sykes'. The South Croydon instruments were adapted so that they would operate in conjunction with Harpers Block instruments at the other end of the section.

There were now 33 signal boxes controlling the routes from Victoria and London Bridge to Brighton via the Quarry line (11 of which opened only for shunting etc.) compared with 46 in 1948 when B.R. was set up and 86 in 1923 upon the formation of the Southern Railway.

From 1955 modernisation of signalling on B.R. Southern Region was switched to other areas, principally the lines serving the Kent Coast and Hampshire. As a result the Borough saw only minor re-signalling over the next 13½ years.

From 1st June 1958 the 'down' relief line (the most easterly) between Windmill Bridge Junction and South Croydon was signalled as a 'reversible' line. Any 'down' train could run over it as before, plus Oxted line trains only in the 'up' direction as it had no connection from the 'up' main lines. Nevertheless this did reduce the number of trains formerly using the 'up' 'through' line leaving paths available for additional trains consequent upon the re-opening of Gatwick Airport as a major international airport. East Croydon had overall control of the reversible working, releasing the signals at Gloucester Road Junction and South Croydon. Trains could be run onto or leave the reversible line at East Croydon if so desired.

Kenley signal box was dispensed with upon the closure of the station goods yard from 10th June 1961, whilst a reduction in race traffic permitted Woodmansterne signal box to be put out of use from 1st May 1963, and the closure of the spur made Norwood Spur Junction signal box surplus to requirements from 30th October 1966.

To assist with the ever increasing Gatwick Airport traffic the 'up local' (No.1) platform line at East Croydon was signalled to permit 'down' terminating services to run direct into that line to reverse, from 30th April 1967.

Above: Norwood Spur Junction signal box.

L.R. Hollands Collection

Left: South Croydon signal box. One of the architecturally pleasing designs introduced in the 1950s.

Author

THE ROUTE SETTING AGE

Progress in the electrical field had, by 1960, greatly increased the distance that electrically operated points could be controlled from, and more importantly, a revolutionary new method of signalling had been developed.

Known as route setting it was based on the track circuit block system with colour light signals, albeit with a new type of subsidiary and shunting signal with two or three miniature lights - officially termed 'position light'. The essential differences were in the electrical circuitry and the action on the part of the signalman. Hitherto the latter had operated a lever for each set of points (and facing point lock in the case of manual points) followed by the signal lever. Under the new system he was provided with an operating panel bearing a diagram depicting the layout under his control with, in early installations thumb switches, and later buttons. Sometimes the track circuit indications and/or switches/buttons were geographically positioned on the panel and sometimes were separate. All interlocking was electrical.

To operate a signal the relevant switch had to be turned for the route required, or in the case of buttons those at two consecutive signals along the intended route of the train had to be pressed. In either case this instigated a route from one signal to the next and provided the route was available, all points (no matter how many sets) between the two signals and for an overlap distance beyond the second would move to the position required. Upon everything being electrically proven - all track circuits clear, all points correctly set, with no equipment failures, the signal would clear. Should there be, say, three signals worked by the one signalman which needed to be operated for the complete running of the train through his area of control, three switch operations or six button pushes only would be required instead of perhaps a dozen or more lever movements under previous methods of signalling.

Train describing had also been modernised. Each train was now shown in the Staff Working Timetables with its own individual number consisting of four digits - the first number indicating the class of train, the second (a letter) its destination or route ('down' trains) or its originating station or route ('up' trains), and the last two numbers identified which train it was. For example 2 T 17 would be a Class 2 (ordinary passenger) Tattenham Corner/Caterham train, number 17.

In many of the route setting panel signal boxes being introduced, the four digit description was initiated at the starting point, to appear on the illuminated track circuit diagram alongside the indication of the train occupying the track circuit. It would then move along the diagram with the progress of the train. Provided the next box was similarly equipped it would automatically transfer forward to the diagram there without any action on the part of the signalman.

It will be realised that the physical work of the signalman was further reduced, enabling him to take on an even bigger area of control, albeit with a consequently bigger responsibility when things go wrong. Moreover, the miniaturisation of the equipment meant that more could be accommodated in one building, and the more there was in one location the better the regulation of the running of trains could be monitored.

A small route setting panel was installed above, and in addition to, the miniature lever frame in Norwood Junction signal box from 1st January 1969. This was without four digit description equipment, but the magazine type descriptions were automatically transferred from and to adjoining signal boxes. This panel controlled part of the London Bridge main line, including the junction at Sydenham (hitherto worked from Forest Hill), the branch between Sydenham and Crystal Palace, and from west of Bromley Junction through Crystal Palace to Gipsy Hill. Four manual signal boxes were dispensed with. The Bromley Junction area itself was added to the miniature lever frame, thus doing away with the signal box there too.

Norwood Junction signal box now controlled the above panel additionally to its previous area - all lines between Norwood Fork Junction and Sydenham (exclusive), including the connections to and from Norwood 'up' and 'down' yards and the Norwood Junction end of Selhurst Depot.

The signalling of East Croydon 'up local' (No.1) platform line was altered again on 11th May 1969, permitting 'down' trains to be run through it, instead of being limited to terminating therein.

Norwood Junction and New Cross Gate signal box control areas were extended to meet one another from 1st June. This dispensed with Forest Hill signal box.

On 8th June a crossover was brought into use from the 'down local' to 'down through' line north of Coulsdon North, controlled from Coulsdon North signal box. This permitted trains for the Redhill line to be run on the 'down local' to that point.

With the closure of the goods yards the intermediate signal boxes on the Tattenham Corner line were gradually put out of use. Within the Borough, Smitham signal box went on 18th June 1970. Track circuit block working was introduced throughout the branch on 29th November, worked from the existing lever frames at Purley and Tattenham Corner. There were now no intermediate signal boxes where a decade earlier there had been 8 (4 of which were used on Race Days only).

West Croydon to Sutton was converted to track circuit block working on 20th November 1972, again worked from the existing lever frames at West Croydon 'B' and Sutton Junction signal boxes. Wallington and Waddon signal boxes were dispensed with, the latter being within the Borough.

During the early 1970s, the Harpers instruments on the Oxted line were replaced by B.R. Standard block instruments, the 'Silent Sykes' at South Croydon signal box being removed, a specially designed illuminated 'standard' instrument being set into the 'console'.

A large route setting panel signal box (or Signalling Centre as such installations are now termed) was commissioned at London Bridge in stages during 1975 and 1976. This controls 47 route miles and 147 single track miles of railway, including some of the busiest routes in the world. Its area embraced from Charing Cross, Cannon Street and London Bridge to Elmstead Woods on the Dover main line, Woolwich, Falconwood and Mottingham on the three routes to Dartford, East Dulwich on the Tulse Hill line, Clapham on the South London line, to Hayes via the Mid Kent line, and so far as the Borough is concerned approximately to its boundary between Anerley and Norwood Junction (including some of the Sydenham - Crystal Palace line) on the Brighton main line and between Elmers End and Woodside on the Mid Kent line. The latter two stages were commissioned on 20th July and 28th September 1975 respectively.

Sixteen signal boxes (some among the busiest in the world) were no longer required. None were within the Borough, although Norwood Junction lost the Sydenham - Forest Hill area.

Other sophisticated equipment installed included automatic train recording, platform indicators and tape recorded announcements at various stations along the routes, all worked automatically by the movement of the train as it occupies relevant track circuits, the associated four digital train number displayed actuating the appropriate information applicable to the train of that number.

Above: Interior of Coulsdon North signal box, illustrating a manual lever frame, magazine train describers and a standard block instrument. *Author's Collection*

Left: Interior of East Croydon signal box, illustrating a miniature lever frame, magazine train describers – and Christmas decorations! *Author's Collection*

Visual display units are also installed at selected places in the signalling centre and on certain stations. These consist of a TV-type screen with typewriter style keyboard. By typing appropriate codes any section of the signalling diagram can be displayed for perusal or alternatively the digital number of a particular train can be requested, whereupon the apparatus will immediately establish which area that train is running within and display that section of the diagram, a flashing light highlighting its position. This considerably reduces telephone calls to the signalling centre enquiring the whereabouts of trains, particularly on days of disruption.

The goods yard having closed and the points between 'through' and 'local' lines at Thornton Heath having been put out of use, the signal box at that station was no longer needed. It was dispensed with on 19th December 1976, the signals being converted to automatic working. The signal box structure remained in situ, gradually deteriorating, until it was demolished during July 1982.

A signalling method new to the Borough was introduced between Waddon Marsh and Mitcham Junction on 14th September 1980. This was 'Track Circuit Block on Single Lines', whereby the entire single line section is track circuited dispensing with the need for a train staff to be carried by the driver of each train.

Another signalling centre, with similar sophisticated apparatus as London Bridge, and more recent developments as well, was introduced between 1980 and June 1983. Situated at Clapham Junction, but officially titled 'Victoria', it controls an even greater distance - some 270 single track miles - consisting of all lines from Victoria and Holborn Viaduct to just short of Longfield, Borough Green and Sevenoaks in Kent (via Herne Hill, Catford or Crystal Palace), East Dulwich to Ewell East, Epsom Downs and Wimbledon via Streatham, the various spur lines at Chislehurst, Tulse Hill and Streatham Junction, the Wimbledon - West Croydon, Sutton - Waddon (exclusive), and Wimbledon - Sutton lines, the low level lines through Stewarts Lane to the South Eastern main line, Pouparts Junction and the West London line, also the Brighton main line southwards just into the Borough at Norbury. 70 stations are within its area of control. Of the 36 signal boxes superseded, once again including some of the busiest in the world, only two were within the Borough - Waddon Marsh and West Croydon 'B'.

So far as the portions affecting the Borough are concerned, the Norbury area was commissioned on 28th June 1981. This completed the resignalling throughout from Victoria to Norbury on the Brighton main line, all now controlled from the new 'Victoria Signalling Centre'. On 9th August control of the Gipsy Hill/Crystal Palace/Bromley Junction area was taken on. This meant that having lost all the additions put onto the box in 1969 to either London Bridge or Victoria signalling centres, Norwood Junction signal box had reverted to approximately its original area of control.

During 1981 TV screen style Visual Display Units (VDUs) were installed between Purley/West Croydon and Norwood Junction in place of the magazine train describers. These were linked to the four digital describing systems in London Bridge and Victoria signalling centres enabling the descriptions to transfer automatically between the two systems, and from box to box within the combined areas. It was also arranged for certain places other than signal boxes to be linked into the system with VDU screens to assist them in ascertaining the whereabouts of trains.

West Croydon 'B' signal box was dispensed with on 18th October 1981, its work being taken over by West Croydon 'A' (consequently renamed West Croydon). This resulted in the loss of the last conventional Sykes block instruments within the Borough - between the two boxes - and also the 'separated' train staff instruments - the single line to Waddon Marsh being converted to the 'Track Circuit Block on Single Lines' system.

The entire line from West Croydon to Wimbledon came under the control of Victoria Signalling Centre on 23rd May 1982, dispensing with Waddon Marsh signal box within the Borough, and on 3rd October the line between Sutton and Waddon (exclusive) was taken over, West Croydon box losing some of what it had taken on during the previous year.

After its singling on 9th January 1983 the Bromley Junction - Beckenham Junction line continued to be controlled from Beckenham Junction signal box until being transferred to the Victoria Signalling Centre on 13th February, completing all the actual resignalling work within the Borough, although the ancillary equipment (train indicators, announcements, etc.) had yet to be provided.

A major improvement introduced on to the Borough's lines for the first time with the introduction of the signalling centres was the Automatic Warning System (A.W.S.). This comprises of a magnetic ramp situated between the rails on the approach side of each signal which is energised and de-energised as appropriate according to the indication exhibited by the signal. As the train passes over, the driver receives an audible indication - a bell if the signal is green, a horn if at any other colour. The latter must be cancelled by the driver by operating a button. Should he fail to respond, the brakes on the train will automatically be applied.

All the many safeguards provided give a near perfect method of train operation. With the advanced electrical interlocking a signal will not clear for a train unless:- (a) all relevant track circuits are clear, (b) all points and other relevant apparatus are correctly set and electrically proven, (c) the signal next ahead has been electrically proven to have returned to red behind the previous train, (d) that signal is electrically proven to be illuminated and (e) no conflicting route has been set up.

Should any of these conditions fail to be maintained whilst the signal is clear it will immediately revert to danger.

Once a signal is cleared, all equipment in the route is electrically locked, and no conflicting route can be set until the train has passed, although of course, the signalman can replace a signal to danger in an emergency without releasing the interlocking.

The speed of trains round diverging junctions etc. is also controlled by arranging the interlocking so that the track circuit approaching a signal must be occupied by the train for a calculated pre-determined period before the signal will clear.

All this is in addition to the driver's visual sight of the signal and his braking skills, the safeguards of the A.W.S. and the driver's safety device (popularly known as the 'deadmans handle') whereby the brakes are applied should a driver release his pressure on the controls.

Overlapping in timescale with the Victoria signalling centre project was another similar scheme known as the 'Brighton Line Re-Signalling Scheme' with its signalling centre located at Three Bridges to control all lines from Norbury and Norwood Junction to Brighton, plus the branch lines to Caterham and Tattenham Corner, to beyond Upper Warlingham, nearly to Godstone, Reigate, Horsham and Lewes, to beyond Hove, the various spur lines at Gloucester Road Junction and the line thence to beyond Waddon. The centre, which will eventually control 113 route miles and 280 single track miles, supersedes 33 signal boxes, and one shunting box. Within the Borough, Norwood Junction, Gloucester Road Junction, West Croydon (formerly 'A'), East Croydon, South Croydon, Purley, Coulsdon

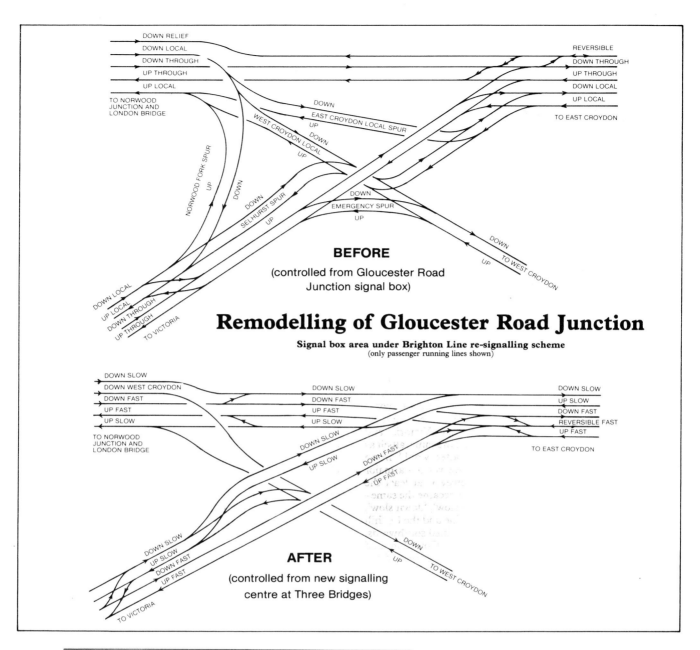

DOWN RELIEF
DOWN LOCAL
DOWN THROUGH
UP THROUGH
UP LOCAL

REVERSIBLE
DOWN THROUGH
UP THROUGH
DOWN LOCAL
UP LOCAL

TO NORWOOD
JUNCTION AND
LONDON BRIDGE

TO EAST CROYDON

DOWN
EAST CROYDON LOCAL SPUR
UP

WEST CROYDON LOCAL
DOWN
UP

NORWOOD FORK SPUR

UP
DOWN

SELHURST SPUR
DOWN
UP

DOWN
EMERGENCY SPUR
UP

DOWN
TO WEST CROYDON
UP

BEFORE

(controlled from Gloucester Road
Junction signal box)

DOWN LOCAL
UP LOCAL
DOWN THROUGH
UP THROUGH
TO VICTORIA

Remodelling of Gloucester Road Junction

Signal box area under Brighton Line re-signalling scheme
(only passenger running lines shown)

DOWN SLOW
DOWN WEST CROYDON
DOWN FAST
UP FAST
UP SLOW

DOWN SLOW
DOWN FAST
UP FAST
UP SLOW

DOWN SLOW
UP SLOW
DOWN FAST
REVERSIBLE FAST
UP FAST

TO NORWOOD
JUNCTION AND
LONDON BRIDGE

TO EAST CROYDON

DOWN SLOW
UP SLOW

DOWN FAST
UP FAST

DOWN SLOW
UP SLOW
DOWN FAST
UP FAST
TO VICTORIA

DOWN
UP
TO WEST CROYDON

AFTER

(controlled from new signalling
centre at Three Bridges)

Overall view of operating floor at Victoria
Signalling Centre.

GEC-General Signal Limited

North, Selsdon and Sanderstead signal boxes plus Coulsdon North shunting box, were to disappear.

In association with the scheme considerable rationalisation and remodelling of track layouts was carried out, much of it within the Borough, with a view to adapting them to present day requirements, some lines becoming bi-directional. Opportunity was being taken to rectify long standing operating anomalies, some of which still reflected the former rivalry between companies and the piecemeal manner in which the routes were developed. For example, prior to the scheme, the order of running lines on the main line north of Coulsdon reading West to East were:-

Coulsdon to Windmill Bridge Junction - 'up local', 'down local', 'up through', 'down through'.

Selhurst to Victoria - 'up through', 'down through', 'up local',. 'down local'.

Norwood Junction to London Bridge - 'up local', 'up through', 'down through', 'down local'.

With such a lack of consistency even the provision of some flyovers at the Gloucester Road Junction intersection of these routes did not preclude some flat junctions, involving trains crossing one anothers paths, undesirable at such a heavily trafficked place.

In an all-out bid to remedy this the whole Gloucester Road Junction complex was redesigned and other considerable layout alterations and other improvements southwards to Coulsdon were carried out. The names of the 'through' and 'local' lines between Coulsdon and Windmill Bridge Junction were transposed to become the 'slow' and 'fast' lines (using modern terminology) respectively. The lines between Selhurst and Victoria and Norwood Junction and London Bridge remain the same, albeit as 'fast' and 'slow' lines. To rearrange the latter would mean changing 'up' lines into 'down' lines and vice versa - a major alteration which could not be justified. However, at least the order of lines between Coulsdon and Victoria became the same - from West to East - 'up fast', 'down fast', 'up slow', 'down slow', and considering the Quarry line as the 'fast' line and the Redhill line as the 'slow' line the consistency is maintained southwards.

The transposing of the lines between Coulsdon and Windmill Bridge Junction was logical anyway. Because of the geographical layout features and the fact that this section deals with Victoria and London Bridge trains, all lines had been used by fast and slow trains intermingled, an unusual and undesirable state of affairs. The illogical situation existed whereby the only stopping services south of East Croydon using the 'local' lines had latterly been the Coulsdon North trains during peak hours only, (and when that station closed these disappeared) whilst generally the other stopping services, serving the Oxted, Tattenham Corner/Caterham and Redhill lines ran on the 'through' lines. Express trains were scheduled to run fairly evenly over all lines! In the future the 'fast' lines need not be used by stopping services under normal working.

Most stages of the scheme, albeit controlled from the existing signal boxes for a period until transfer to the signalling centre have been carried out. The Caterham line was converted to track circuit block working on 15th March 1981, resulting in the abolition of the last 'silent' Sykes instrument. New crossovers between Purley and Coulsdon North were provided in April of that year, providing connections between 'through' and 'local' lines for 'up' and 'down' trains, thereby permitting 'up' Redhill line trains to use the 'up local' line and Coulsdon North services, while they lasted, the 'through' lines north of this point for the first time. An old name was resurrected to identify the location - Stoats Nest Junction.

Most of the new track layouts at East Croydon and Purley were laid in and brought into use, stage by stage, during 1981 and 1982, resulting in additional bi-directional working through East Croydon platforms with connections to and from the 'through' and 'local' lines at either end and additional crossover facilities between 'through' and 'local' lines at the north end of Purley. The new layouts were designed not only to improve train operation but also to allow extension, widening and straightening of the platforms at both stations to be carried out concurrently.

Most connections between 'through' and 'local' lines for the eventual layout were then in use. As South Croydon layout was, as yet, unaltered there were the original 'up' and 'down' facilities between 'through' and 'local' lines there as well. This might be considered as over provision but was, in fact, deliberate planning, for when from 3rd October 1982 the heavily used junction between the 'up' and 'down' Victoria and London Bridge 'through' lines at Windmill Bridge Junction disappeared, to permit the extensive earthworks and bridge building associated with the redesigned Gloucester Road Junction complex to commence in earnest, all Victoria services were obliged to run on the 'local' lines north of East Croydon, and such restricted working demanded improved flexibility elsewhere. For example, trains from Victoria to the Redhill line had to join the 'down through' line before Coulsdon North and those which formerly would have gained that line at Windmill Bridge Junction now had the option of crossing from 'down local' to 'down through' line either at the north end of East Croydon, the south end of East Croydon, at South Croydon, at Purley, or at Stoats Nest Junction, whichever suited the timetable, or the actual running of trains at the time, bearing in mind that the 'up through' line had to be crossed.

The work in the Gloucester Road area involved the building of a new embankment and flyover facilities to take a new connection from the Victoria line at Selhurst over the West Croydon - London Bridge line and the London Bridge - East Croydon main lines to connect with the eastern side of the latter at Windmill Bridge Junction, to take the place of the missing flat junction, and other considerable re-routing of tracks. Mining waste from Betteshanger Colliery in Kent was used for the new embankments and a considerable amount of major earth moving was involved. During the period of the work huge mounds of mining waste, earth and ballast, intermingled with contractors' huts, cranes, floodlights, grabs, pile drivers and other machinery appeared between the various railway tracks, the passengers view of the site rapidly changing from one of grass wasteland, sometimes beautified by the presence of numerous blooms of stray lupins, to a cross between a large building site and a colliery!

Track circuit block working was introduced on the Coulsdon - Redhill line from 26th February 1983, controlled from a route setting panel in Redhill 'A' signal box until its eventual transfer to the new Brighton line signalling centre. This superseded B.R. standard block instruments which had replaced Sykes during the late 1970s on this route.

Additional bi-directional working was introduced through Purley platforms during June and the crossovers to enable trains to turn round in either platform at Smitham, were laid in by the end of July.

Purley signal box took on additional work from 25th September, temporary route setting panels replacing the miniature lever frame, to control the area previously worked from Purley, Caterham, Tattenham Corner and Coulsdon North signal boxes. In the case of the latter the connections between the quarry and 'through' lines were taken out of use, and only the layout that would exist after Coulsdon North station closed was worked from the temporary panels at Purley. Coulsdon North signal box remained at this stage, albeit reduced in status, and released by Purley, to signal movements in and out of the terminus in conjunction with the shunting box.

On 1st October, after the closure of Coulsdon North station, the nomenclature of the lines north of Stoats Nest Junction were transposed, the former 'through' and 'local' lines becoming the 'slow' and 'fast' lines respectively. On this and the following day much of the eventual layout in the Gloucester Road Junction/Windmill Bridge Junction area, including the new flyover and its connections was brought into use. The former 'local' lines between the two junctions were taken out of use, the new 'slow' lines having taken their place. The emergency spur was, however, retained as the compensatory connections between 'fast' and 'slow' lines at Selhurst were not yet provided. At East Croydon No.5 platform became bi-directional, No.6 platform losing its facility to depart towards London.

These alterations were encompassed by extensive alterations to the interlocking of the miniature lever frames at Gloucester Road Junction and East Croydon.

Coulsdon North signal box and shunting box were put out of use on 9th October, and the temporary panels at Purley were superseded by the Brighton line signalling centre from 14th January 1984.

The provision of the outstanding track layouts in the East Croydon/Selhurst area took place early in 1984 in time for the hectic month of April, South Croydon and Selsdon signal boxes being abolished on the 1st, East Croydon and Gloucester Road Junction on the 8th, West Croydon on the 9th and Norwood Junction on the 28th. In conjunction the 'down slow' line between East Croydon and South Croydon became reversible in place of the previous reversible line, and the emergency spur was taken out of use. This meant that the Victoria/London Bridge to Brighton line (via the quarry line) almost to Preston Park

(Sussex) was now controlled from 3 signalling centres – Victoria (at Clapham Junction), London Bridge and Brighton line (at Three Bridges), and the route of the new Gatwick Express by only two.

Not associated with the scheme, Woodside signal box was abolished during the weekend of 23rd/24th June, its work being taken over by Addiscombe and London Bridge.

Work continued on the remainder of the scheme. On 14th October a crossover between the 'down' and 'up' slow lines north of Selhurst was brought into use. This allowed 'down' trains to erminate in the 'up' slow platform. The revised layout at Norwood Junction was completed by the end of the year.

The transfer of the Coulsdon South-Redhill signalling from the panel in Redhill 'A' signal box to the signalling centre at Three Bridges took place, along with the resignalling of the Redhill area, on 10th May 1985.

All that remains to be carried out within the Borough, under the Brighton line re-signalling, is from Sanderstead towards Oxted, with its associated closure of Sanderstead signal box. When it disappears in 1986 the only signal box within the Borough will be Addiscombe, an isolated oasis of semaphore signals surrounded on all sides by the most sophisticated route setting centres. It seems logical that it will be taken over by London Bridge signalling centre in due course.

In that event this would result in the Borough, which in 1923, when the Southern Railway was formed, had within its present boundaries, 38 signal boxes, and upon Nationalisation in 1948 still had 30, and at the start of 1983, 12, becoming entirely devoid of such structures.

Work in progress on a bridge to take the new flyover over the West Croydon lines at Gloucester Road junction. *Author's Collection*

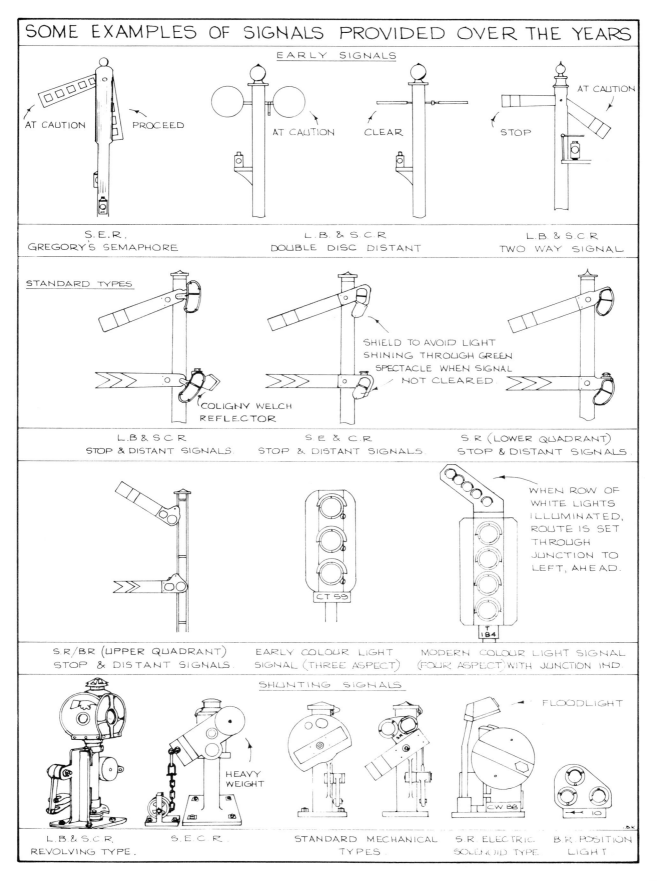

SOME EXAMPLES OF SIGNALS PROVIDED OVER THE YEARS

EARLY SIGNALS

AT CAUTION   PROCEED

AT CAUTION   CLEAR

STOP   AT CAUTION

S.E.R.
GREGORY'S SEMAPHORE

L.B.&S.C.R
DOUBLE DISC DISTANT

L.B.&S.C.R
TWO WAY SIGNAL

STANDARD TYPES

COLIGNY WELCH REFLECTOR

SHIELD TO AVOID LIGHT SHINING THROUGH GREEN SPECTACLE WHEN SIGNAL NOT CLEARED

L.B.&S.C.R
STOP & DISTANT SIGNALS.

S.E.&C.R
STOP & DISTANT SIGNALS.

S.R (LOWER QUADRANT)
STOP & DISTANT SIGNALS.

WHEN ROW OF WHITE LIGHTS ILLUMINATED, ROUTE IS SET THROUGH JUNCTION TO LEFT, AHEAD.

CT 59

T 184

S.R/BR (UPPER QUADRANT)
STOP & DISTANT SIGNALS.

EARLY COLOUR LIGHT
SIGNAL (THREE ASPECT)

MODERN COLOUR LIGHT SIGNAL
(FOUR ASPECT) WITH JUNCTION IND.

SHUNTING SIGNALS

FLOODLIGHT

HEAVY WEIGHT

CW 88

10

L.B.&S.C.R
REVOLVING TYPE.

S.E.C.R.

STANDARD MECHANICAL
TYPES.

S.R. ELECTRIC
SOLENOID TYPE

B.R. POSITION
LIGHT

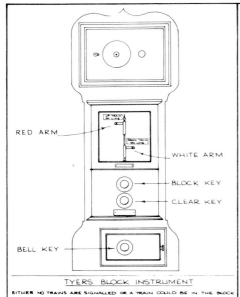

RED ARM

WHITE ARM

BLOCK KEY

CLEAR KEY

BELL KEY

TYERS BLOCK INSTRUMENT
EITHER NO TRAINS ARE SIGNALLED OR A TRAIN COULD BE IN THE BLOCK
SECTION ON EITHER OR BOTH UP&DOWN LINES THE INDICATIONS ARE SIMILAR

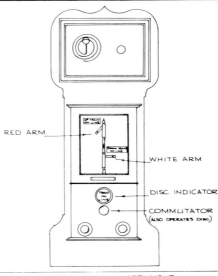

RED ARM

WHITE ARM

DISC INDICATOR

COMMUTATOR
(ALSO OPERATES DISC)

HARPERS BLOCK INSTRUMENT
A TRAIN IS IN THE SECTION FROM THE SIGNAL BOX IN REAR
A TRAIN IN THE OPPOSITE DIRECTION HAS BEEN ACCEPTED BY THAT BOX

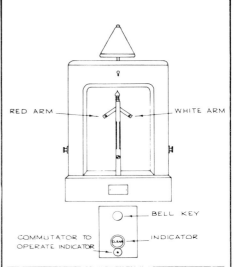

RED ARM

WHITE ARM

BELL KEY

COMMUTATOR TO
OPERATE INDICATOR

INDICATOR

WALKERS BLOCK INSTRUMENT
A TRAIN HAS BEEN ACCEPTED FROM SIGNAL BOX IN REAR
A TRAIN IN THE OPPOSITE DIRECTION HAS ALSO BEEN ACCEPTED BY THAT BOX

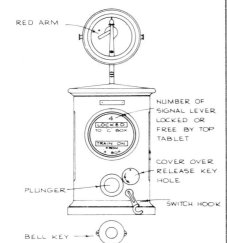

RED ARM

NUMBER OF
SIGNAL LEVER
LOCKED OR
FREE BY TOP
TABLET

COVER OVER
RELEASE KEY
HOLE

PLUNGER

SWITCH HOOK

BELL KEY

SYKES LOCK & BLOCK INSTRUMENT
A TRAIN HAS BEEN ACCEPTED FROM A SIGNAL BOX IN THE REAR
BUT HAS NOT YET BEEN OFFERED TO 'C' SIGNAL BOX AHEAD

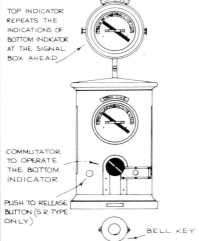

TOP INDICATOR
REPEATS THE
INDICATIONS OF
BOTTOM INDICATOR
AT THE SIGNAL
BOX AHEAD

COMMUTATOR
TO OPERATE
THE BOTTOM
INDICATOR

PUSH TO RELEASE
BUTTON (S R TYPE
ONLY)

BELL KEY

S R STANDARD BLOCK INSTRUMENT
A TRAIN IS OCCUPYING THE UP & DOWN SECTIONS
BETWEEN TWO SIGNAL BOXES

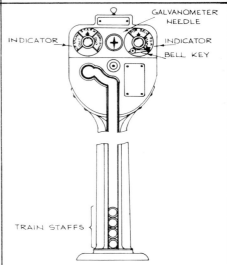

GALVANOMETER
NEEDLE

INDICATOR

INDICATOR

BELL KEY

TRAIN STAFFS

ELECTRIC TRAIN STAFF INSTRUMENT
TOP STAFF WITHDRAWN BY PASSING IT UP SLOT, THROUGH LOCK
WHEN RELEASED AND OUT THROUGH LARGE HOLE AT END OF SLOT.

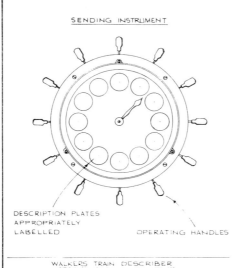

SENDING INSTRUMENT

DESCRIPTION PLATES
APPROPRIATELY
LABELLED

OPERATING HANDLES

WALKERS TRAIN DESCRIBER
(RECEIVING INSTRUMENT SIMILAR BUT WITHOUT
HANDLES AND WITH THIN STRAIGHT POINTER HAND)

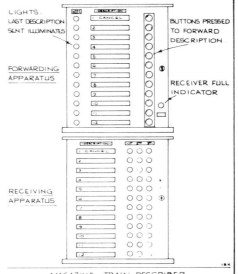

LIGHTS.
LAST DESCRIPTION
SENT ILLUMINATES

FORWARDING
APPARATUS

BUTTONS PRESSED
TO FORWARD
DESCRIPTION.

RECEIVER FULL
INDICATOR

RECEIVING
APPARATUS

MAGAZINE TRAIN DESCRIBER
WHEN 24 DESCRIPTIONS NECESSARY, TWO ROWS OF
12 SIDE BY SIDE, PROVIDED IN ONE APPARATUS CASE.

Location of Signal Boxes 1st January 1923

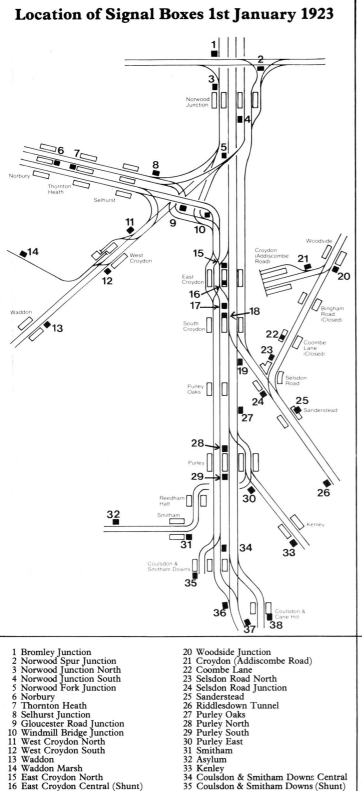

Location of Signal Boxes 1st January 1948

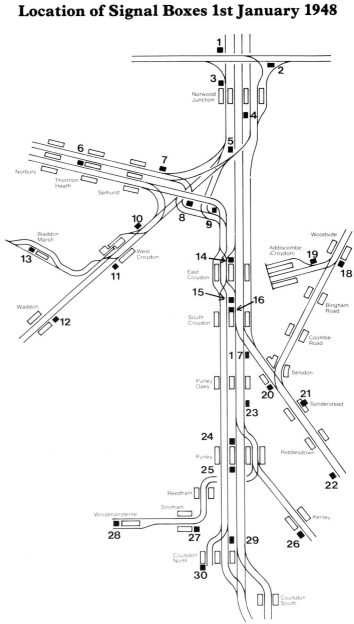

1 Bromley Junction	20 Woodside Junction
2 Norwood Spur Junction	21 Croydon (Addiscombe Road)
3 Norwood Junction North	22 Coombe Lane
4 Norwood Junction South	23 Selsdon Road North
5 Norwood Fork Junction	24 Selsdon Road Junction
6 Norbury	25 Sanderstead
7 Thornton Heath	26 Riddlesdown Tunnel
8 Selhurst Junction	27 Purley Oaks
9 Gloucester Road Junction	28 Purley North
10 Windmill Bridge Junction	29 Purley South
11 West Croydon North	30 Purley East
12 West Croydon South	31 Smitham
13 Waddon	32 Asylum
14 Waddon Marsh	33 Kenley
15 East Croydon North	34 Coulsdon & Smitham Downs Central
16 East Croydon Central (Shunt)	35 Coulsdon & Smitham Downs (Shunt)
17 East Croydon South	36 Coulsdon & Smitham Downs South
18 South Croydon Station	37 Cane Hill
19 South Croydon Junction	38 Coulsdon (S.E.C.R.)

1 Bromley Junction	16 South Croydon Station
2 Norwood Spur Junction	17 South Croydon Junction
3 Norwood Junction North	18 Woodside
4 Norwood Junction South	19 Addiscombe (Croydon)
5 Norwood Fork Junction	20 Selsdon
6 Thornton Heath	21 Sanderstead
7 Selhurst Junction	22 Riddlesdown Tunnel
8 Gloucester Road Junction	23 Purley Oaks
9 Windmill Bridge Junction	24 Purley North
10 West Croydon North	25 Purley South
11 West Croydon South	26 Kenley
12 Waddon	27 Smitham
13 Waddon Marsh	28 Woodmansterne
14 East Croydon North	29 Coulsdon North
15 East Croydon South	30 Coulsdon North (Shunt)

NOTE: Full track layouts not shown, only sufficient to identify position of signal boxes.

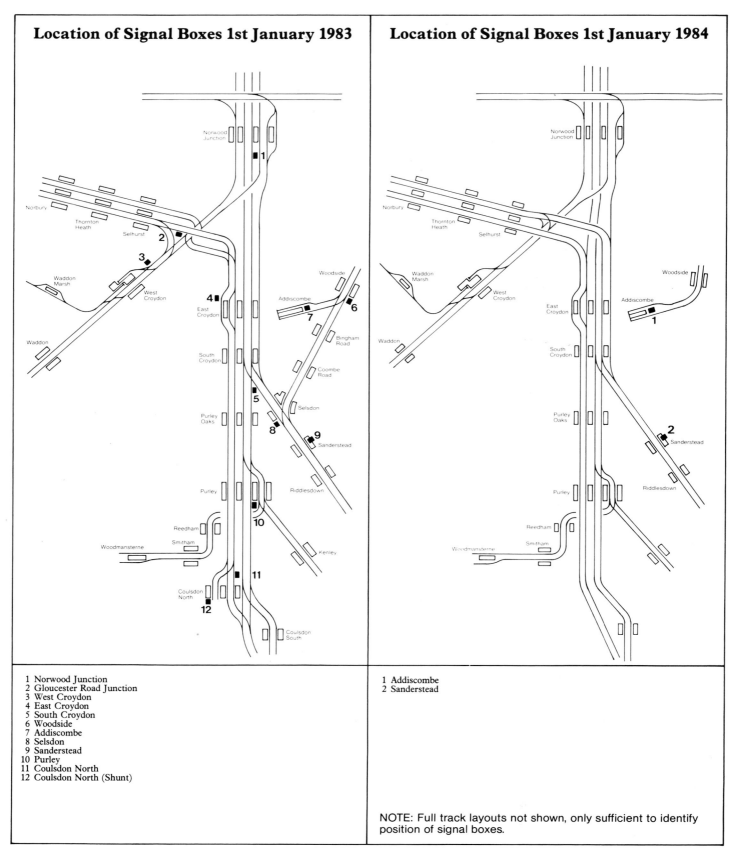

Location of Signal Boxes 1st January 1983

Norwood Junction ■1

Norbury

Thornton Heath

Selhurst ■2

West Croydon

Waddon Marsh ♦3

Waddon

East Croydon ■4

South Croydon

Woodside

Addiscombe ■7 ■6

Bingham Road

Coombe Road

■5

Selsdon

Purley Oaks

■8

■9 Sanderstead

Purley

Riddlesdown

■10

Reedham

Woodmansterne

Smitham

Kenley

■11

Coulsdon North

■12

Coulsdon South

1 Norwood Junction
2 Gloucester Road Junction
3 West Croydon
4 East Croydon
5 South Croydon
6 Woodside
7 Addiscombe
8 Selsdon
9 Sanderstead
10 Purley
11 Coulsdon North
12 Coulsdon North (Shunt)

Location of Signal Boxes 1st January 1984

Norwood Junction

Norbury

Thornton Heath

Selhurst

Waddon Marsh

West Croydon

East Croydon

Waddon

South Croydon

Woodside

Addiscombe ■1

Purley Oaks

■2 Sanderstead

Riddlesdown

Purley

Reedham

Woodmansterne

Smitham

1 Addiscombe
2 Sanderstead

NOTE: Full track layouts not shown, only sufficient to identify position of signal boxes.

Area covered by Victoria, London Bridge and Brighton Line Signalling Centres when current schemes are completed

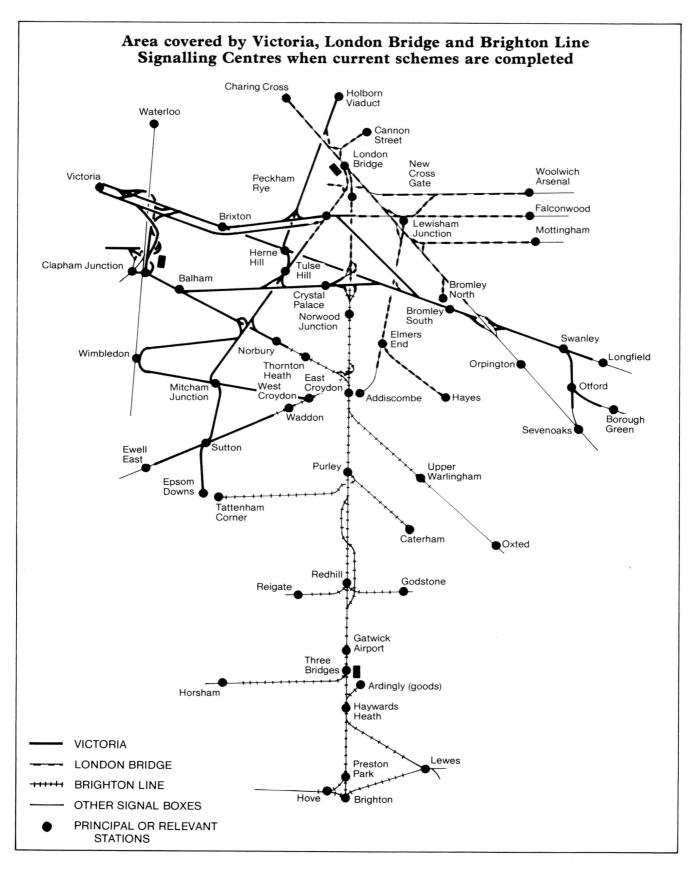

VICTORIA

LONDON BRIDGE

BRIGHTON LINE

OTHER SIGNAL BOXES

PRINCIPAL OR RELEVANT STATIONS

Chapter Four

Accidents
Part One - **19th Century**

The previous chapter showed how, once the train collision hazard was realised, methods of signalling were invented and improved upon over the years.

That was, however, by no means the only factor involved in safe railway operation. Train braking systems received similar attention, vital, since braking with highly polished wheels on highly polished rails can never provide the friction and adhesion achieved by treaded rubber tyre on rough surfaced road. Moreover, trains cannot swerve to avoid another train or obstruction.

Equally important is the standard of maintenance of track, trains and signalling apparatus, as faulty equipment can cause accidents or be contributory.

There is also the human factor. A slight relaxation in concentration can lead to such lapses as a driver passing a signal at danger, a signalman moving points or using a release at the wrong time or a maintenance worker failing to observe a fault or omitting to tighten a vital nut - all potential causes of accidents.

Because this was recognised at an early date it has always been a feature of railway practice that equipment be designed to fail safe (e.g. signals revert to danger, brakes to be applied) and for all accidents and irregularities, no matter how trivial or irrelevant they may seem, to be investigated with a view to taking all possible action to avoid a repetition.

The early railwaymen had little previous experience to guide them, but from the lessons learned by experience and from the investigations, books of 'Rules, Regulations and Instructions', catering for working in all kinds of weather and in all conditions of apparatus failure, etc. were produced. Wherever possible these were designed so that more than one person must err before a potentially dangerous situation could be set up. They were constantly amended to cater for changed circumstances or as a result of yet another lesson learned, so that today they have become extremely comprehensive.

Despite a high degree of adherance to these guidelines, accidents, irregularities and incidents still occur, albeit the serious ones extremely rarely. It must, however, be accepted that all the efforts made by the railways to combat the problem has achieved the highest possible standards of safety throughout B.R. In recent times there have been several complete years without a single fatality to passengers as a result of train accidents over the whole B.R. system!

Although some of the worlds busiest lines are within the Borough's boundaries the safety record throughout their long history is second to none.

This chapter reviews the more important accidents and irregularities and several of the lesser ones. The fact that the details of the latter survive, only highlights the serious way in which safety on the railways was developed.

The diversity of cause is interesting, whilst some of the minor incidents, although without doubt treated seriously at the time, do provide a degree of humorous reading when viewed in the past tense!

One of the first recorded incidents was an atmospheric train which failed to brake in time on wet rails and ran into a carriage at the Croydon terminus on 1st April 1846. Four passengers and one member of the railway staff were injured. On 29th July of the same year a derailment at Norwood Junction was attributed to the condition of the London & Croydon Company's track.

A derailment at Stoats Nest on 4th January 1847 was caused by a fracture of an axle on the 08.45 express from Brighton to London Bridge (later to become the City Limited) on only the fourth day it had run.

A near collision occurred at Brighton Junction on 28th of the month and another at East Croydon on 13th July when an L.B. & S.C.R. locomotive on trial was nearly run into by a S.E.R. train, whilst on 24th August an L.B. & S.C.R. passenger train was derailed at Brighton Junction. No casualties were reported.

A coupling chain broke as an Epsom Race Special left Croydon (West) on 23rd May 1849. The rear portion ran back some 50 to 60 yards whereupon a following Race Special came into slight collision with it. Three persons were slightly hurt.

On 1st March 1850 a London - Croydon train took both routes at Brighton Junction due to a defect in the points. The locomotive proceeded towards the main line and the carriages took the Croydon (West) line. Derailment resulted, one carriage being on its side. There were five injuries.

At East Croydon the original loop lines serving the platforms were removed in the early 1850s and new platforms were being built on either side of the main lines. In connection with this work trucks of ballast to form the platforms were being horse drawn from the sidings on to the 'up' and 'down' lines during intervals between trains. At 13.00 on 11th February 1852 the Foreman of Works, having ascertained that the signals were at 'stop', commenced such work with 9 or 10 trucks, no train being due until 13.55. As the trucks were being shunted back into the sidings at about 13.53 they were struck by the S.E.R.'s 13.30 train from London Bridge running a couple of minutes early, which had passed the protecting signal at danger. Both the driver and fireman alleged that upon sighting the distant signal it was showing 'clear' so they did not slow down, but it was reversed before they passed it and they were unable to stop in time. The driver was, however, blamed for the incident, other members of the staff having confirmed that they had seen it at 'caution' shortly before the approach of the train. Comment was also passed by the Inspecting Officer that the speed of the train was likely to have been excessive.

On 9th May 1853 a horsebox on a S.E.R. train was derailed between Stoats Nest and East Croydon; there were no injuries. The S.E.R. blamed the state of the L.B. & S.C.R. track!

A more serious collision occurred at East Croydon on 21st August 1854. An S.E.R. special train from Dover to Crystal Palace had attracted so many passengers that the number of carriages necessary to carry them made the train too long to be accommodated at the stations. It was, therefore, split into two separate trains at Ashford (Kent). This fact was telegraphed forward to East Croydon but after the first train passed it was forgotten and an L.B. & S.C.R. ballast locomotive was allowed on to the 'up' main line to take water. In the absence of interlocking the East Croydon distant signal was showing 'clear' although the signal on the approach to the station was showing 'stop'. The second train did not have to slow down upon sighting the former and when the latter was observed the driver was unable to stop. Fortunately the ballast locomotive driver noticed the special approaching and started his locomotive in an unsuccessful attempt to run away from it; a collision occurring north of the station. Three passengers were killed and thirty two injured.

On 4th December 1861 there was a slight collision between a passenger train and a preceding freight train near Norwood Junction. No one was hurt.

An S.E.R. locomotive standing at a signal on the 'up' main line at the south end of East Croydon was run into by the 09.10 passenger train from Hastings on 17th November 1862. The latter had been irregularly admitted into the occupied block section at Caterham Junction. A form of block working was in force but it was of a primitive nature and the Inspecting Officer recommended that an improved system of block working should be provided on this busy line. He also commented that the driver of the passenger train should have been able to stop short of the locomotive had he been keeping a good lookout, as it would have been visible for a considerable distance on this straight stretch of line. No one was hurt.

On 30th April 1866 the 20.00 from Brighton ran into chalk wagons at Caterham Junction due to a signalman's error. Three or four passengers were killed, the locomotive and a first class carriage plunging down an embankment.

A somewhat similar incident occurred at Norwood Junction on 24th March 1871. A passenger train from London Bridge to Victoria via Norwood Junction and Selhurst was in collision with four trucks. Sixteen passengers were injured. Hand points were still in use and the points within the goods yard had remained set towards the passenger lines. The trucks had moved on the falling gradient and run from the Yard out on to the passenger lines and remained there, without the knowledge of the shunters or the signalman.

There was a slight collision at East Croydon on 7th December 1871, one passenger receiving cuts, and on 25th April 1872 at that station it had been the intention to attach a horsebox for Victoria to the rear of the 'up' train from Hastings and Portsmouth to London Bridge and Victoria due at 19.28. When the pilot engine propelling the horsebox arrived at the rear of the train it was discovered that there were two horseboxes to be detached first. These were attached and the pilot shunted them to the dock siding via the 'down' line. Upon returning to the 'up' line with the horsebox to attach, the driver somehow gained the impression that he was to propel it right up to the north end of the station for a Victoria locomotive to pick up as was often the practice. Shouts from the platform caused him to apply the brake but not in time and the train was hit at about 5 mph. Fortunately the London Bridge portion had gone and the locomotive for the Victoria portion had not yet come on to the train, so the carriages were able to move forward and lessen the effect of the impact. No one was injured.

On 30th September 1872 an axle broke on a wagon of a freight train near Caterham Junction, derailing six or seven wagons. This was attributed to the wagon being overloaded. Again no one was hurt.

A locomotive crank axle breakage occurred between Norwood Junction and Selhurst on 14th January 1873. 0-6-0 Goods locomotive No. 211 was working the 11.15 Kensington Freight train, consisting of 34 wagons and 2 brake vans at the time. No serious damage resulted.

Locomotive No. 133 *Penge* was damaged in a slight collision at Windmill Bridge Junction on 18th July 1873.

Another breakage of a locomotive axle occurred at East Croydon on 22nd March 1874. Locomotive No. 238 *Shoreham* was the culprit, when working the 21.30 Brighton to London Bridge.

On 17th January 1875 a South Eastern Railway freight train ran into the L.B. & S.C.R. pilot locomotive which was standing on the 'up' main line at Norwood Junction, due to the L.B. & S.C.R. signalman's forgetfulness. The guard of the freight train was injured.

At West Croydon the second half of that year was eventful. As the empty stock of the 18.15 from Victoria was being shunted to the sidings on 14th July the following 18.48 passenger train from Crystal Palace ran into it. The signalman had omitted to put up his signal after the passing of the Victoria train and had accepted the Crystal Palace train and permitted the shunt movement to take place with the signal still at clear, no interlocking being provided to prevent him doing so. Two passengers were injured and three carriages of the empty train were derailed.

On 25th September a freight train was being held at the signal leading from the Wimbledon single line into the station. The following passenger train, the midnight from Victoria to West Croydon via Wimbledon, was consequently being held at the previous signal box. Lightning struck the telegraph wires giving a clear line, whereupon the passenger train was admitted into the occupied section. It collided with the rear of the freight train causing two guards and one passenger to be shaken.

0-4-2 tank locomotive No.18 *Stockwell* sustained slight damage in the locomotive shed on 11th October. Although this occurred in the early hours of the morning the driver was found to be drunk. The matter remained a mystery until several months later when the foreman caught the head cleaner dispensing an excellent quality rum in a storeroom which he sold as a sideline!

A week later, on 20th October, another passenger train, this time from Victoria, collided with an empty train, owing to an experienced signalman's forgetfulness. Four passengers were injured.

A train was derailed and overturned at Gloucester Road Junction on 8th June 1876. Miraculously, there were no casualties.

At Norwood Junction on 10th December 1876, 0-6-0 saddle tank locomotive No. 228 with a freight train was accidentally routed into buffer stops instead of out on to the main line. After demolishing the buffer stops No. 228 continued on to Portland Road underline bridge. The cast iron girders gave way and the locomotive slowly descended into the roadway below. The only injury was a broken arm sustained by the driver.

Locomotive No. 166 was derailed near Sanderstead (obviously on the Brighton line in the vicinity of the present Purley Oaks station, the Oxted line not yet being open) on 11th January 1877, due to an obstruction placed on the line by boys. Vandalism on the railways is obviously not a recent problem!

On 28th July 1877 the 14.55 from New Croydon conveyed two additional carriages on the rear loaded with troops for Chatham. These were to be detached on the 'up' main line at Norwood Junction, whence the pilot locomotive would haul them to the 'down' line prior to propelling them on to the Beckenham Junction train, whose platform was on the 'down' side. Upon gaining the 'down' line the shunter decided to change his mind and detached the carriages from the pilot, got the driver to give them a start and then let them run on to the Beckenham Junction train. Unfortunately, hand points in the route had not been correctly set and the two carriages went into a short siding instead, where they collided with a couple of wagon loads of rails. One officer and thirteen other ranks were shaken or bruised.

One passenger was shaken when a slight collision occurred at East Croydon on 22nd December 1879, the 12.00 from Hastings being run into the 'up' main platform by a locomotive from a 'down' train en route from the south end of the station to the sidings at the north end. There was dense fog with about 20 yards visibility at the time, so the driver of the locomotive would have had little chance of stopping upon seeing the train ahead. It

Above: The leading end of the 'City Limited' following the collapse of Portland Road underline bridge, 1st May 1891. 'Gladstone' class No. 175 *Hayling* (only six months old at this time) was clearly in deep trouble. It cost £54 to repair. *Croydon Libraries*

Left: Some of the rear coaches at the bridge. *R.C. Riley Collection*

was the Inspecting Officers opinion that the signalman would not have intentionally run the locomotive to the rear of the train in dense fog without at least cautioning the driver, and considered that it had been the intention to run it via the 'up' loop line which was clear, but the signalman had set up the wrong route. He was blamed for the incident.

The 17.05 from Hastings was one of the trains which split at East Croydon into portions for London Bridge and Victoria. On 9th September 1884 after the London Bridge portion had gone the tank locomotive to work the Victoria portion forward set back along the 'up' main line but did not stop in time, striking the train with considerable force, causing eight passengers to be shaken or bruised. This was attributed to the drivers' want of care.

On 17th December 1884 the driver of the 17.50 passenger train from Sutton irregularly passed the last signal at Waddon which was at danger owing to the 15.05 freight train from Epsom being in the block section ahead. On the approach to West Croydon a collision occurred. Two guards on the freight train were badly injured, whilst eight passengers and the guard of the passenger train sustained slight injuries.

Another case of the Victoria portion locomotive backing on to the train with considerable force at East Croydon occurred on 22nd November 1885. This time the train involved was the 17.35 from Hastings. Eight passengers were again shaken or bruised. There was a slight variation on this occasion though. After the London Bridge portion had departed the station staff had pushed the Victoria portion forward to facilitate the loading and unloading of parcels so the driver found the train sooner than expected. He was, however, held responsible in that he should have been keeping a good lookout, and the person in charge of the platform was criticised for not proceeding along the platform to caution the driver.

On 31st December 1888, in the vicinity of Tennison Road overline bridge just south of Norwood Junction, in dense fog, the rearmost vehicle of the 19.00 passenger train from London Bridge to Hastings was struck by a locomotive crossing from the 'up' sidings to the 'down local' line en route to West Croydon shed. Eighteen passengers were injured. Norwood Junction South signal box's last signal was situated just beyond Tennison Road overline bridge. The driver of the 19.00 drove the train cautiously, peering for this signal through the fog. Being unable to locate it he stopped his train and got off his locomotive to try to find it on foot. The position in which the train stood left the rear carriage astride the crossover road from the 'up' to the 'down' side. Some 3 or 4 minutes later the locomotive was ready for West Croydon, so the signalman having no equipment to assist him and as, in fact, the signal for the passenger train had been clear, considered that it would now be well beyond the crossover road and he consequently signalled the locomotive to cross. The driver of the latter did not see the position of the train through the fog until it was too late. No one was held responsible for the incident. The Inspecting Officer could not criticise the driver of the locomotive owing to the limited visibility, or the driver of the 19.00 for being conscientious and stopping to check the position of the signal, or the signalman who had allowed plenty of time for the 19.00 to have cleared the crossover road. Certain signals were, however, listed in the staff publications to be left in the clear position and not used during fog. The signal in question was so listed and the signalman expected the driver to be aware of this and could not have anticipated that the driver would stop to search for it.

On 10th December 1890 the 17.40 Victoria to Brighton and Eastbourne was in collision with a wagon inadvertently left on the 'down' line at Stoats Nest during shunting in darkness and fog. Seven carriages were derailed and there were 18 injuries.

The cast iron girders of Portland Road underline bridge at Norwood Junction failed again on 1st May 1891 as the 08.45 Brighton to London Bridge 'City Limited' express passed on to it. 'Gladstone' class locomotive No. 175 *Hayling* and its train was derailed, the rearmost vehicle dropping into the resultant hole. Fortunately there were no fatal injuries. The subsequent enquiry criticised the L.B. & S.C.R. for not having learned a lesson from the previous collapse.

An 'up' special train conveying Ardingly schoolboys was run into by the 06.55 Hastings to London Bridge passenger train at Norwood Fork Junction on 17th December 1891, one vehicle being derailed. Forty one passengers were injured, none of them seriously. Once again this occurred in dense fog. The signalman at Windmill Bridge Junction was responsible. When the Ardingly train passed his box he omitted to forward the bell signal to Norwood Fork Junction to indicate that the train had entered the section. In consequence the signalman there did not alter the block instrument or signal the train forward, neither was he aware that it had arrived at his signal as he could not see it. The signalman at Windmill Bridge Junction then accepted the Hastings train from East Croydon and, noticing that the block instrument was showing an acceptance from Norwood Fork Junction (the original acceptance of the Ardingly train), assumed this to be for the Hastings train and, in the absence of interlocking, was able to operate his signals for it to enter the occupied section.

Six passengers were injured when a light locomotive ran into a Caterham train at Purley on 22nd December 1894, and on 4th July 1895 the driver of L.B. & S.C.R. 'Terrier' No. 36 *Bramley*, working the 18.05 from Wimbledon, experienced difficulty in braking on wet rails and ran into the buffers at West Croydon, injuring two passengers.

On 31st August 1895 as the 17.05 London Bridge to Eastbourne passenger train, formed of a locomotive and 14 vehicles, was approaching East Croydon 10 vehicles left the rails. Eleven passengers and two guards were slightly injured. The evidence presented at the ensuing enquiry proved inconclusive and the Inspecting Officer was obliged to pass conjective comments. He considered that the most likely cause was a light van between two heavy vehicles having jumped due to oscillation when passing over the 'V' of a trailing crossover road, the other vehicles being forced into derailment.

At South Croydon Junction on 24th April 1896 the brake van of the 22.30 freight train from Norwood to Newhaven was struck by the 23.28 East Grinstead to Victoria passenger train. Little damage resulted. The freight train was standing at a main line signal at danger with its brake van just foul of the 'up' Oxted line. The signalman failed to check whether or not it was clear before signalling the East Grinstead train. He left the company prior to the enquiry which, nevertheless, found him responsible.

Also at South Croydon Junction a deliberate derailment of a locomotive occurred on 14th April 1899. L.B. & S.C.R. tank locomotive No. 139 *Lombardy* had been involved in a slight collision at New Cross (L.B. & S.C.R.), the force of which had resulted in it running away in steam down the main line, the crew having obviously jumped off upon seeing the collision coming. Despite the continuous rising gradient it did not stop, so the signalman at South Croydon Junction set his Oxted Junction points half way to derail it. Had it continued further either towards Oxted, Caterham, Kingswood or Redhill it would have reached S.E.C.R. or shared territory. No doubt this played a part in deciding the point of derailment.

THE STOATS NEST DISASTER 29th JANUARY 1910

Left: A breakdown train lifts the coach which mounted the platform.

Centre: Some of the coaches and wagons containing the discarded bogie wheels.

The damaged platform after the clearance of the derailed vehicle.

Part Two - 20th Century

On 9th July 1902 the 10.30 London Bridge to Bognor passenger train was derailed as it approached West Croydon. The train was composed of the locomotive and five vehicles. When the derailment occurred the locomotive broke away from the rest of the train and remained on the rails. The leading two coaches, however, fell on their sides. Forty five passengers were injured, some seriously.

The enquiry revealed that the ganger had found defects when gauging the track and had set about rectifying them. In order to do so he had loosened some rail chairs which allowed the rails to move under the train, spreading to 1½ inches wider apart than normal, allowing the carriage wheels to drop into derailment. The carriages were tipped over when points were reached.

The 05.45 Norwood to Crawley freight train, consisting of tank locomotive No. 417, 31 wagons and a brake van, parted between the 11th and 12th wagon on the rising gradient near Purley on 17th March 1907. The front portion carried on, but the rear portion ran back towards Croydon. Fortunately the guard was able to stop it before any damage resulted.

The new silent movie films were all the rage at this time, the Clarendon Film Company based at Croydon being one of the pioneers. During 1907 the station master at Stoats Nest permitted them to film at that station without official sanction and unfortunately for him a fatal accident occurred. The film required a man to be laid across the rails with a train approaching in the best traditions of early thrillers. His dog was to rescue him at the last moment. A Mr. Zeitz was the actor and locomotive No. 379 *Sanderstead* was run slowly towards him. Unfortunately something went wrong and it did not stop short of him as planned and he was killed. The station master was reduced in grade and sent to Horsted Keynes in Sussex.

On 10th July 1909 the 06.30 empty stock train from New Cross was in collision with a shunting locomotive on the 'down relief' line at East Croydon. The locomotive was on its way into Halls Sidings when the empty train passed the protecting signal at danger. The driver of the empty train, who was held responsible, and both firemen were injured, and the driver of the shunting locomotive was killed. The signalman was also criticised for accepting the empty train without the proper distance ahead of the signal being clear.

A far more serious disaster occurred at Stoats Nest, where on 29th January 1910, the 15.40 fast train from Brighton, hauled by 4-4-2. locomotive No. 41, was derailed. A leading wheel on one of the coaches had shifted an inch on the axle and had milled against the bogie frame. It derailed at the junction points, whereupon the train divided ahead of the derailed coach. The rear portion swung round and mounted the platform ramp, struck a water column and turned over, minus its bogies. Five passengers, plus two persons on the platform who were crushed by the wreckage, lost their lives and forty two were injured.

On 10th July 1910 tank locomotive No.370, working a train of London and North Western Railway stock, broke an axle at

The collision at East Croydon on 10th July 1909, when an E.C.S. train collided with a shunting engine on its way to Hall & Co. sidings.

South Croydon Junction and leaned on goods locomotive No. 308 on the adjoining line. No one was hurt, the driver and fireman of the latter being able to take evasive action.

A military train from Bricklayers Arms had just passed Coulsdon and Cane Hill on 23rd May 1915, when the train crew noticed that a wagon of petrol in wooden and steel barrels was on fire, probably ignited by a spark from a locomotive. They stopped the train and split it into three parts, leaving the burning wagon isolated, to prevent the fire spreading to the other wagons. They were rewarded for their efforts. The wagon was totally destroyed.

A derailment occurred at Windmill Bridge Junction on 13th November 1922 which in itself was not serious. It could

informed him that the train on the 'up' main line was the 08.42 from Coulsdon & Smitham Downs, and that on the 'up local' line was the 08.10 Pullman express from Brighton. He decided that the Pullman should be given preference, changed his points and operated his signals for it to run to the Victoria main line. He did not, however, set the 'up' main line points towards London Bridge as he should have done to re-create a proper clearance distance for the Coulsdon train should it not stop at the junction signal. The Coulsdon train left East Croydon before the 'Pullman' and having received a 'caution' indication at the distant signal was approaching Windmill Bridge Junction slowly. The signals in this area were high up on bridges and gantries because of space

A breakdown crane sets about rerailing 'Gladstone' class No. 172 *Littlehampton*, derailed at Windmill Bridge Junction on 13th November 1922.

easily have been a major disaster, however, for it happened right in the path of an approaching express in dense fog. The signalman at Windmill Bridge Junction first accepted an 'up' Victoria passenger train from East Croydon North signalman on the 'up' main line. He set his points towards Victoria but did not signal the train forward, not at this time being certain of its identity. Shortly afterwards, he was offered another 'up' Victoria passenger train on the 'up local' line which he also accepted, being able to set his points via the 'local' line towards Gloucester Road Junction, thus providing both trains with proper clearance in the event of either or both trains failing to stop at the signals. The signalman at East Croydon North then

restrictions and consequently were impossible to observe from the footplate in dense fog, the handsignals given by fog-signalmen, who were provided with repeating signals, being the only indications received by the locomotive crews. The fireman of the Coulsdon train was attempting to locate the fog-signalman appointed to the junction signals. Upon sighting him through the gloom but being unable to see any handsignal he shouted a question - 'Alright?' His driver heard this and assumed that it was his fireman informing him that it was alright to proceed, whereupon he opened up the regulator. Before his fireman could rectify matters, the locomotive - a 'Gladstone' - and some of the coaches were derailed at a moveable diamond crossing, right into the path of the approaching 'Pullman'. Fortunately the signalman was resourceful enough to replace his signals to danger in front of the 'Pullman' and set his points towards Gloucester Road Junction, thus diverting it away from the obstructed route. No one was injured.

The 16.44 from Tattenham Corner did not stop in time when running into Purley to couple on to the 16.53 from Caterham on 16th December 1929. A minor collision resulted, injuring four passengers.

On 10th December 1932 an express train from Brighton divided into two portions as it passed South Croydon, the automatic brakes bringing it to a stand. The passengers were transferred to the front portion which continued to East Croydon.

In fog and wartime blackout on 4th November 1942 the 06.15 West Croydon to Holborn Viaduct (via Sutton) ran into the 05.34 London Bridge to Epsom in Waddon station, the driver of the 06.15 and one passenger being killed. The blame was attributed to misuse of the Sykes release key by the Waddon signalman.

The Borough's worst every railway disaster was also a result of the misuse of the Sykes release key in dense fog. On 24th October 1947 the 07.33 passenger train from Haywards Heath to London Bridge had been held for several minutes at Purley Oaks awaiting acceptance by South Croydon Junction. The signalman at Purley North signal box had the 08.04 passenger

Above and below: Two photographs of the Borough's worst ever railway disaster at South Croydon on 24th October 1947 in which thirty-two people perished. *Times Newspapers*

train from Tattenham Corner to London Bridge ready to leave and telephoned the signalman at Purley Oaks to question how much longer it would be before the 'Train out of Section' bell signal would be received for the 07.33. The latter man, who had only worked at Purley Oaks for four months, normally rostered to cover the off-peak period between the morning and afternoon peak period signalmen, and who had never worked in dense fog before, became confused, overlooked the presence of the 07.33 out of sight from his box, used the release key, forwarded the 'Train out of Section' bell signal and accepted the 08.04. Unfortunately at this critical moment the South Croydon Junction signalman was able to accept the 07.33 whereupon the Purley Oaks signalman operated all his signals, as he thought, for the 08.04. The 07.33 moved slowly away, being gradually caught up by the 08.04 which was running at speed having sighted the distant signal at clear. Approaching South Croydon the inevitable collision occurred. Being at the height of the peak hours there were some 1,800 passengers in the two trains. Of these the driver of the 08.04 and thirty one passengers were killed and there were fifty-eight injuries.

During preparatory work in connection with re-signalling in the early 1950s the last passenger train from Victoria via Crystal Palace became derailed at the north end of Norwood Junction. Points had been disconnected and hand signalling was being carried out. At such times it is necessary to secure facing points to prevent them moving. Obviously the men carrying out

Rerailing in progress following the collision at Gloucester Road Junction on 4th March 1958. The vans of the parcels train have been taken away.
Times Newspapers

the securing were under the impression that the two switches were still connected for although the closed point switch was secured with a point clip, a wooden plug had not been inserted in the open switch. However, the switches had been disconnected from one another and the vibration of the train caused the open switch to gradually close. As a result the middle of the train tried to take both routes, resulting in derailment.

Another train which tried to take two routes was the 08.09 Littlehampton to London Bridge on 13th February 1954 on the 'up' main line at Windmill Bridge Junction. This train was not booked to call at East Croydon and, being derailed at speed, all six coaches left the rails. However, no one was hurt, the only complaint being in respect of a broken gramophone record! The enquiry found that the driver had irregularly passed the junction signal at danger. The signalman had just put a 'down' train from Victoria across the junction and was changing the route for the 08.09. As he was moving the junction facing points the leading wheels had reached them. The physical damage caused included half a dozen new electric point machines, installed ready for the re-signalling of the area, but not yet brought into use, which had to be written off.

On 4th March 1958 a slow speed collision occurred at Gloucester Road Junction where the local lines from East and West Croydon converged. A parcels train from Brighton to London Bridge passed a signal at danger and collided with the 12.55 West Croydon to Victoria via Crystal Palace. Five passengers and the guard were slightly hurt.

Another signal passed at danger resulted in a collision between passenger trains in the 'up local' platform at Norwood Junction on 31st December 1968. The 16.57 from Coulsdon North to London Bridge was the offending train which ran into the 16.45 from London Bridge to London Bridge via Streatham, Selhurst and Norwood Junction. Two drivers and one guard were slightly hurt. Sixteen passengers went to hospital but none were detained.

On 30th March 1974 the driver and guard of an early morning train from Caterham left the train unattended in Caterham platform without adequately securing the brakes. After a while the train started to move on the falling gradient and set off along the 'up' line. Fortunately the signalman was able to contact the crossing keepers at Whyteleafe South and Whyteleafe so that the level crossing gates could be opened. At Purley the question was posed whether to divert the runaway into the siding at the north end of the station where a train crew were preparing a train, or to let it out on to the main line. It was considered that the former would have probably resulted in a heavy collision that would have damaged the two trains, blocked the through lines and perhaps killed or injured the train crew on the train in the siding. It was, therefore, decided to allow it on to the main line which was kept clear. It carried on through Purley Oaks, South Croydon and East Croydon and at Windmill Bridge Junction it was put through Teetotallers Siding and into Norwood Yard. It passed right through the yard and at the northern end ran into the buffer stops at the south end of Norwood Junction No. 1 platform, demolishing them and derailing the train. Railway staff had attempted to board it at Purley, East Croydon and Norwood yard but it was travelling too fast - not surprising since it had travelled 8¼ miles overall, all on a down gradient!

Two collisions attributable to passing a signal at danger occurred in fairly close succession. On 13th November 1981 six passengers were slightly injured when the 08.22 from West Croydon to London Bridge via Crystal Palace and Tulse Hill was in collision with the 08.23 from Beckenham Junction to Victoria at the confluence of the lines at Bromley Junction. The enquiry heard that the driver was suffering from a slight migraine and had

A glancing blow! The collision at Bromley Junction on 13th November 1981. The 'offending' train from West Croydon is leaning precariously towards the embankment side.

Times Newspapers

a painful wisdom tooth. His mother was seriously ill in hospital and his wife and new born baby were due to be collected from hospital later that day. He had consequently only managed to get five hours sleep and had taken a slight overdose of a mild analgesic-cum-tranquilliser, and the Inspecting Officer concluded that a combination of all these features had reduced the driver's alertness.

The other was on 16th January 1982 when an engineers train from Three Bridges to New Cross Gate ran into a stationary parcels train in No.1 platform at East Croydon. The driver, who it was considered had fallen asleep, was seriously injured, losing part of his leg after being trapped for seven hours and other staff were slightly injured.

Other minor derailments and incidents have occurred over the years and for a variety of reasons. The majority of them were within yards, sidings, and depots during shunting, but some occurred on, or obstructed the running lines.

Within the Borough in the last twenty years there have been isolated cases of trains being derailed as a result of human errors by drivers or signalmen, whilst a passenger train was derailed at Windmill Bridge Junction in the evening peak period on 30th November 1970, following the relaying of the entire junction. During a period when, for technical reasons, short wheelbase wagons on freight trains were becoming

derailed frequently nationwide, instances occurred at Purley, Norwood Junction and Norbury. By coincidence one on the 'down local' line at the latter station, and a passenger train derailed on the 'up through' line opposite as a result of running over a fallen poplar tree, put two of the four lines out of use at the same time for different reasons! During shunting at Waddon Marsh a freight brake van ran away unmanned along the goods siding on a falling gradient until becoming derailed at the end of the siding at Beddington Lane. By sheer coincidence this was within weeks of the Caterham runaway. Near Waddon Marsh, a car careered off the roadway onto the passenger line. At Coulsdon North during shunting with a train of aviation oil, some tank wagons ran away along the siding and demolished the buffer stops just south of Old Lodge Lane underline bridge, becoming derailed and also springing a leak. Because of the latter hazard, trains on all lines had to be stopped for several hours. Occurring on a Saturday as it did would normally have proved to be advantageous, with no peak hour traffic to be dealt with. However, it happened to be the one Saturday when holders of 'Senior Citizens Railcards' were invited to travel anywhere free and considerable crowds had to be transported by alternative bus services!

At West Croydon a different sort of accident affected the train service. A stockpile of oxy-acetylene and propane gas cylinders caught fire. Some of them exploded, others took off like shells and shrapnel flew for a considerable distance in all directions. An engineers office was destroyed by fire and other buildings on the station (including most of the glass on the platform awnings) were damaged. The signalling cable between the two signal boxes was burnt. Trains were halted for several hours whilst the fire was extinguished and the area declared safe, and were delayed afterwards until the signalling cable was fully restored.

Whilst in essence only a simple minor derailment, an incident between Purley and Purley Oaks on 21st October 1983 proved to be quite spectacular, and could well have resulted in a major disaster. A wagon on a freight train on the 'up fast' line derailed, dragging others into derailment. These struck and demolished the abutment of the bridge over Purley Downs Road forcing rubble onto the roadway below. 'Jack-knifing' of the derailed wagons resulted, and whereas they had previously veered away from the railway, they now also fouled the 'down fast' line, where the 15.36 passenger train from London Bridge to Brighton struck them, two passenger coaches being derailed. Other freight wagons went down the embankment. At some stage the derailed vehicles struck one of the new signal gantries recently brought into use under the Brighton line re-signalling which spanned the four tracks, bringing it down, thus blocking all four tracks. The only injury to persons was minor, a passer-by on the roadway below being struck by a piece of rubble.

Both good and bad luck feature in this incident. Bad luck turned a simple derailment into a complete blockage of four lines by reason of the bridge abutment and signal gantry being struck. It was also bad luck that one of the new signal gantries was involved rather than   the superseded ones which were awaiting demolition   an unofficial strike of certain railway staff at the time and a very reduced train service was operating, so it was also bad luck that not only was there a passenger train in the vicinity, but it was in such close proximity. Had it been running a minute or two later the derailed wagons would have touched the rails of the 'down fast' line, operated the track circuit and reverted the signal in rear to red, allowing the driver to stop short of the obstruction. By the same token it was good luck that had it not been for the strike there might well have been other trains in the vicinity which might also have collided with the derailed vehicles or fallen gantry. As the incident occurred at about 1600 it was also good luck that the local schools were on half term holiday, otherwise flocks of homegoing school-children could have been passing under the bridge.

Notwithstanding such events the success of the efforts to obtain near perfection in rail safety can be gauged from the fact that so far as the author can ascertain only five fatal train accidents (collision or derailment) have occurred within the present Borough boundaries throughout its long railway history, 45 or 46 passengers having lost their lives.

In proportion to the many millions of trains that have been run and the countless billions of passengers conveyed, this reflects much credit on those responsible for ensuring that safety methods were improved to keep up with increases in the speed and frequency of trains, the technical staff who design, provide and maintain the track, rolling stock and signalling equipment and the operating staff who run the trains.

Without the constant standard of vigilance and disciplined adherence to safety requirements by all these dedicated personnel through the years such a record could certainly not have been achieved.

The 'runaway' train from Caterham being re-railed at Norwood Junction, 30th March 1974.   *Author*

Chapter Five
Miscellaneous Section

There are certain features which do not logically fall within the scope of any of the previous sections, yet are of sufficient interest for inclusion. They are varied, and are listed under various sub headings:-

SELHURST DEPOT

Within this depot, opened in 1911 and extended during the 1920s, and which covers several acres, there are numerous sidings for trains to be stabled in, and also large sheds where carriage cleaning, fuelling, inspection of the trains, minor and major repairs, general overhauls, including lifting trains to change their wheels, motors, etc., and painting are performed. Most of the Southern Region Central Division suburban trains are allocated to Selhurst for their maintenance and repairs. Main line trains are also dealt with, also locomotives and the Waterloo & City Underground trains (operated by B.R.). The latter have to be routed via Wimbledon and West Croydon owing to gauge restrictions, and have to be locomotive hauled. An Engineers School is also situated within the Depot. Work on enlarging and modernising the Depot began early in 1984 and is scheduled for completion in 1986.

ELECTRIC STABLING SIDINGS

Other stations within the Borough which have electrified sidings, thus allowing electric trains to be stabled when not required in service are:- West Croydon, Purley and Addiscombe, the latter having a carriage shed. Coulsdon North was in the list until the station was closed.

DISTRIBUTION OF ELECTRIC CURRENT

When the Overhead A.C. electric trains commenced, the current was obtained from the London Electric Supply Corporation's Power House at Deptford at 6,700 volts to a switch cabin at Queens Road, Peckham, thence via numerous switch cabins to the wires. When the extension was made from Balham to Coulsdon North and Sutton the current was received at 6,700 volts at New Cross Gate where it was stepped up to 64,000 volts and transmitted through four 32,000 volt cables to a switch cabin at Gloucester Road, Croydon. Here it was changed back to 6,700 volts and distributed to other switch cabins, thence to the wires.

Upon the Mid Kent lines being electrified supply for the conductor rails was received at a distribution switch room at Lewisham at 11,000 volts A.C. It was transmitted to various substations where it was converted to 660 volts D.C., and supplied to the conductor rails.

Lewisham distribution switch room was extended to similarly accommodate the supply of current for the Central Division suburban conductor rail system.

A more modern arrangement applied when the Brighton line south of Purley was electrified. Current was taken at 33,000 volts from the Central Electricity Board at three places – two in Sussex and the other at Croydon, being transmitted to various substations where it was converted to 660 volts, thence to the conductor rails. These substations were unmanned, the whole area being remotely supervised from a control room at Three Bridges.

After the Second World War the replacement of the suburban power supply network with Control Rooms remotely supervising unmanned substations was progressed. So far as the Borough's lines were concerned this resulted in the Mid Kent lines to Addiscombe and Sanderstead being controlled from

Lewisham, the Coulsdon area, as hitherto, from Three Bridges, and the remainder from a new control room at Selhurst. Equipment was provided to take a rail voltage of 750 volts which has been introduced in stages and should be completed soon.

The control rooms resemble a modern route panel signalling centre. In the operations room a large diagram showing the many miles of lines under the electrical controller's supervision is provided in such a position that he can observe it all from his desk. On the diagram there are coloured lights, audible buzzers, switches, etc., and mounted on his desk are numerous dials.

By means of these and by keeping a detailed log the controller is able to monitor the position throughout his extensive area so far as electrical current supply and distribution is concerned. He can establish how much current is being taken from the National Grid, how much is being used at various places, and, should a short circuit occur, circuit breakers will operate automatically, lights on the diagram will flash and audible warnings sound. The controller will operate the switches as required to either restore the current or maintain the isolation as appropriate.

His switches allow him to isolate an entire section of line between various given points either in planned circumstances or emergencies, and he has strict procedures to follow according to circumstances. Should it be necessary to lessen the extent of an isolation to allow more flexible movement of trains it is necessary for switches inserted at selected places in the actual conductor rails to be operated manually by staff on the ground using special poles.

No matter which method is used an isolation or recharging of the current must only be made with the consent of the electrical controller, thus ensuring that at all times he is fully aware of the state of his area so far as the supply of current is concerned and he is, as a result, in a position to advise where current is available and where it is not – a very necessary essential where such a dangerous commodity is involved.

He also has means, in the event of a power supply failure, to switch over to alternative supply points thus keeping the system running.

The electrical supply for much of the colour light signalling apparatus is also provided via the control rooms.

TUNNELS

The Borough's railways are fortunate in that there are few tunnels. The longest, at 837 yards, and indeed the only one from May 1983, is at Riddlesdown on the Oxted line. The other three were previously on the now closed Woodside – Selsdon line. They were Woodside (266 yards), Park Hill (122 yards) and Coombe Lane (157 yards).

Until is was opened up in 1954 the Cane Hill 'covered way' at Coulsdon (see chapter one), although not a tunnel in the true sense, was classified as one for the purposes of safety rules, etc. This was 417 yards in length.

The lengths quoted are Southern Railway/B.R. figures. There appears to have been elastic tape measures used at some stage, for the L.B. & S.C.R. quote the lengths as:- Riddlesdown (836 yards), Woodside (264 yards), Park Hill (121 yards), Coombe Lane (157 yards) and Cane Hill covered way (411 yards 2 feet)!

LEVEL CROSSINGS

Level crossings are another undesirable feature which can be a source of hindrance to the running of both road and rail traffic, particularly nowadays with the vast increase in both types of traffic compared with the early days when they were originally provided, and every effort is focused on abolishing them at the first opportunity.

There were two level crossings within the Borough from the opening of the London and Croydon Railway. One, where Brighton Junction (later Norwood Ford Junction) was to be located a few years later, allowed the occupants of Selhurst (then spelt Sellhurst) Farm to cross the line. When the flyover was added on the east side a small bridge had to be provided under it, immediately at the end of the level crossing, for the farm traffic to pass through. The level crossing was closed about 1860 but the bridge remains. Just over ½ mile nearer (West) Croydon the second took Brighton Road (Croydon) (later renamed Gloucester Road) over the railway. An overline bridge was later provided so the crossing was dispensed with.

At Stoats Nest from the early days a level crossing took Stoats Nest Road across the London – Brighton line whilst it was double track only. It was abolished just prior to the widening works which towards the turn of the century gradually resulted in virtually six widely spread tracks at this point – the four Brighton lines and the parallel Chipstead Valley double line. The road was diverted by an inverted 'S' bend to pass through underline bridges.

There was a private road level crossing just north of where Selhurst station was later built from the opening of the line in 1862 for a couple of years or so until it could be abolished.

Another level crossing was just south of Norbury station. This was across the original double line, and was superseded by the present footbridge which spanned four tracks and a middle siding, just prior to the quadrupling of the line in 1903.

At Waddon Marsh there was a level crossing at the site of the old signal box until 1930 when it was abolished, along with the signal box, in conjunction with the remodelling, electrification and provision of a goods line and halt.

From that date there were no level crossings over running lines within the Borough. There were, however, two level crossings immediately adjacent to one another taking private sidings over Hospital Road at Waddon Marsh until the sidings were closed in recent years.

Two railway departmental level crossings were later installed. One, over the single 'down' line between Bromley Junction and Norwood Junction, permits vehicles to enter and leave the Regional Mechanical and Electrical Engineers Depot which is situated on the site of the former Norwood Junction locomotive depot. It is unusual in that it consists of one gate and one lifting barrier worked by hand.

Another level crossing with hand barriers allowed vehicles to pass over the single line connecting Selhurst station and Selhurst Depot, the main workshops complex and the paint shops in the Depot being on opposite sides. Under the current modernisation of the Depot it was superseded by electrically operated barriers over two new 'in and out' lines during June 1984. A temporary addition was provided in connection with the major remodelling and earthworks in the Gloucester Road Junction, area. It connected the working site, which was rail locked, with Tait Road by passing over the former two 'local' lines between Windmill Bridge Junction and Gloucester Road Junction, and consisted of electrically operated lifting barriers. It was removed upon completion of the work.

All these crossings are or were opened and closed by railway staff, under the authority of the signalman concerned.

HEADQUARTERS OFFICES

Croydon, being from the start of railways one of the principal towns in the South of England, it is hardly surprising that it appealed as a desirable centre for headquarters offices.

The London and Croydon Railway offices were at (West) Croydon in a building on the 'down' side, later to become the station masters house, which was abolished when the station was rebuilt in the 1930s, whilst the L.B. & S.C.R. District Superintendent's office was located at East Croydon for many years.

The former locomotive shed at Purley was for some years the headquarters of the District Permanent Way Engineer.

The major development of Croydon as an office complex centre from the late 1950s, together with its excellent train services, attracted many large firms to base themselves in the town; B.R. were no exception, Essex House in College Road becoming the Southern Region Central Division Offices. This accommodated most of the Divisional Headquarters staff covering all functions, and included the Traffic Control Office and the Divisional Mechanical and Electrical Engineer, until the Division was dispensed with during 1984. The Divisional Civil Engineer and Divisional Signal & Telecommunications Engineer and their staffs were, however, located in Southern House, off George Street, a building which otherwise was mainly occupied by Southern Region head office personnel whose responsibilities embrace the entire Region. Many departments have based their offices there, as diverse as the Chief Civil Engineer, Chief Signal & Telecommunications Engineer, Chief Mechanical and Electrical Engineer, Personnel, Architect, Audit, Finance, Medical, Stores, Shipping & International and Services sections, as well as the aforementioned Central Division Engineers plus the Divisional Signal & Telecommunications Engineers for the South Eastern and South Western Divisions, until their demise during 1984. Area Management which took over from the Divisions are based there too.

Also located in the building is another control office, known as 'Maintrol', whose function is to monitor the whereabouts and performance of all types of rolling stock and to ensure that maintenance and overhaul schedules are adhered to.

Train emerging from Coombe Lane Tunnel. *Pamlin Prints, Croydon*